Immigration and America's Future:

A NEW CHAPTER

Report of the Independent Task Force on
Immigration and America's Future

Spencer Abraham and Lee H. Hamilton, Co-Chairs

Doris Meissner

Deborah W. Meyers

Demetrios G. Papademetriou

Michael Fix

SEPTEMBER 2006

Cataloging-in-Publication Data is available from the Library of Congress.
ISBN 0-9742819-3-X, 978-0-9742819-3-3

Cover and Design by Sally James of Cutting Edge Design, Inc.

CONTENTS

SUPPLEMENTARY DOCUMENTS

TABLES

APPENDICES

FOREWORD

FEW POLICY AREAS AFFECT A SOCIETY as directly or as deeply as do immigration and immigration policy. Large-scale immigration magnifies those effects enormously.

The United States has been taking in unprecedented numbers of immigrants — legal and illegal — for over a decade now. Including those who come into the country both within and outside the parameters of the permanent immigration system and stay for extended periods of time, annual US immigration today totals about 1.8 million. Temporary immigrants entering legally on visas that do not require proof of an intention to return home and foreigners who enter and/or stay without authorization comprise the difference between the annual legal flows, which have averaged nearly one million in recent years, and the "actual inflow" figure estimated at 1.8 million.

No country can afford to have an immigration system that either ignores or otherwise merely ratifies the facts on the ground. Yet, that is what the United States has been doing for a while now. The result is a challenge to the most basic rules of governance; a hit-or-miss relationship between immigration policy and crucial US economic and social priorities; and an exceptional degree of political attention, not all of which has been thoughtful or productive. For these reasons, the Migration Policy Institute (MPI) organized the bipartisan Independent Task Force on Immigration and America's Future. This volume presents the results of the Task Force's effort to understand the key challenges and opportunities that immigration represents for the nation and the group's proposals for sensible but fundamental solutions.

Under the steady leadership of two distinguished American public servants, Spencer Abraham and Lee H. Hamilton, the Task Force recommendations articulate a vision that promotes US global competitiveness in the context of post-9/11 security imperatives, while also grappling with many of the technical details that have made immigration such an intractable public policy problem. The resultant proposals call for a flexible system that meets US economic interests now and in the future, promotes longstanding social goals and priorities, respects core US values, and dramatically improves the government's ability to advance the rule of law, a standard no longer being met by the status quo.

As with most efforts to fundamentally re-think complex and deeply ingrained systems and practices, the ideas the Task Force is presenting will require thoughtful debate and time for thorough assessment. The members of the Task Force, my MPI colleagues, and I are pleased to contribute the new thinking the Task Force has generated to the national immigration conversation now underway.

Demetrios G. Papademetriou
PRESIDENT, MIGRATION POLICY INSTITUTE

ACKNOWLEDGMENTS

THIS REPORT IS THE CULMINATION of the efforts of many skilled, effective individuals. We begin by expressing our gratitude to Spencer Abraham and Lee Hamilton for agreeing to serve as co-chairs of the Task Force. They have presided over the project with steady hands and seasoned judgments about the issues at stake in today's immigration debate. We are also grateful to the members of the Task Force for engaging in the process of dialogue and debate that took place during Task Force meetings and for committing time and imagination to grappling with the truly complex, wide-ranging issues addressed in this report. Our partners in convening the Task Force were the Manhattan Institute (MI) and the US Studies program and the Mexico Institute of the Woodrow Wilson International Center for Scholars (WWIC). We thank Tamar Jacoby, Andrew Selee, and Philippa Strum from those organizations for helping to organize the Task Force. Finally, the background information and perspectives provided by the ex officio members of the Task Force broadened the scope of the issues in valuable ways.

The idea for the Task Force dates back almost three years. Throughout its gestation, funding, research, meetings, and preparation of publications, all of our MPI colleagues have supported the initiative in varying ways. We have worked extremely well together in a spirit of warm collegiality preparing for Task Force meetings and bringing this report to fruition. We want especially to recognize Julia Gelatt, whose attention to detail, quantitative contributions, and tenacity in tracking down information have been indispensable. Her many contributions include tables, graphs, citations, and sidebars; Marc Rosenblum for intellectual ingenuity and persistent "drilling-down" on several key issues in the report; and Lisa Dixon for smooth liaison with members and funders, professionally managed meetings, and an excellent sixth sense for preventing things from falling through the cracks. Finally, our colleague Muzaffar Chishti added important perspectives and suggestions on a range of pertinent topics. Their work and dedication were exceptional.

The report reflects a great deal of research and analysis for which we also thank current and former MPI staff members Jeanne Batalova, Betsy Cooper, David Dixon, Kevin Jernegan, Julie Murray, and Kevin O'Neil, with assistance from interns Megan Davy, Shirin Hakimzadeh, Mary Helen Johnson, and Eliot Turner. We are indebted to Colleen Coffey and Meg Weaver for outstanding help with communications, copyediting, and publications tasks and to Ben Rhodes of the Woodrow Wilson Center for deft editing and editorial advice in the writing of the report.

Present and former US government officials were particularly helpful in supplying technical information. For that we thank Steve Fischel, Jeff Gorsky, and Charlie Oppenheim of the State Department; staff of the Office of Immigration Statistics; and Lisa Roney of the Department of Homeland Security. Staff of the members of Congress who served on the Task Force played similarly important roles. Our thanks, therefore, goes to Esther Olavarria, Margaret Klessig, Julia Massimino, and Rebecca Jensen.

The quality of discussion at Task Force meetings was sparked by excellent briefings and written analyses. In particular, we wish to thank Frank Bean, David Ellwood, Susan Ginsburg, Leighton Ku, James Loy, David Martin, Susan Martin, and Jeffrey Passel. Many additional authors also contributed importantly to the project. The papers they prepared were, or are being, published to contribute solid information and analysis to the ongoing debate. A full list of Task Force publications and authors appears in the appendix.

Finally, we are extremely grateful to the Carnegie Corporation, Charles Evans Hughes Foundation, Ford Foundation, Haas Foundation, JEHT Foundation, JM Kaplan Fund, and Open Society Institute for their confidence in and financial support for this project.

Doris Meissner, Task Force Director
Deborah W. Meyers
Demetrios G. Papademetriou
Michael Fix

LIST OF TASK FORCE MEMBERS

Co-Chairs

Spencer Abraham
Chairman and CEO,
The Abraham Group, LLC;
Distinguished Visiting Fellow,
Hoover Institution
Former Secretary of Energy and Senator
(R) from Michigan

Lee H. Hamilton
President and Director, Woodrow Wilson
International Center for Scholars;
Former Vice Chair, 9/11 Commission and
Member of Congress (D) from Indiana

Director

Doris Meissner
Senior Fellow, Migration Policy Institute;
Former Commissioner, US Immigration
and Naturalization Service (INS)

Members

T. Alexander Aleinikoff
Dean of the Law Center and Executive
Vice President for Law Center Affairs,
Georgetown University;
Former General Counsel, US Immigration
and Naturalization Service (INS)

Howard Berman*
(D) Member of Congress, California

Oscar A. Chacón
Director, Enlaces América,
Heartland Alliance for Human Needs
and Human Rights

Thomas J. Donohue
President and CEO, United States
Chamber of Commerce

Jeff Flake*
(R) Member of Congress, Arizona

Fernando Garcia
Executive Director,
Border Network for Human Rights

Bill Ong Hing
Professor of Law and Asian American
Studies, University of California, Davis

Tamar Jacoby
Senior Fellow, Manhattan Institute

Juliette Kayyem
Lecturer in Public Policy at
the John F. Kennedy School of
Government at Harvard University;
Former member of the National
Commission on Terrorism

Edward Kennedy*
(D) Senator, Massachusetts

John McCain*
(R) Senator, Arizona

Janet Murguía
President and CEO,
National Council of La Raza

Leon Panetta
Director, Leon and Sylvia Panetta
Institute for Public Policy, California
State University at Monterey Bay;
Former Chief of Staff to the President;
Former Director, Office of Management
and Budget (OMB)

Steven J. Rauschenberger
Senator, State of Illinois;
Immediate Past President, National
Conference of State Legislatures;
Deputy Republican Leader and Former
Chairman, Illinois Senate Appropriations
Committee

Robert Reischauer
President, Urban Institute;
Former Director,
Congressional Budget Office (CBO)

Kurt L. Schmoke
Dean, Howard University School of Law
Former Mayor, Baltimore, MD

Frank Sharry
Executive Director,
National Immigration Forum

Debra W. Stewart
President, Council of Graduate Schools;
Former Vice Chancellor and Dean of the
Graduate School, North Carolina State
University

C. Stewart Verdery, Jr.
Principal at Mehlman Vogel
Castagnetti, Inc.;
Adjunct Fellow, Center for Strategic and
International Studies (CSIS);
Former Assistant Secretary, Department
of Homeland Security

John W. Wilhelm
President, Hospitality Industry of
UNITE HERE

James W. Ziglar
President and CEO, Cross Match
Technologies, Inc.;
Former Commissioner, United States
Immigration and Naturalization Service
(INS)

Ex officio members

Malcolm Brown
Assistant Deputy Minister, Strategic
and Program Policy, Citizenship and
Immigration Canada

Jean Louis De Brouwer
Director, Directorate B - Immigration,
Asylum, and Borders, European
Commission Directorate General for
Justice, Freedom and Security

Jeff Gorsky
Chief, Legal Advisory Opinion Section,
Visa Office, US Department of State

Gerónimo Gutiérrez Fernández
Undersecretary for North America,
Ministry of Foreign Affairs, Mexico

Observers

Thor Arne Aass
Director General, Department of
Migration, Ministry of Labour and Social
Inclusion, Norway

Carlos de Icaza
Ambassador to the United States
of America, Mexico

Alexandros Zavos
President, Hellenic Migration Policy
Institute

* Because of their legislative roles, currently serving members of Congress were not asked to endorse the Task Force recommendations.

Note: Some Task Force members submitted additional comments that appear at the end of the report. One member submitted a dissenting comment.

EXECUTIVE SUMMARY

IMMIGRATION IS THE OLDEST AND NEWEST story of the American experience. The same dreams of freedom and opportunity that galvanized people to cross the ocean hundreds of years ago draw people to America today. Immigration has enabled America's growth and prosperity, and helped shape our dynamic American society. Yet just as it has been a vital ingredient in America's success, immigration generates changes that can be unsettling and divisive.

Immigration is essential to advancing vital American interests in the 21st century. To maximize the benefits and mitigate the strains caused by immigration, the United States needs a new immigration policy and system for a new era.

Three times in our history, the United States has experienced "peak periods" of large-scale immigration that coincided with transformative economic change. Today, we are living through a fourth peak period, as globalization prompts the United States to complete the transformation from a manufacturing to a knowledge-based economy. With over 14 million newcomers, legal and illegal, the 1990s ranks numerically as the highest immigration decade in American history; the current decade will almost certainly surpass it.[1]

As with previous peak periods, immigration is helping the United States respond to shifting economic realities, while also enriching American society. At the same time, communities across the country are experiencing rapid change and new challenges in integrating diverse new populations. In particular, the United States is faced with an unprecedented level of illegal immigration. Demands for greater border control, an immigration system that can meet neither workforce requirements nor the need for families to unify, and government agencies at all levels that are struggling to manage immigration mandates are all signs that our policy is broken and outdated.

The American people are deeply divided about whether immigration helps or hurts the country. They recognize the imperative for change, but often give contradictory answers when asked to choose among various policy options.[2] Legislative action has mirrored this division. The House of Representatives passed a bill in December 2005 that focused on tough new enforcement measures at the border and in the interior of the country. The Senate passed a bill in May 2006 that complements stringent enforcement measures with substantially expanded opportunities for legal immigration and earned legal status with a "path to citizenship" for unauthorized immigrants.

The Independent Task Force on Immigration and America's Future welcomes the national dialogue on immigration. We applaud Congress for taking action, but believe that both the House and Senate bills are insufficient. The House bill will not fix the problem because it fails to address the economic forces driving immigration. The Senate bill is preferable because it is more comprehensive and bipartisan, but the bill is overly complex to implement and fails to correct systemic problems in immigration law and policy.

The Task Force report is based upon a careful analysis of the economic, social, and demographic factors driving today's large-scale immigration. In crafting recommendations, we sought to design a new and simplified system that averts illegal immigration, while also harnessing the benefits of immigration for the future.

THE BENEFITS OF IMMIGRATION

Immigration offers the United States unique benefits that will allow us to be a more productive, competitive, and successful nation in the 21st century.

Productivity

Immigration augments and complements the workforce exceptionally well because the US economy is creating more jobs than can be filled by native-born workers. In the 1990s, half of the growth in the US labor force came from new immigrants.[3] That share is projected to grow. This demand for foreign labor is evident across the skills spectrum. At a time when Japan and most European countries are less competitive and face mounting social welfare costs because of declining working-age populations, infusions of young, taxpaying immigrants are helping the United States overcome worker, skills, and entitlement program shortfalls. Without immigration, we cannot sustain the growth and prosperity to which we have become accustomed.

Competitiveness

Immigrants are helping the United States maintain a competitive edge. In the critical fields of science and engineering, immigrants play a pivotal role. To take just one example, in 2004, 50 percent of students enrolled in engineering graduate programs in the US higher education system were foreign-born.[4] At a time when China and India are increasingly competitive, the United States must continue to attract the world's best and brightest — or risk losing an important resource to other nations.

Immigration also propels entrepreneurship. Immigrants are more likely to be self-employed than native-born Americans.[5] The number of Hispanic-owned businesses has grown at three times the national average.[6] And one quarter of Silicon Valley start-ups were established at least in part by immigrants, including Intel, Sun Microsystems, and Google.[7] These and countless immigrant-owned businesses across the country are creating jobs, revitalizing neighborhoods, and helping the US economy adapt to changing global market conditions.

Dynamism

Immigration remains a driving force behind the dynamism of American society. The impact of immigration on daily life is evident in the food we eat, the entertainment we watch, the houses of worship we attend, and the sports we play. Prominent immigrants have won Nobel Prizes, built soaring skyscrapers, written or performed masterpieces, and served at the highest levels of government. Classic indicators such as employment, education, military service, intermarriage, and home ownership show that today's immigrants are successfully integrating into American society.

In an age of globalization, America's openness to immigrants is also an important foreign policy asset. Those who live, study, or emigrate to the United States learn first-hand about our values of freedom, opportunity, individual rights, and the rule of law. And in a global economy that increasingly demands global interaction, exposure to a diversity of people and experiences is a unique resource for Americans.

THE CHALLENGES OF IMMIGRATION

Despite these substantial benefits, America's immigration system has been overwhelmed by myriad challenges. Many of these challenges are tied to illegal immigration and the resulting population of unauthorized immigrants in the United States.

Illegal immigration

The most dramatic manifestation of the breakdown of America's immigration system is that a large and growing share of today's immigration is illegal. According to recent estimates, 11.5 to 12 million unauthorized immigrants are in the United States — nearly one-third of the country's foreign-born population.[8] For a nation of immigrants that is also a nation of laws, this level of illegal immigration is unacceptable. Illegal immigration generates insecurity about America's borders, carries economic and fiscal costs, and risks the creation of an isolated underclass. The prevalence of illegal immigration also generates disturbing social and cultural tensions, and causes a decline in Americans' support for immigration more generally.

Temporary immigration

Along with illegal immigration, nonimmigrant (temporary) immigration programs constitute the primary ways immigration has adapted to new conditions and labor market demands. Temporary immigration programs have increasingly been used as a step to permanent immigration and are filling standing, ongoing labor market needs. The result is that illegal immigration is meeting the nation's low-skill demands, and temporary visa programs are meeting the demands for mostly high-skilled immigration.

An over-burdened system

Illegal immigration occurs within the bounds of a broader immigration system that is over-burdened and no longer serves the nation's needs. The primary engines of immigration — family unification and employment — generate far more demand than the immigration system can meet. Individuals who apply to immigrate legally — on a temporary or permanent basis — face overly complex procedures, unreasonable delays, and inflexible statutory ceilings that dictate levels of immigration to the United States.

Native-born workforce

Immigration — particularly illegal immigration — also presents challenges to the native-born workforce. While the net economic impact of immigration is beneficial to the US economy, today's immigration also has some troubling consequences. Illegal immigration can have negative impacts on wages at the bottom end of the pay scale. And immigrant labor, particularly of unauthorized immigrants, can lead to declining labor standards that undercut the position of native-born workers.

[handwritten margin notes: net effect for country not for all workers]

Integration

The sheer number of today's immigrants — and the fact that many are unauthorized — presents substantial integration challenges. Many of the costs and responsibilities associated with integration are borne by states and localities. Large numbers of immigrants are now settling in states such as Georgia, North Carolina, and Nebraska that do not have recent traditions of immigrant integration. Unauthorized immigrants by definition cannot be integrated into American society, complicating integration further. And at the local level, communities are often faced with demands for services from unauthorized immigrants, particularly for education and health care, which are costly and engender resentment.

[handwritten margin notes: well, not legally]

Security

Despite more than a decade of unprecedented growth in resources for border security, the number of unauthorized immigrants residing in the United States has led to a sense that the government lacks the ability and will to secure its borders. Many border communities feel besieged, and citizens across the country are calling increasingly for strengthened border enforcement. Within the country, rules against employers hiring unauthorized immigrants are easily broken, manipulated, or simply under-enforced.

While the overwhelming majority of migrants entering the United States do not represent a threat to national security, the borders must be the front line for security. In a post-9/11 environment, Americans are particularly concerned about terrorists crossing a permeable border or fraudulently gaining admittance to the country at legal ports of entry. In addition, increases in smuggling, dangerous border crossing patterns that have led to tragic migrant deaths, and vigilantism all pose risks to migrants and border communities alike.

AN IMMIGRATION POLICY FOR THE 21ST CENTURY

The Independent Task Force on Immigration and America's Future believes America has entered a new era of immigration, and thus needs a new framework for immigration policy. Our recommendations integrate economic, security, and social concerns. We make proposals that are comprehensive, and governed by rules that are simplified, fair, practical, and enforceable. Above all, we have sought to build for the future upon a firm foundation of America's values and traditions of successful immigration.

Attracting the immigrants the United States wants and needs

The Task Force recommends the simplification and fundamental redesign of the nation's immigration system to accomplish timely family unification and to attract the immigrant workers required for the United States to compete in a new economy.

A re-designed system

Immigration should take place through three new streams: temporary, provisional, and permanent. Temporary visas would be issued for short-term stays and work assignments, such as seasonal employment. Provisional visas would allow employers to recruit foreign-born workers for permanent jobs and possible future immigration after a testing period of several years. A combination of such temporary and provisional visas, based on the nature of the job, is preferable to a bracero-like guest-worker program, which ties workers to individual employers and provides no opportunity for permanent residence. Finally, permanent immigration would be available both to those who apply directly, and those who "graduate" from provisional status.

temp
provis
perm

The proposed system would initially set annual immigration levels at about 1.5 million, approximately 300,000 less than the actual annual number of immigrants — legal and illegal — being absorbed into the labor market and the country today. The system would simplify many visa categories and procedures, so that US immigration is better able to meet family unification and labor market goals. Special visa categories would be created, such as "strategic growth visas" for individuals in strategically important disciplines.

Standing Commission

An independent, federal agency called the Standing Commission on Immigration and Labor Markets should be created. The Standing Commission would make recommendations to Congress every two years for adjusting immigration levels. Its recommendations would be based on analyses of labor market needs, unemployment patterns, and changing economic and demographic trends. In adjusting immigration levels to be flexible to changing market conditions and ongoing review, the Standing Commission would provide an important tool for policymaking, much as the Federal Reserve does for monetary policy.

Executive branch

To bolster the government's capacity to implement immigration policy, the president should: 1) name a White House coordinator for immigration policy;

2) issue an executive order establishing an interagency cabinet committee for immigration policy; and 3) strengthen the capacity of executive branch agencies to implement major new immigration mandates.

Enforcing the rules

People cross the border illegally or overstay their visas because of the availability of jobs in the United States and the absence of legal immigration opportunities. Any strategy to reduce illegal immigration must therefore increase the numbers of workers admitted legally, and then effectively and credibly punish employers who continue to hire unauthorized workers. The new bargain must be that with increased employment-based immigration, employers be given the tools to reliably hire only authorized workers, and be held to high standards of compliance with immigration and other labor standards laws.

Employer enforcement

Mandatory employer verification and workplace enforcement should be at the center of more effective immigration enforcement reforms. Without them, other reforms — including border enforcement — cannot succeed. Electronic verification is a major undertaking that relies on upgrading several massive federal databases. Government agencies must be given sufficient, sustained resources and support to upgrade databases and establish privacy and anti-discrimination safeguards. To assist in the process, the Department of Homeland Security should create a Workplace Enforcement Advisory Board to help build support for new employer enforcement policies, and monitor the progress of new measures.

Secure documents

A secure Social Security card is necessary to combat fraud, enable individuals to establish their eligibility to work, and allow employers to easily verify the documents presented by legally authorized workers — US citizens and non-citizens alike. A secure, biometric Social Security card should be developed to replace existing non-secure cards. Along with "green" cards and immigration work authorization cards — which are already secure, biometric documents — the three cards should eventually be the only documents used to verify work eligibility.

Border enforcement

Border enforcement must accomplish a number of intertwined goals: restricting the illegal entry of people and goods; regulating the flows of people and goods that the United States wishes to admit; protecting against terrorism and other national security threats; and protecting against criminality, violence, and other threats to the quality of life.

■ *Smart borders.* To accomplish these goals, implementation of "smart border" measures that combine personnel, equipment, and technology should be accelerated. The administration should submit an annual report to Congress and the American people that establishes measures of effectiveness for border enforcement and reports progress in meeting them. Three particular areas that need to be closely monitored are Border Patrol staffing and support, the effectiveness of technology, and civil rights protections of migrants and border community residents. Border enforcement efforts have received substantial resources in recent years with uncertain results. In implementing border enforcement policies, Congress and the public need better information to assess the effectiveness of those investments.

■ *Ports of entry.* Immigration enforcement in other areas of border security should continue to be strengthened, especially legal ports of entry and overseas visa issuance. As southwest border enforcement increases, incentives for individuals to use legal ports of entry to gain admittance to the United States will continue to grow. Legal immigration admissions procedures must not become "weak links" in border protection. Sustained attention to document security and vigilance in the issuance of overseas visas will continue to be of key importance. Meanwhile, security must be balanced with efficiency, as facilitating legitimate trade and travel are essential to economic prosperity and US engagement around the world.

■ *Counter-terrorism.* Terrorist travel and transportation tactics should be aggressively targeted with the same depth and urgency as terrorist communications and finance. International terrorists depend upon mobility. Every time a terrorist crosses an international border, he must make contact with an enforcement official. This represents a significant vulnerability for terrorists, and a vital opportunity for counter-terrorism officials. The tracking and disruption of terrorist travel demands higher priority and resources. Border officials must have ready access to information, such as real-time intelligence and law enforcement watch-lists, to enable them to promptly identify terrorism suspects.

Labor market protections

A re-designed immigration system must not diminish employment opportunities or wages of native-born US workers. Furthermore, increased levels of immigration must not be accompanied by declining labor standards — for US workers or for foreign-born workers.

■ *Labor certification.* The existing case-by-case labor certification system should be replaced with a system that provides for pre-certified employers, designates shortage occupations for blanket certifications, and uses a streamlined individual certification process for non-shortage occupations. Pre-certifications would require employers to file sworn attestations that no qualified US workers are available to do the job, that no striking workers are being replaced, and that prevailing wages will be paid.

■ *Worker flexibility.* Temporary and provisional workers should have the right to change employers after an initial period without jeopardizing their immigration status, and to exercise labor rights comparable to those of similarly employed US workers.

Immigrant integration

US immigration policies are specified in great detail in US laws, but integration policies are skeletal, ad hoc, and under-funded. Immigrant integration is an essential dimension of successful immigration, especially in a period of large-scale immigration. Currently, there is no focal point for leadership in the federal government to promote immigrant integration. Individual, family, and state and local efforts accomplish a great deal, but they could be better leveraged to achieve important national goals.

Office of Immigrant Integration

A National Office on Immigrant Integration should be created to provide leadership, visibility, and a focal point at the federal level for integration policy. The office would establish goals for immigrant integration, and measure the degree to which these goals are met. The office would assess and coordinate federal policies and agencies related to integration, and serve as an intermediary with state and local governments. As a principal priority, the office should examine the supply of and demand for English-language instruction among limited English-proficient groups, and provide leadership and expertise for public and private sector initiatives and resources to meet that demand.

The unauthorized population

An earned path to permanent legal status is the most urgent immigrant integration need at this time and should be provided for unauthorized immigrants currently in the United States. The requirements for earning legal status should be the same for all eligible applicants. A legalization process should be simple, with an eligibility date that is as recent as possible. The process should include registration for work eligibility in the United States, accompanied by a background security check, English-language requirements, and payment of a substantial fine for illegally entering the United States. Earned legal status should occur within the context of broad, comprehensive immigration reform.

The Region

Illegal migration is a regional issue. Nearly 80 percent of the unauthorized population in the United States is from Latin America, primarily from Mexico and Central America. The flow of remittance earnings from migrants in the United States to families and communities in their home countries has reached record amounts. The United States must engage Mexico and Canada in longer-term initiatives that result in viable economies and higher standards of living throughout the region.

Conclusion

America's ability to effectively manage and take advantage of our current period of large-scale immigration constitutes a new chapter in the nation's immigration experiences that will play a large part in shaping our nation in the 21st century. Will we be able to compete effectively? Will we be secure? Will we maintain our tradition of openness? The Task Force strongly believes that the United States can answer each of these questions in the affirmative, but only if we adopt a simplified, comprehensive, and new approach to immigration that addresses the American people's sense of crisis about illegal immigration, as well as the opportunities that immigration provides for the United States in a new era.

PREFACE

INTERNATIONAL MIGRATION IS TRANSFORMING not only the United States, but also more countries than at any time in history. The United States has long been a world leader in welcoming and integrating newcomers. Yet, our nation's official immigration policies are increasingly disconnected from the economic and social forces that drive immigration.

The nation's attention is focused on illegal immigration. Americans are deeply divided in their opinions about the impact of immigration on the country, and anger about illegal immigration colors public attitudes about all aspects of immigration, illegal or otherwise. Confronting the problem of illegal immigration is long overdue. Still, illegal immigration is but one aspect of immigration. Today's debate side-steps the broader question that looms for America's future: What kind of immigration policy and system would harness the benefits of immigration to advance US national interests in the 21st century?

The Independent Task Force on Immigration and America's Future was convened by the Migration Policy Institute (MPI) to grapple with that question. Its report and recommendations are based on careful analysis of the economic, social, and demographic factors driving today's large-scale immigration, illegal and legal. Its core conclusion is that the benefits of immigration far outweigh its disadvantages and that immigration is essential to US national interests and will become even more so in the years ahead. But to harness the benefits, the United States must fundamentally rethink its policies and overhaul its system for managing immigration.

The Task Force is a bipartisan group of leaders and experts from key sectors concerned with immigration. The co-chairs are Spencer Abraham, Principal, The Abraham Group, former Secretary of Energy and Senator from Michigan, who chaired the Subcommittee on Immigration of the Committee on the Judiciary; and Lee Hamilton, President and Director of the Woodrow Wilson International Center for Scholars (WWIC), former Vice-Chair of the 9/11 Commission and Representative from Indiana who chaired the House Committee on Foreign Relations. The Division of United States Studies and the Mexico Institute of the Woodrow Wilson Center and Manhattan Institute have collaborated with MPI in convening the Task Force.

The Task Force first met in May 2005. Research and analyses prepared for it have been released at regular intervals during the past year to inform policymakers, the press, and the public about critical issues.[9] Since the first meeting, legislative debate suddenly accelerated in the Congress. Because of their legislative roles, currently serving members of Congress were not asked to endorse the Task Force recommendations. Many Task Force members have been actively engaged in advocacy on behalf of key constituencies. Their support for the recommendations in the report in no way alters positions they may have taken on pending legislation and does not necessarily imply agreement with every aspect of the report.

This report is the culmination of the work of the Task Force. It addresses issues in the current debate and beyond. The Task Force hopes it will serve as a durable foundation upon which to build the discourse and policies that can meet the challenges and opportunities immigration poses for the 21st century.

TASK FORCE REPORT

I. Introduction

IMMIGRATION IS THE OLDEST and newest story of the American experience. The same dreams of freedom and opportunity that galvanized people to cross the ocean hundreds of years ago draw people to America today. Immigration has helped define the United States, enabled our growth and prosperity, and shaped our dynamic American society. Yet just as it has been a vital ingredient in America's success, it generates changes that can be unsettling and divisive.

Although immigration has occurred throughout American history, large-scale immigration has occurred during just three peak periods: the peopling of the original colonies, westward expansion during the middle of the 19th century, and the rise of cities at the turn of the 20th century. We are currently living through a fourth peak period of immigration that began in the 1980s and continues today.

These peak immigration periods have coincided with fundamental transformations of the American economy. The first saw the dawn of European settlement in the Americas. The second allowed the young United States to transition from a colonial to an agricultural economy. The industrial revolution gave rise to a manufacturing economy during the third peak period, propelling America's rise to become the leading power in the world. Today's large-scale immigration coincides with globalization and the last stages of transformation from a manufacturing economy to a 21st-century knowledge-based economy. As before, immigration has been prompted by economic transformation, just as it is helping the United States adapt to new economic realities.

With more than 14 million newcomers (legal and illegal), the 1990s rank numerically as the decade of highest immigration in US history[10] (see Figure 1). The current decade is poised to exceed 15 million. Foreign-born Americans comprise a wide range of national, racial, religious, and ethnic groups. African-Americans — the only group whose immigration was involuntary — have been superseded by Latinos as America's largest minority population.[11] A nation that has had a European-origin majority with one principal minority is becoming the most diverse society in history. One commentator describes America as "the first universal nation."[12]

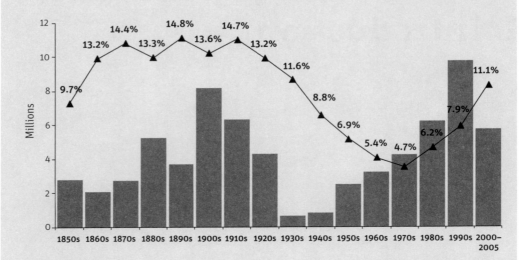

FIGURE 1. Number of New Lawful Permanent Residents by Decade and Foreign-Born Share of US Population, 1850s to 2000s

Note: Percentages show foreign-born share of the total US population in the year of the decennial census, so 1850s data shows the immigrant share of the population in 1850, for example. While the foreign-born made up 11.1 percent of the US population in 2000, that share grew to 12 percent by 2005.

Sources: US Department of Homeland Security, Office of Immigration Statistics, *Yearbook of Immigration Statistics, 2005*, Table 1 (Washington, DC: US Department of Homeland Security Office of Immigration Statistics, 2006); Campbell J. Gibson and Emily Lennon, "Historical Census Statistics on the Foreign-born Population of the United States: 1850–1990," Population Division Working Paper No. 29 (Washington, DC: US Bureau of the Census, February 1999); US Census 2000.

Americans take great pride in their nation-of-immigrants heritage. Most know and readily recount their families' history of immigration. Indeed, there is no more American story than the journey to a new land by sea, land or rail; the first job in a farm, factory, or shop; the child of immigrants reaching new heights of educational and economic opportunity.

Still, Americans approach immigration with deep unease. Each peak era of immigration has unleashed tumultuous social changes and political reactions. Each peak era has had far-reaching consequences in shaping the American character, identity, economy, and society. Yet each era has resulted in dramatic improvements in America's prosperity and well-being that would not have been possible without large-scale immigration.

The United States is now a mature, settled nation. Many believe that large-scale immigration is no longer needed, and is harming the country. Congestion, sprawl, pollution, crime, deficits, failing schools, falling wages, health care costs, housing shortages, border security, and terrorism all worry Americans. Immigration taps into such anxieties and raises complex questions about job competition, the integration of millions of newcomers, language, culture, and, above all, America's national identity.

As we grapple with today's era of immigration, we do so with an appreciation of the magnitude of the questions before America: Who are we and who are we becoming?

II. Why Is Immigration Important?

THE TASK FORCE HAS EXAMINED the economic, social, and security dimensions of today's immigration and has concluded that immigration is a unique and vital asset to the nation for the reasons outlined below.

THE ECONOMY AND DEMOGRAPHY OF THE 21ST CENTURY

Despite popular misgivings, immigration continues to be a critical resource for the US economy in the 21st century. At a time when Japan and most European countries are less competitive and facing increasingly severe social welfare burdens because of declining working-age populations — a trend that will become more acute in the next decade — immigration is allowing the US population and workforce to grow at a moderate and healthy rate, and is providing the American economy with needed skills, entrepreneurship, and innovation.

The worker gap

Immigration is necessary to keep up with the pace of job creation in the US economy.

A massive increase in native-born 25- to 54-year-old workers, particularly women and baby boomers, came into the workforce during the last 35 years. As Table 1 shows, this age group accounted for the majority of labor force growth between 1980 and 2000. However, between 2000 and 2020, there will be no net increase in native-born workers aged 25 to 54.[13] About 50 percent of the growth in the US labor force between 1990 and 2000 was due to new immigrants; a share that increased to 60 percent between 2000 and 2004.[14] While new native-born workers are projected to continue entering the workforce in sufficient numbers to replace retiring workers, the growth in the labor force will not be met by such workers. In the future, net increases of workers will come from only two sources — older workers and immigrants.[15]

TABLE 1. Growth in the Size of the Native- and Foreign-Born Labor Force Aged 25 and Over, 1980 to 2020

Nativity and Age	Labor Force 1980 (millions)	Growth 1980 to 2000 (millions)	Labor Force 2000 (millions)	Growth 2000 to 2020 (millions)	Labor Force 2020 (millions)
Native-born, Aged 25 to 54	60.1	26.7	86.8	0.0	86.8
Native-born, Aged 55+	13.8	2.7	16.5	13.3	29.8
Foreign-born	5.9	9.3	15.2	6.0	21.3
Total	79.8	38.7	118.5	19.4	137.9

Note: The projected growth in the foreign-born labor force between 2000 and 2020 is based on US Census Bureau projections of future immigration flows, which assume a continuation of current immigration law.

Source: David Ellwood, "How We Got Here," in *Grow Faster Together. Or Grow Slowly Apart* (Washington, DC: The Aspen Institute Domestic Strategy Group, 2002).

Immigration cannot forestall looming strains on social assistance programs for the elderly. It would take millions more and younger immigrants over a long period to change the demographic structure of the population.[16] However, infusions of young, tax-paying immigrants are an important part of addressing the shortfalls that lie ahead in terms of numbers of high- and low-skilled workers and in social insurance programs.[17]

Immigration is critical to sustaining the vitality of the US economy. The workforce is aging, there are fewer new native-born workers entering the labor market, and the economy is continuing to create new jobs. Satisfying future workforce needs will rest heavily on two factors: first, producing well-educated and properly trained workers (an increasing proportion of whom will be the

FIGURE 2. Aging US Population: Size and Share of US Population Aged 55 and Older, 2000 to 2030

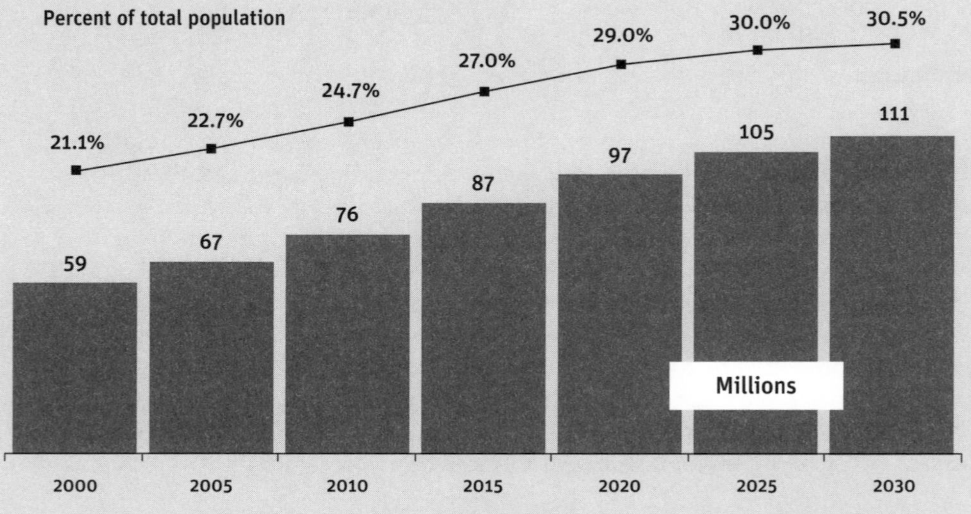

Source: David Dixon, "America's Emigrants: US Retirement Migration to Panama and Mexico," Presentation at the Migration Policy Institute, June 29, 2006.

children of today's immigrants) that will allow the US economy to maintain its productivity and competitive edge; and second, selecting the numbers and types of immigrants needed to supplement and enhance the qualifications of US workers.

The skills gap

Immigration is filling in gaps in the American workforce across the skills spectrum — from the lowest skilled jobs to the highest skilled fields.

Between 1980 and 2000, the proportion of native-born workers with high school and college degrees increased significantly, and the quality of the domestic labor force rose dramatically (see Table 2). Educational attainment will continue to increase, but the skill levels of the domestic labor force will not grow nearly as much. There will be fewer native-born workers available for low-skilled jobs due both to the demography of aging, and higher educational levels among native-born workers.[18]

TABLE 2. Education Characteristics of the Labor Force Aged 25 and Over, 1980, 2000, 2020

	Labor Force 1980	Labor Force 2000	Labor Force 2020
With More than High School Education	38.9%	58.0%	62.1%
With College Degree	21.6%	30.2%	33.6%

Source: David Ellwood, "How We Got Here," in *Grow Faster Together. Or Grow Slowly Apart* (Washington, DC: The Aspen Institute Domestic Strategy Group, 2002).

Immigration complements labor market gaps very well. High-skilled workers are a critical resource for a knowledge-driven economy. This is especially so in science and engineering, which have high concentrations of immigrants (see Table 3). At the same time, 11 of the 15 occupations projected to have the largest absolute job growth between 2004 and 2014 require less than a bachelor's degree[19] (see Table 4). While about one-quarter of the foreign-born in the United States have a bachelor's degree or more, one-third have not completed high school, and thus become the labor pool for the hundreds of thousands of essential jobs that require relatively few skills.[20]

From the standpoint of economic growth and competitiveness, building a system that taps the contributions of both high- and low-skilled immigrants is an asset for the nation.

Entrepreneurship

Immigration helps fuel the entrepreneurship that is essential to national economic success.

A high degree of entrepreneurship has helped make the US economy the most successful in the world. Entrepreneurs are a primary source of innovation, and small businesses generate two out of every three new jobs in the US economy.[21] Entrepreneurs also account for many of the adaptations to changing market conditions that keep the economy flexible and competitive. In a fast-paced global marketplace, entrepreneur-driven flexibility in the United States is a major

TABLE 3. The 15 Occupations Projected to Grow Fastest (In Percent Growth), 2004 to 2014

Occupation	Employment (thousands)		Change		Most significant source of post-secondary education or training	Immigrant share of workforce in 2000
	2004	2014	Number (thousands)	Percent		
Network Systems, Data Communication Analysts	231	357	126	55	Bachelor's degree	12%
Physician Assistants	62	93	31	50	Bachelor's degree	11%
Computer Software Engineers	800	1,168	368	46	Bachelor's degree	27%
Dental Hygienists	158	226	68	43	Associate degree	5%
Dental Assistants	267	382	114	43	Moderate-term on-the-job training	12%
Personal and Home Care Aides	701	988	287	41	Short-term on-the-job training	18%
Physical Therapist Assistants and Aides	102	142	40	39	Short-term on-the-job training/associate degree	8%
Occupational Therapist Assistants and Aides	26	36	10	38	Short-term on-the-job training/associate degree	5%
Network and Computer Systems Administrators	278	385	107	38	Bachelor's degree	11%
Database Administrators	104	144	40	38	Bachelor's degree	17%
Physical Therapists	155	211	57	37	Master's degree	12%
Medical Assistants, Healthcare Support	861	1,162	301	35	Short/moderate-term on-the-job training/ vocational degree	10%
Medical Scientists	77	103	26	34	Master's/doctoral degree	45%
Occupational Therapists	92	123	31	34	Master's degree	7%
Postsecondary Teachers	1,628	2,153	524	32	Doctoral degree	17%

Source: B. Lindsay Lowell, Julia Gelatt, and Jeanne Batalova, "Immigrants and Labor Force Trends: The Future, Past, and Present," Task Force Insight No. 17 (Washington, DC: Migration Policy Institute, July 2006). Data drawn from occupational projections from the US Department of Labor, Bureau of Labor Statistics, and tabulations of the 2000 Census 5 percent Public Use Microdata Sample (PUMS).

TABLE 4. The 15 Occupations Projected to Undergo the Largest Job Growth (In Absolute Numbers), 2004 to 2014

Occupation	Employment (thousands)		Change		Most significant source of post-secondary education or training	Immigrant share of workforce in 2000
	2004	2014	Number (thousands)	Percent		
Retail Salespersons	4,256	4,992	736	17	Short-term on-the-job training	10%
Registered Nurses	2,394	3,096	703	29	Associate degree	11%
Nursing, Psychiatric, Home Health Aides	2,138	2,816	678	32	Short-term on-the-job training/vocational degree	17%
Postsecondary Teachers	1,628	2,153	524	32	Doctoral degree	17%
Customer Service Representatives	2,063	2,534	471	23	Moderate-term on-the-job training	9%
Driver/Sales Workers and Truck Drivers	3,231	3,681	450	14	Short/moderate-term on-the-job training	10%
Janitors and Building Cleaners	2,389	2,831	442	19	Short-term on-the-job training	20%
Waiters and Waitresses	2,252	2,627	376	17	Short-term on-the-job training	13%
Computer Software Engineers	800	1,168	368	46	Bachelor's degree	27%
Food Preparation, Serving Workers	2,150	2,516	367	17	Short-term on-the-job training	10%
Elementary and Middle School Teachers	2,102	2,452	350	17	Bachelor's degree/bachelor's or higher, plus experience	5%
General and Operations Managers	1,807	2,115	308	17	Bachelor's or higher, plus experience	9%
Medical Assistants, Healthcare Support	861	1,162	301	35	Short/moderate-term on-the-job training/vocational degree	10%
Personal and Home Care Aides	701	988	287	41	Short-term on-the-job training	18%
Cooks	2,121	2,395	274	13	Short/moderate/long-term on-the-job training	23%

Source: B. Lindsay Lowell, Julia Gelatt, and Jeanne Batalova, "Immigrants and Labor Force Trends: The Future, Past, and Present," Task Force Insight No. 17 (Washington, DC: Migration Policy Institute, July 2006). Data drawn from occupational projections from the US Department of Labor, Bureau of Labor Statistics, and tabulations of the 2000 Census 5 percent Public Use Microdata Sample (PUMS).

advantage over other advanced industrial nations that are typically heavily regulated, with large enterprises that are slow to change.

The risk-taking that motivates people to migrate frequently translates into entrepreneurship. Immigrants are more likely to be self-employed than the native-born.[22] The four countries with the highest per-capita creation of new companies are the United States, Canada, Israel, and Australia — all countries with high rates of immigration.[23] In the United States, the number of Hispanic owned businesses has grown at three times the national average, while the number of Asian-owned businesses has grown at twice the national average.[24]

To an extent, immigrant entrepreneurship is a survival strategy emanating from barriers to mainstream employment. At the same time, the relatively open nature of the US economy has provided fertile ground for immigrant-run businesses. One-quarter of Silicon Valley start-ups were established by immigrants, including companies such as Intel, Sun Microsystems, and Google that have helped maintain America's technological leadership.[25] Then there are the countless quiet stories of immigrant entrepreneurs who establish cleaning businesses, restaurants, construction companies, medical practices, transportation services, engineering firms, and myriad other establishments that create jobs, boost tax revenues, pay rent, and generate valuable goods and services. Neighborhoods on the brink of decay in many of the nation's cities are being revitalized by these immigrant businesses.

Innovation and technology leadership

Immigration helps the United States maintain its leadership in science and technological innovation, which has traditionally been a foundation of American economic power and performance.

Some of the world's most talented people are attracted to the United States for schooling, work, and freedom. The attraction often springs from the American higher education system, which provides an unrivalled teaching and research infrastructure. Seventeen of the top 20 universities considered to be the best in the world are in the United States.[26] This higher education system sustains US leadership in the global marketplace, and undergirds US superiority in critical national security sectors such as defense and intelligence.

Science and engineering specialties are particularly essential to national security and economic success, and here immigrants play a substantial role. While 12 percent of the population and 14 percent of the workforce were foreign-born in 2003, between 16 and 19 percent of bachelor's degree holders in science and engineering occupations were foreign-born; between 29 and 32 percent of scientists and engineers holding master's degrees were foreign-born; and between 36 and 40 percent of those holding doctoral degrees were foreign-born.[27] In 2004, graduate enrollments in engineering were 50 percent foreign-born; in the physical sciences, they were 41 percent. In contrast, the two largest graduate fields chosen by native-born students are education and business.[28]

Yet America's position of dominance in higher education is being challenged. For the first time, there is an emerging global competition for the world's best and brightest. China and India — the source of many such students — are beginning to bid heavily to retain them. China now graduates over two and a half times as many students with bachelor's degrees in engineering, computer science, and information technology as the United States.[29] And both China and

India are successfully implementing ambitious plans to invest heavily in higher education.[30] Other industrialized countries and emerging economies have also begun to compete vigorously for talent — whether their own or from abroad, and are adjusting their immigration and employment laws as part of their efforts.

In the 2006 State of the Union address, President Bush announced the *American Competitiveness Initiative,* an ambitious math and science education program that funds increased training to maintain American leadership in innovation.[31] At the same time, foreign students and professionals will continue to play a key role in maintaining the country's edge in the global economy. And,

Global Competition for Talent

For the past 50 years, the United States has comfortably enjoyed its position as the top destination for international students and scholars. However, the United States's share of international students has fallen since the mid-1990s, while Australia, Japan, New Zealand, and several European countries have seen large growth in their shares of the $30 billion per year higher education market.

The United States is facing increasing international competition in the training of new science and technology professionals. Only 7 percent of the world's engineering graduates worldwide come from the United States, and US high school students had among the lowest math and sciences scores of the 30 countries in the Organization of Economic Co-operation and Development (OECD). Europe produced twice as many science and engineering PhDs in 2000 as the United States while Asia has taken the lead in graduating science and engineering students. If current trends continue, 90 percent of the world's PhD-holding scientists and engineers will live in Asia by 2010.

Countries around the world have enhanced their efforts to attract global talent. The European Union has recently mounted a concerted effort to streamline the EU's educational system. Several countries, including France, Germany, and Hungary have increased courses offered in English. The United Kingdom launched a marketing campaign in 1999 to draw international students to UK universities, which has brought an additional 118,000 students. Prime Minister Tony Blair recently announced plans to draw 100,000 more international students over the next five years. Canada has also developed strategies to increase its number of foreign students, including changing its laws to allow foreign students to work off campus.

China and India, which together are the source of 25 percent of the international students in the United States, are working to encourage students to study at home, investing in education and transforming their top universities and research institutes into some of the world's best. China intends to increase its number of undergraduates and doctoral candidates fivefold in the next ten years, and Indian professionals increasingly remain in their home country, or return after migrating to the United States. The Returned Non-Resident Indian Association (RNRI) estimates that between 30,000 and 40,000 Indian expatriates have returned to Bangalore in the last decade alone.

Sources: "Lesson in Selling: International Students Have Plenty to Choose From," *The Financial Times,* September 14, 2005; National Science Foundation, Division of Science Resources Statistics, National Science Board, *Science and Engineering Indicators 2004* (Arlington, VA: National Science Foundation, Division of Science Resources Statistics, May 2004); "Foreigners Returning to US Schools," Reuters, March 25, 2006; NAFSA: National Association of International Educators, "Restoring U.S. Competitiveness for International Students and Scholars" (Washington, DC: NAFSA, June 2006); "Survey: A World of Opportunity," *The Economist* 376, no. 8443 (Sept 10, 2005); Stephen Yale-Loehr, Demetrios G. Papademetriou, and Betsy Cooper, *Secure Borders, Open Doors: Visa Procedures in the Post-September 11 Era* (Washington, DC: Migration Policy Institute, August 2005).

given the global nature of science and technology research and development, workers in these careers will likely always be mobile and international.

Effective, predictable, and welcoming immigration regimes are becoming important factors in a newly competitive global environment. The United States thus has a strong interest in building an immigration system that provides opportunities for the highly skilled and their families to travel, work, and live here.

The economic impact of immigration on native workers

Despite these substantial economic advantages, immigration — particularly illegal immigration — can have a mixed impact on the economic well-being of some native-born Americans.

The belief that immigrants take jobs from American workers and depress their wages is one of the most widely felt fears about immigration, according to opinion surveys.[32] Whether at the top or the bottom of the job ladder, unchecked or illegal immigration can drive down wages and undermine working conditions. The best available evidence remains inconclusive regarding immigration's effects on the work opportunities of native-born Americans, including the less skilled and minorities. There is, however, evidence that in some sectors of the economy and parts of the country, immigrants may adversely affect the job opportunities and wage scales of native workers.[33]

The broad consensus among economists is that immigrants have very modest negative effects on the employment of less-educated American workers, but that immigration has other broad, positive economic effects, including lower prices for goods such as food and housing, increased demand for US-made products, increased capital investment, and higher wages and employment for US workers.[34] To the extent that immigrants can have negative economic effects, however modest, illegal immigration intensifies the problem, especially for vulnerable groups.

The wage gap

There is a growing wage gap between the high- and low-skilled ends of the labor market. During the 1960s, workers experienced the same percentage of increases in income regardless of whether they were at the high or low end of

Immigration Facts

The US foreign-born are:
- One in eight people living in the United States
- One in seven workers
- One in five low-wage workers
- One in two new workers in the past ten years
- Two in five workers with less than a high school degree
- Three in four workers with less than a ninth grade education

One in five children in the United States has a foreign-born parent.
One in four children living in low-income families has a foreign-born parent.

Sources: US Census Bureau, Census 2000; Tabulations from the US Census Bureau, Current Population Survey, various years.

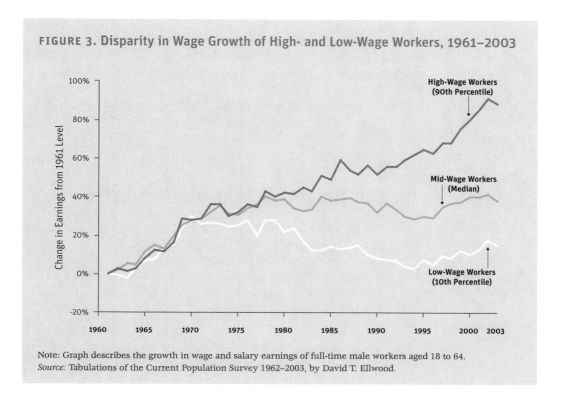

FIGURE 3. Disparity in Wage Growth of High- and Low-Wage Workers, 1961–2003

Note: Graph describes the growth in wage and salary earnings of full-time male workers aged 18 to 64.
Source: Tabulations of the Current Population Survey 1962–2003, by David T. Ellwood.

the labor market. Beginning in the 1970s, wages flattened out. Since then, the highest paid workers have seen dramatic increases in their pay, while the wages of the lowest-paid bottomed out, in relative terms, during the 1980s and 1990s [35] (see Figure 3).

Immigration has almost certainly contributed to the wage gap, particularly in low-wage occupations. One in seven workers is foreign-born. For low-wage workers, the ratio is one in five.[36] Illegal immigration in particular drives down wages at the bottom end of the pay scale. So, the problems faced by low-skilled workers are serious and represent important challenges for economic policymaking. Nevertheless, larger forces, especially trade, are responsible for most of the wage gap. Changes far beyond the scope of immigration, such as tax policy, for example, could have an effect on wage distribution, the wage gap, and declining real wages. Simply limiting the influx of foreign-born workers will not cure the problem.

Labor standards

High immigration levels invite another concern deeply rooted in the nation's history and associated with earlier peak immigration periods: declining labor standards. Images of industrial sweatshops and harvests of shame are dark chapters in America's past. Important government agencies responsible for enforcing labor protection laws have experienced steady reductions in resources for the past 25 years.[37]

Without renewed vigor in labor standards enforcement, immigration policy can enable the importation of labor that is vulnerable to exploitation, and to an undercutting of the competitive position of native workers. The immigration selection and labor regulation systems must assure that qualified US workers are not denied the opportunity to compete for a job, and that immigrants are not hired at less than competitive wages.

A related challenge is better preparing native workers for jobs in fields where they are currently less qualified than immigrant workers. Such deficiencies are pronounced in science, math, and engineering fields. The premium for job success in today's economy is on education, training, and skills. Immigration of the highly skilled must not be allowed to undercut education and retraining of — and incentives for — American workers to compete successfully for good jobs in a knowledge-based economy.

IMMIGRATION AND THE IDENTITY OF THE COUNTRY

Immigration infuses American society with a dynamism that is unique in human history. The comparatively welcoming immigration policies of the United States embody many of our core values: opportunity, hard work, sacrifice, tolerance, and pluralism. The successful integration of successive waves of newcomers in turn depends upon and revitalizes our social, cultural, and political institutions.

Dynamism

The dynamic impact of immigration is evident in daily life across the United States. Salsa now outsells ketchup; dying heartland towns are being reborn; business and government seek the foreign-language skills of first-generation Americans; political parties are vying for newly naturalized voters; baseball and basketball teams compete to sign foreign-born players; and the faith of new immigrants is contributing to the robustness of religion in the country today.[38]

The contributions of immigrants can be found in every aspect of American life. Martina Navratilova, Albert Pujols, Patrick Ewing, and Mario Andretti are esteemed sports figures; cityscapes gleam with designs by I. M. Pei and Cesar Pelli; audiences thrill to the music of Yo-Yo Ma, Placido Domingo, Zubin Mehta, and Seiji Ozawa; literature is enriched by Isabel Allende and Frank McCourt; Liz Claiborne and Oscar de la Renta are fashion icons; stellar contributions to public service have been made by John Shalikashvili, Henry Kissinger, Madeleine Albright, and Zalmay Khalilzad; Max Frankel and Peter Jennings rose to the highest echelons of journalism; Bob Hope, Mikhail Baryshnikov, Elizabeth Taylor, and Michael Fox have entertained millions; John Kenneth Galbraith and Vartan Gregorian were awarded Presidential Medals of Freedom; George Soros inspired a new era of personal philanthropy; Elie Wiesel is among many Nobel prize winners who made the United States their home; and the founders or chief executives of McDonalds, eBay, United Airlines, Coca Cola, Pfizer, Eli Lilly, Yahoo!, Kellogg, and McKinsey and Company are all immigrants.

The story of immigration encompasses much more than famous names. Immigration succeeds in large part as immigrants and their families work hard, defer gratification, and sacrifice for their children. In so doing, they play essential roles in an economy and society that values and grows through their efforts. Basic rights for all persons, including non-citizens, provide an environment that enables exceptional achievement that is unmatched by any other country.

Integration

A profusion of individual, family, and institutional initiatives provide support for integrating America's immigrant population.

A century ago, government, private organizations, and philanthropy engaged in ambitious programs of civic education, English instruction, and "Americanization" to smooth the road to full economic and social participation by immigrants. These efforts had extensive collateral benefits for the public good, including quality public schools, the adult-education system, public libraries in every community, and the settlement-house movement that established social work as a profession.[39] Society as a whole has been enriched as it has assisted immigrants.

at what cost

This revitalization continues today as immigrants, helped by strong family and kinship networks, strive to become part of the mainstream. In addition, churches, schools, libraries, hospitals, social service organizations, law enforcement, and local officials remain deeply engaged in adapting services to immigrants. The enduring good sense of this tradition is that immigrants, in turn, work hard and adopt the American civic creed and democratic values that bind us as a nation. In the process, immigrants inject new energy and patriotism into American society, serving as an ongoing source of renewal and striving.

Today's immigrants

Today's immigrants are continuing the tradition of dynamic integration into American society.

Critics argue that today's immigrants are different: They stay connected to their home countries for too long, continue to speak native languages, and do not want to assimilate into American society. It is true that many immigrants maintain close ties to the community, economy, and culture of their home countries through remittances and regular digital communication, for instance. However, these connections to a native country have been prevalent throughout the history of immigration; technology and the interdependence that is characteristic of globalization simply enables these connections to take new forms.

ok—but

In fact, the classic indicators of integration — labor force participation, language acquisition, education, military service, naturalization application rates, voting, intermarriage, and home ownership — are reassuring. Immigrants are learning English at historically high rates and continue to embrace American values, habits, and beliefs. Mexican-born men are in the labor force at higher rates than native-born Americans.[40] Over half of all immigrants own their own homes.[41] And today's immigrants intermarry at higher rates and faster than earlier ethnic groups.[42] By the second generation, most immigrants are improving their job status, paying taxes, and speaking English.[43]

indic of integ

This pattern is fully consistent with the experience of earlier waves of immigration. Still, today's large-scale immigration is generating rapid and profound social and cultural change in growing numbers of communities, almost literally before people's eyes. Not only are the sheer numbers of immigrants unprecedented, but — drawn by jobs and family ties — immigrants are now settling in medium-size cities or semi-rural areas in nearly every state in the nation. Most of these localities have not had traditions of immigration since the early decades of the 20th century.[44] Both public and private sector institutions are struggling to

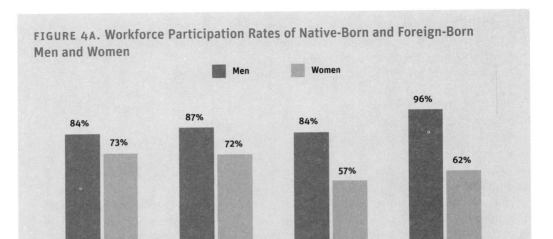

FIGURE 4A. Workforce Participation Rates of Native-Born and Foreign-Born Men and Women

Note: This graph describes an average of participation rates from 2001 and 2002.

Source: Drawn from Jeffrey S. Passel, Randolph Capps, and Michael Fix, "Undocumented Immigrants: Facts and Figures" (Washington DC: Urban Institute, January 2004).

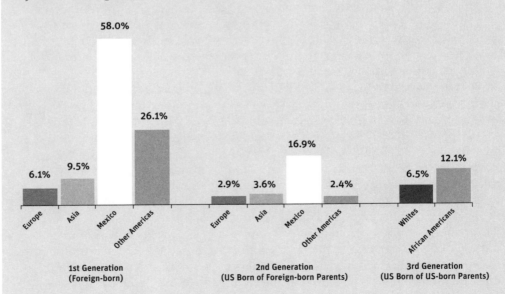

FIGURE 4B. Percent Adults (Ages 25 to 65) with Less than a High School Education by Place of Origin and Generation, 2004

Note: Europe refers to Europe, Canada, and Australia.

Source: Roger Waldinger and Renee Reichl, "Today's Second Generation: Getting Ahead or Falling Behind?" in *Securing the Future: The US Immigrant Integration Policy Agenda,* ed. Michael Fix (Washington, DC: Migration Policy Institute, forthcoming 2006).

respond, but their efforts are often complicated by the fact that a large proportion of the immigration is illegal.

It should not be surprising that social strains caused by immigration are intensifying. These tensions point to substantial challenges for immigrant integration, an often-ignored aspect of immigration policy. Yet in spite of the difficulties, the abiding story — the American Dream — of starting at the bottom of the ladder and moving up to create a better life for one's children is playing itself out as it has throughout American history. The context is a new economy in a different time.

FOREIGN POLICY AND NATIONAL SECURITY

Immigration plays an important role in the advancement of US foreign policy goals and the protection of national security. In a world in which people move more freely and easily across borders, immigration policy can enhance US prestige and influence in the world, while helping to keep bad people and things from crossing our borders.

Terrorism and criminality

The events of 9/11 tragically demonstrated how America's immigration laws can be violated or manipulated to cause terrible harm, while also signaling that immigration policy can be an important tool in stopping or monitoring terrorists and criminals.

Terrorist and criminal networks are global. Tens of millions of people enter the United States every year. The vast majority come and go properly with honest intentions. But because the United States is an open society, travel and immigration systems can be exploited by the infrastructure of smuggling, trafficking, and false document production that supports unauthorized immigration.

Sensible and effective immigration measures and tough controls are thus essential to safeguarding national security. Every time a terrorist or criminal crosses a border, an opportunity presents itself to apprehend somebody intending to do harm. Furthermore, effectively tracking the travel and smuggling patterns of terrorists and criminals can enable government officials to learn about and break up dangerous networks. In so doing, a critical challenge of the post-9/11 world is to reconcile the competing claims of security and openness.

Foreign policy

Immigration can be an important and effective tool of American foreign policy.

Immigration is an invaluable "soft power" resource that helps the United States win political influence around the world. Those who live, study, or emigrate to the United States often build up a reservoir of goodwill toward America, and learn first-hand about the American values of individual rights, personal responsibility, opportunity, freedom, pluralism, the rule of law, democratic principles, and civil society. When they return to their home countries, they help spread these values.

Indeed, educating foreign students may be one of the best long-term investments the United States makes in pursuit of international peace and prosperity,

Heads of State Educated in the United States

ANTIGUA & BARBUDA Lester Bird, Prime Minister (former)

ARGENTINA Raul Ricardo Alfonsin, President (former)

BAHRAIN Shaikh Salman bin Hamad Al Khalifa, Crown Prince and Commander-in-Chief of the Defense Force

BANGLADESH Iajuddin Ahmed, President

BOLIVIA Eduardo Rodriguez Veltze, President (former); Jorge Quiroga Ramirez, President (former); Gonzalo Sanchez de Lozada Bustamante, President (former)

CANADA Pierre Elliot Trudeau, Prime Minister (former)

CHILE Ricardo Lagos Escobar, President (former)

COSTA RICA Abel Pacheco, President; Jose Maria Figueres Olsen, President (former)

DOMINICA Roosevelt Skerrit, Prime Minister

ECUADOR Jamil Mahuad Witt, President (former)

EGYPT Atef Muhammad Muhammad Ebid, Prime Minister (former); Kamal Ahmed al-Ganzuri, Prime Minister (former)

EL SALVADOR Alfredo Felix Cristiani, President (former)

FRANCE Jacques Chirac, President

GEORGIA Mikhail Saakashvili, President

GERMANY Ernst Carl Julius Albrecht, Prime Minister (former)

GHANA Kwame Nkrumah, President (former)

GREECE Andreas George Papandreou, Prime Minister (former)

GUYANA Janet Jagan, President (former)

HONDURAS Ricardo Maduro, President; Carlos Roberto Flores, President (former)

INDONESIA Susilo Bambang Yudhoyono, President; Megawati Sukarnoputri, President (former)

IRELAND Mary Robinson, President (former), UN High Commissioner for Human Rights (former)

ISRAEL Moshe Katzav, President; Ehud Barak, Prime Minister (former); Benjamin Netanyahu, Prime Minister (former); Shimon Peres, Prime Minister (former)

JAMAICA Portia Simpson Miller, Prime Minister

JORDAN Abdullah Bin Al-Hussein, King of Jordan; Ali Abul Ragheb, Prime Minister (former); Sharif Zeid Ben Shaker, Prime Minister (former)

KAZAKHSTAN Nurlan Balgimbayev, Prime Minister (former)

LATVIA Aigars Kalvitis, Prime Minister

LEBANON Emile Lahoud, President

LIBYA Shukri Ghanem, Prime Minister (former)

LITHUANIA Valdas Adamkus, President

MALAWI Bingu wa Mutharika, President and Minister of Defense; Ngwazi Kamuzu Banda, President (former); Mahathir bin Mohammed, Prime Minister (former)

MALAYSIA Mahathir bin Mohammed, Prime Minister (former)

MEXICO Vicente Fox Quesada, President; Carlos Salinas de Gortari, President (former)

MICRONESIA Joseph J. Urusemal, President; Bailey Olter, President (former)

MONGOLIA Tsakhia Elbegdorj, Prime Minister (former)

NAMIBIA Hopelong Ipinge, Ambassador to the United States (former); Hage Gottfried Geingob, Prime Minister (former)

NEPAL Birendra Bir Birkram Shah Dev, King

NEW ZEALAND Geoffrey Palmer, Prime Minister (former)

NIGERIA Haakon Magnus, Crown Prince; Gro Harlem Brundtland, Prime Minister (former)

PAKISTAN Benazir Bhutto, President of Pakistan (former)

PALAU Tommy Remengesau, President

PANAMA Martin Torrijos, President; Ernesto Balladares, President (former); Eric Arturo Delvalle Henriquez, President (former)

PERU Alejandro Toledo, President; Alberto Fujimori, President (former); Beatriz Merino, Prime Minister (former)

PHILIPPINES Gloria Macapagal Arroyo, President; Corazon Cojuangco Aquino, President (former); Fidel V. Ramos, President (former)

SOUTH AFRICA F. W. DeKlerk, President (former)

SOUTH KOREA Kang Young Hoon, Prime Minister (former)

TAIWAN Lee Teng Hui, President (former)

TANZANIA Benjamin W. Mkapa, President (former)

THAILAND Thaksin Shinawatra-a, Prime Minister

TOGO Faure Gnassingbe, President

TONGA Prince Ulukalala Lavaka Ata, Prime Minister

TUNISIA Zine El Abidine Ben Ali, President

TURKEY Suleyman Demirel, President (former); Tansu Ciller, Prime Minister (former)

UNITED KINGDOM Tony Blair, Prime Minister

YEMEN Abdul-Aziz Abdul-Ghani, Prime Minister (former)

Sources: American International Education Foundation, http://www.ief-usa.org; American Immigration Law Foundation, "Foreign Students on Campus, An Asset to Our Nation," Immigration Policy Focus 2, Issue 1 (Washington, DC: AILF, February 2003); US Department of State, "Foreign Students Yesterday, World Leaders Today," http://exchanges.state.gov/education/educationusa/leaders.htm; US Central Intelligence Agency, "Chiefs of State and Cabinet Members of Foreign Governments."

while also bringing billions of dollars into the US economy — $13.3 billion in the 2004–2005 school year.[45] Thousands of young people — often the most talented in their societies — have studied in the United States and become leaders in politics, government, business, media, religion, and social and cultural institutions in every nation of the world. Their experiences of life in a free, open society are transmitted through that leadership, a process that advances US interests abroad in deep, long-lasting ways. Such experiences also facilitate the conduct of personal diplomacy: It is easier for an American diplomat to sit across the negotiating table from someone who lived, worked, or studied in the United States.

Issuing visas is also among the most recognizable features of American diplomacy. Visa-granting communicates respect and openness to other cultures, a commitment to economic development, and support for education and exchange. Conversely, stringent visa requirements can be a point of consternation in our relations with other countries. During the Cold War, one of the key ways the United States advanced its interests was through a comprehensive policy of international education and exchange. The policy enlisted a wide range of immigration programs to encourage foreign students to study in the United States, and to encourage exchange of scholars and citizens at all levels of society.

The administration has announced public diplomacy goals aimed at "winning hearts and minds" of people across the globe, particularly in the Islamic world. Immigration is a critical tool in accomplishing such goals. Yet changes in visa practices since 9/11 have led to fewer people coming to the United States to travel, study, and participate in conferences and exchanges.[46] Recent signs of recovery are strong, but there are key exceptions: Reports persist in the predominantly Muslim countries of the Middle East and South Asia that potential students, scholars, and other visitors are unwilling to undergo current visa procedures and no longer view the United States as a welcoming nation.[47] Such attitudes and perceptions undermine important national security interests.

In January 2006, Secretary of Homeland Security Michael Chertoff and Secretary of State Condoleezza Rice announced that the demands of security must be balanced with the need to remain an open society that welcomes international travelers, global businesses, and foreign students to advance key national economic, political, and foreign policy interests.[48] This is — and will continue to be — an important challenge for US immigration policy in a post-9/11 world.

III. What Is Wrong with US Immigration Policy and Practice?

DESPITE THE CONSIDERABLE BENEFITS of immigration, the US immigration system is broken and outdated. The most dramatic manifestation of this breakdown is that a large and growing share of today's immigration is illegal.

ILLEGAL IMMIGRATION

Illegal immigration has created a sense of crisis in much of the country.

There are approximately 37 million foreign-born persons living in the country. About 11.5 million are naturalized citizens, about 11.8 million are lawful permanent residents (LPRs), about 1.3 million have temporary or other immigrant status, and more than 11 million are unauthorized[49] (see Figure 5). Thus, nearly one-third of the foreign-born population is not authorized to be in the United States.

The size of the unauthorized population is estimated to be growing by about 500,000 per year. In recent years, annual levels of illegal immigration sometimes may have exceeded those of legal permanent immigration, and best estimates show that in 15 states, the unauthorized population is about as large, or even exceeds, the size of the legal immigrant population.[50] Two-thirds of the more than 11 million persons illegally in the country are believed to have been here for ten years or less.[51]

Illegal immigration is primarily a response to laws of supply and demand — workers filling workforce openings — that have proven more powerful than immigration enforcement. Two-thirds of the total unauthorized population is working, accounting for slightly less than five percent of the labor force nationwide. More than three out of five unauthorized women and 96 percent of men are employed. The unauthorized population is overrepresented in a growing number of occupations. For instance, unauthorized workers comprise 24 percent of workers in farming occupations, 17 percent in cleaning services, 14 percent in construction, and 12 percent in food preparation.[52] The majority of the jobs are year-round and not limited to occupations traditionally associated with illegal immigration, such as seasonal agricultural work. Meanwhile, spiraling numbers of deaths at the border are an ongoing humanitarian crisis, and the unprecedented fivefold increase in resources aimed at enforcement along the southwest border

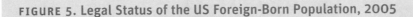

FIGURE 5. Legal Status of the US Foreign-Born Population, 2005

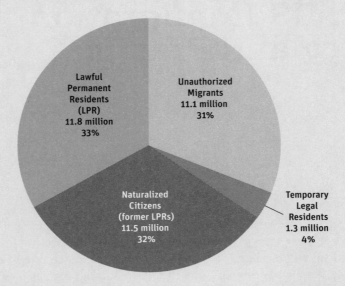

Lawful Permanent Residents (LPR)
11.8 million
33%

Unauthorized Migrants
11.1 million
31%

Naturalized Citizens (former LPRs)
11.5 million
32%

Temporary Legal Residents
1.3 million
4%

Note: While the unauthorized population was estimated at 11.1 million in 2005, the estimate for 2006 is 11.5 to 12 million, which is the number used elsewhere in this report.
Source: Jeffrey S. Passel, "The Size and Characteristics of the Unauthorized Migrant Population in the U.S." (Washington, DC: Pew Hispanic Center, March 2006).

over the last two decades has failed to slow high levels of illegal immigration[53] (see Figure 6).

Illegal immigration is not a new phenomenon. In 1986, when the unauthorized population was estimated to be four to six million, Congress enacted legislation that for the first time made it illegal for employers to hire immigrants who were not authorized to work. Combined with border control and legalization of the illegal population that had been in the country for at least five years, the goal was to "wipe the slate clean" for effective immigration control.

In practice, the legislation failed to solve the problem of illegal immigration. Employer enforcement has proven difficult, in large part because fraudulent documents became readily available, and the legislation did not mandate a reliable way for employers to verify the legal status of those they were hiring. Serious efforts to strengthen border enforcement did not begin until a decade later. Although legalization resulted in about 2.8 million people being able to obtain legal status and ultimately permanent residency, those who were here for less than five years stayed and became the nucleus of today's unauthorized population. The 1986 law did not anticipate the deep changes in labor markets, demographics, and the pace of globalization that were just ahead.

For a nation of immigrants that is also a nation of laws, the current level of unauthorized immigrant flows is indefensible and dangerous. Illegal immigration has fueled deep resentment of immigration more generally, and has led to widespread skepticism about the capacity of the government to secure the southern border and manage immigration, especially in ways that promote the nation's security, economic success, and social and cultural well-being.

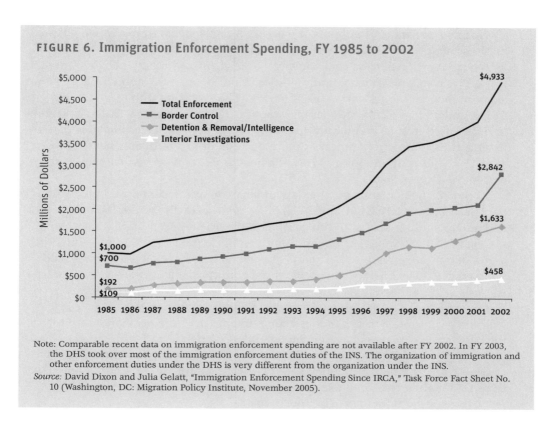

FIGURE 6. Immigration Enforcement Spending, FY 1985 to 2002

Note: Comparable recent data on immigration enforcement spending are not available after FY 2002. In FY 2003, the DHS took over most of the immigration enforcement duties of the INS. The organization of immigration and other enforcement duties under the DHS is very different from the organization under the INS.

Source: David Dixon and Julia Gelatt, "Immigration Enforcement Spending Since IRCA," Task Force Fact Sheet No. 10 (Washington, DC: Migration Policy Institute, November 2005).

TEMPORARY IMMIGRATION

Along with illegal immigration, nonimmigrant (temporary) immigration programs constitute the primary ways immigration has adapted to meet new conditions and labor market demands.

Temporary immigration programs have increasingly been used as a step to permanent immigration. Traditionally, the purpose of temporary immigration visas has been to meet seasonal or transitory needs and shortages. Increasingly, however, temporary workers and visa categories are meeting standing, ongoing labor market needs and employer preferences. In response, there has been explosive growth in the categories and numbers of temporary immigration programs, creating a patchwork system of visas tailored to specific types of workers or entrants. As a result, illegal immigration is meeting the nation's low-skill demands, and temporary visa programs in the legal immigration system are meeting the demands for mostly high-skilled immigration[54] (see Appendix I: Temporary Visa Categories and Admission Numbers for Fiscal Year 2004).

The scale of the various agricultural, non-agricultural, and high-skilled visa programs that admit temporary workers and their dependents is at an historic high. The number of H and L temporary visas issued more than tripled from 136,000 in FY 1992 to about 440,000 in FY 2005.[55] Demand for H-1B visas, the primary path for high-skilled workers, is so high that the annual cap has typically been met before the fiscal year even begins.[56] The roughly 550,000 temporary work visas for employment in FY 2004 outnumbered by nearly four-fold the cap on employment-based admissions in the current permanent immigration system.[57]

This new reliance on temporary workers reflects global trends in which business adapts to changing market conditions by tapping skilled professionals drawn from a global labor pool. However, this growing dependence on temporary workers is also a response to the rigidities of the permanent immigration system, because most of the jobs are not temporary. The migrants who fill them and their employer sponsors are manipulating the temporary categories as first steps to permanent immigration. And the immigration system accommodates that by having either selectively removed the requirement for "temporariness" or by allowing holders of temporary visas to adjust to permanent visa categories from within the United States.

Of the 980,000 persons granted lawful permanent resident status on average each year between FY 2001 and 2005, 61 percent were already in the country and adjusting their status. In the case of employment-based immigrants, the rate was 80 percent.[58] Thus, permanent immigration to the United States is largely a product of the adjustment of status of persons who have already established strong ties to jobs and labor markets in the country while in various temporary statuses or here illegally.

Employers have learned to rely on the temporary system to gain access to workers because it is faster and less cumbersome than the permanent immigration system. Lawmakers have encouraged that tendency by failing to reconfigure permanent immigration. In turn, the number of temporary immigrants eligible to adjust to permanent residency keeps growing, adding to backlogs of applications for an already inadequate number of permanent slots, and making the permanent system increasingly unresponsive.

THE LEGAL IMMIGRATION SELECTION SYSTEM

The immigration selection system rarely realizes its core goals of meeting family reunification and labor market demands. Immigration critics often call for intending immigrants to "play by the rules." However, the rules do not work effectively.

Immigrants who try to immigrate legally (and family members and employers who sponsor them) quickly are constrained by immigration category caps, as well as caps that limit each country to no more than 7 percent (approximately 25,600) of the total number of annual worldwide visas (see Appendix II: Legal Immigration Preference System). The purpose of the per-country caps is to prevent high-demand countries from dominating others. But it has led to unreasonable delays for employers and family unification applicants from countries such as Mexico, China, India, and the Philippines. For instance, a US citizen sponsoring an unmarried child from Mexico is likely to endure a nearly 14-year wait for unification, and an LPR sponsoring a spouse can expect to wait six years regardless of country of origin. The wait can extend to 23 years for siblings of US citizens from the Philippines (see Table 5). In addition to being inhumane, such waits mean that a large portion of such individuals' productive working years that make immigration a good investment will have passed by the time many ever arrive in the United States.

Delays in employment-based immigration mean that the system often fails to meet labor market needs. Inflexible statutory ceilings, limits in allocation of numbers to high-demand countries, and overly complex procedures all

TABLE 5. Date of Submission of Lawful Permanent Residence Applications Processed July 2006

	Mainland China	India	Mexico	Philippines	All Other Countries
Family					
1st Unmarried Adult Children of Citizens	Jan. 1, 2000	Jan. 1, 2000	May 15, 1992	Sep. 22, 1991	Jan. 1, 2000
2A Spouses/Minor Children of LPRs	Sep. 1, 1999	Sep. 1, 1999	Sep. 1, 1999	Sep. 1, 1999	Sep. 1, 1999
2B Unmarried Adult Children of LPRs	Aug. 22, 1996	Aug. 22, 1996	Dec. 1, 1991	Jul. 8, 1996	Aug. 22, 1996
3rd Married Adult Children of Citizens	Aug. 22, 1998	Aug. 22, 1998	Oct. 15, 1993	Jul. 1, 1988	Aug. 22, 1998
4th Siblings of US Citizens	May 1, 1995	Oct. 1, 1994	Aug. 15, 1993	Dec. 15, 1983	May 1, 1995
Employment					
1st Priority Workers/Persons with Extraordinary Ability	Current	Jan. 1, 2006	Current	Current	Current
2nd Professionals with Advanced Degrees/Persons with Exceptional Ability	Mar. 1, 2005	Jan. 1, 2003	Current	Current	Current
3rd Skilled or Professional Workers	Oct. 1, 2001	Apr. 15, 2001	Apr. 22, 2001	Oct. 1, 2001	Oct. 1, 2001
Schedule A Workers[1]	Current	Current	Current	Current	Current
Other Workers[2]	Unavailable	Unavailable	Unavailable	Unavailable	Unavailable
4th Special Immigrants/Religious Workers	Current	Current	Current	Current	Current
5th Immigrant Investors/Targeted Employment Areas	Current	Current	Current	Current	Current

1 Schedule A workers include physical therapists, nurses, and immigrants of exceptional ability in the sciences and arts (except performing arts). Schedule A is a list of occupations for which the Department of Labor delegates authority to USCIS to approve labor certifications.

2 No visas were available in the "Other Workers" category. "Other workers" includes persons capable of filling positions requiring less than two years' training or experience.

Source: US Department of State, "Visa Bulletin No. 95, Vol. VIII," July 2006.

contribute to employers not getting workers when they need them.[59] Skilled workers and professionals with a job offer may wait five years for a visa. Persons of "exceptional ability" may have to wait over three years for an employment visa if they are from India[60] (see Table 5). Visa supply is also a poor fit with demand. Just 5,000 visas are available worldwide each year for low-skilled workers.[61] Yet as many as 500,000 unauthorized immigrants are added to the nation's population each year, the majority of whom work, mostly in low-wage jobs. Thus, legal channels for meeting important elements of labor market demand are often all but nonexistent.

Delays in processing applications also contribute to difficulties in family reunification and employment. Many applications pass through three separate agencies: Citizenship and Immigration Services (USCIS) at the Department of Homeland Security (DHS), the Department of Labor (DOL), and the Bureau of Consular Affairs at the Department of State. Each has its own applications, processing requirements, fees, backlogs, and information tracking and data systems.

As has historically been the case, individual immigrants continue to be selected because of their sponsorship by employers or family members. However,
permanent immigration has transformed into a ratification of decisions
already made in the marketplace. The system's multiple shortcomings have
led to a loss of integrity in legal immigration processes. These shortcomings
contribute to unauthorized migration when families choose illegal immigration
rather than waiting unreasonable periods for legal entry, and employers hire
unauthorized workers because legal channels are oversubscribed, delayed by
processing backlogs, or simply unavailable. Hallmarks of the system are inflex-
ibility and Congressional behavior that alternates between micromanagement
and inaction. The combination has led to policymaking by exception, and has
stymied the fundamental re-thinking needed to adapt to 21st-century conditions
and needs.

FILLING A VACUUM: STATE AND LOCAL ROLES

The failure of federal immigration policy to adapt to new realities has put an
unsustainable burden on state and local governments, including many without
recent experience integrating immigrant populations.

Integration of immigrants has always occurred primarily through the efforts of
families, employers, schools, and communities at the local level. But immigration
policy has been an issue of exclusive federal authority and responsibility. Today,
a process of devolution of this responsibility is underway because of the failure
of the federal government to address major shortcomings in immigration policy
and practice. The vacuum has forced state and local governments to address
the day-to-day consequences of large-scale immigration in new ways. Federal
failures have also severely eroded public support for immigration, polarized
public opinion, and placed burdens on state and local governments that they are
ill-equipped to handle.

Heightened pressures on states have made immigration an important new issue
facing state legislatures and officials. Immigration is the subject of 540 bills already
in 2006 in 27 states.[62] In 2005, about 300 bills were introduced and 37 became
law.[63] A set of disparate policies is emerging. Georgia has authorized employer
enforcement to combat illegal hiring.[64] Arizona and Colorado have voted to deny
state benefits, including non-emergency health care, to anyone who cannot prove
legal residence.[65] The governors of Arizona and New Mexico declared states of
emergency to tap special funds that would buttress inadequate border enforcement.[66] Ten states are allowing high school graduates who do not have legal status
to attend state colleges and universities at in-state resident tuition rates.[67]

State and local authorities are also coping with new and increasing federal requirements they see as unfunded mandates. The best known is the REAL ID Act
requirement for drivers' licenses, passed by Congress in 2005.[68] The law requires
that states verify the legal status of those to whom they issue drivers' licenses.
If they do not meet federal verification standards, state licenses will not be
considered valid identification for federal purposes — such as boarding airplanes.
Some states, including New Hampshire and Washington, have expressed
strong opposition to this measure.[69] In addition to the REAL ID Act, federal
officials are pressing hard to enlist state and local assistance in immigration law
enforcement.

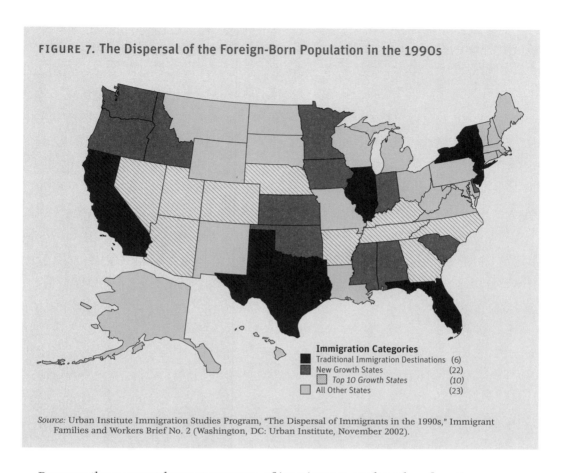

FIGURE 7. The Dispersal of the Foreign-Born Population in the 1990s

Immigration Categories
Traditional Immigration Destinations (6)
New Growth States (22)
Top 10 Growth States (10)
All Other States (23)

Source: Urban Institute Immigration Studies Program, "The Dispersal of Immigrants in the 1990s," Immigrant Families and Workers Brief No. 2 (Washington, DC: Urban Institute, November 2002).

Because the new settlement patterns of immigrants are largely a function of the availability of jobs and slowing growth in the native-born workforce, immigration is no longer an issue for just a few states. The six traditional immigrant-receiving states — California, New York, Texas, Florida, New Jersey, and Illinois — have seen a decline in their share of the immigrant population. States with the most rapidly growing foreign-born populations between 1990 and 2000 included many with traditionally small immigrant populations. They include North Carolina, Georgia, Nevada, Arkansas, Tennessee, Colorado, Arizona, Nebraska, and Utah[70] (see Figure 7). These states have less experience with new immigrant populations and typically lack the infrastructure and civil society institutions that have traditionally been engaged in immigrant integration.

Complicating the process of immigrant integration is the fact that costs and benefits are not evenly felt or allocated. Taxes paid to the federal government and the productivity of the macro economy make immigration a net benefit to the nation. At the local level, however, communities are faced with unanticipated demands for services, particularly in education and health care.[71] These fiscal costs are offset by the taxes immigrants pay, their entrepreneurship, lower prices for goods and services, and new growth and vitality for communities. But the revenues and costs flow to and from different pockets. The mismatch is experienced most acutely at the local level.

At a time when English-language learning, educational attainment, naturalization preparation, and workforce development should be high priority initiatives, state and local governments are severely handicapped in their ability to manage integration tasks due to a federal failure to control unauthorized immigration, and by the additional burdens of responding to matters that have traditionally been uniquely federal responsibilities.

IV. An Immigration Policy and System for the 21st Century

THE IMMIGRATION SYSTEM IS BADLY out of step with and often works at cross-purposes to US interests. The United States will require substantial levels of both high- and low-skilled immigration to sustain a successful 21st-century economy. There is an urgent need for new and comprehensive thinking that incorporates immigration fully into broad national policies. We are in a new era; we need a new immigration policy and system.

THE CURRENT DEBATE

The nation's attention is currently focused on illegal immigration, which colors people's views about all aspects of immigration. Americans are deeply divided and conflicted in their opinions about whether immigration helps or hurts the country, and what policies should be implemented to combat illegal immigration. When asked to choose among various policy options, respondents frequently give contradictory answers. Perceptions of immigrants are more positive in high-immigration locales than in communities less affected by immigration. Yet concern about the scale and burdens of illegal immigration are growing, and Americans do not give the government high marks for managing immigration policy, especially border protection.

Deep divisions and genuine differences of opinion help explain why the country's elected leaders and political system have been unable to produce solutions. At the same time, mounting public frustration has created a harsh political environment that is not conducive to sound policymaking.

The House and Senate bills

The deep divide in how to respond to illegal immigration is reflected in starkly different approaches taken in legislation enacted by the two houses of Congress.

The House of Representatives passed a bill in December 2005 that calls for tough new enforcement measures at the border and in the interior of the country. Its logic is that immigration is fundamentally an issue of national sovereignty and the rule of law. Known as the enforcement-only approach, the bill discounts the economic forces and family connections that drive illegal immigration and have historically proven to be more powerful than law enforcement measures.

The Senate legislation that passed in May 2006 also adopts stringent enforcement measures. Bipartisan and comprehensive, it also expands legal immigration, including the opportunity to earn legal status for most of those currently in the country illegally. Its logic — that illegal immigration is a market phenomenon requiring both increased enforcement and increased immigration — is more realistic and promising. Yet although it is preferable to the House bill, the Senate bill does not address all of the issues that need attention. Illegal immigration is a symptom of deep-seated problems in the immigration system itself. The system cannot be repaired by simply adding visa categories and new programs to an already unwieldy array of temporary and permanent visas and procedures that are overly complex and unsuitable for the conditions that shape immigration flows.

The work of the Task Force

Confronting the problem of illegal immigration is long overdue, but it is not enough. Immigration policies that tap the benefits of immigration are increasingly important for securing the economic future and interests of the United States. The Independent Task Force on Immigration and America's Future was convened to grapple with the issues of illegal immigration and the role of immigration for the future. Its deliberations have led to an approach that is more comprehensive than either the House or Senate has contemplated.

The Task Force recommendations are based on careful analysis of the economic, social, and demographic factors driving today's large-scale immigration flows, illegal and legal. Its core conclusion is that the benefits of immigration significantly advance US national interests in the 21st century. However, harnessing those benefits over the longer term requires fundamentally re-thinking US policies, and overhauling the nation's system for managing immigration.

NEW ASSUMPTIONS

For most of the nation's history, the goals of immigration policy have been family unity, meeting labor market needs, and humanitarian protection.[72] These goals remain sound. However, fundamental policy changes must be made to achieve these goals in practice because of an aging native-born population, a globally interdependent economy, post-9/11 security imperatives, and historic challenges in integrating new immigrants. In addition, the immigration system has become overly complex, with a proliferation of visa categories and mandates that are difficult to enforce. Reforms must include an effort to simplify both the streams through which the United States welcomes immigrants and the enforcement of the rules governing the system, as well as to enable integration policies to be vigorously pursued by all levels of government.

The new assumptions that must guide immigration policymaking are:

- *Continuing large-scale immigration.* Large-scale immigration is likely to continue for the foreseeable future. During earlier peak immigration periods, numerical limits on immigration did not exist as they do today. Thus, enforcing numerical limits during a period of large-scale flows is a new challenge. In addition, the imperative of immigrant integration is unprecedented. Earlier periods of large flows were followed by slow periods that provided time for American society and newcomers to adjust. Moreover, more education and skills are required to succeed in the information age than in earlier manufacturing and agricultural economies. Leaders at all levels must be candid in educating the public about these new circumstances and the capabilities that are needed.

■ *Regulatory approaches.* Fixed, statutory ceilings as the framework for immigration policy must give way to methods that meet changing demand while regulating flows that represent important assets for the nation. The movement of people is different from the movement of information, goods, and capital, but some of the techniques that have been successful in regulating those flows can be applied to immigration. In a global marketplace, talent pools are international and growing numbers of people live in more than one country during the course of their lives. Having the flexibility to take account of increasing mobility is thus a key characteristic of a successful 21st-century immigration policy.

■ *Comprehensive policies.* Immigration is a complex, sprawling area of policy that requires that many different pieces work together. Fixing the immigration system involves border and employer enforcement, increased legal immigration, labor protections for all workers, local initiatives to support integration, and international cooperation. Policymaking and implementation require coordination among many different disciplines, agencies, and the public and private sectors.

■ *Complementarity with other economic and social policies.* Long-term competitiveness calls for immigration policy to be integrated with reforms in education, labor market and workforce preparedness, and international development, among others. Immigration policies should work with, rather than against, such key policy priorities, just as other policy domains face the challenge to incorporate and adapt to immigration. Doing so will demand enticing more of America's most talented young people to pursue math and science careers, which, in turn, must begin to offer some of the rewards available to law and business graduates today. Nor should such efforts focus only on high-level talent. Changing the way in which society views — and rewards — all work, regardless of formal skill and education levels, requires creating opportunity and rewarding effort and hard work throughout the economy, so that various economic sectors do not become dominated with work that "Americans will not do." Immigration should be but one of several key ingredients to ensure competitiveness in the long term. Immigration can augment and complement — not substitute for — sound human capital strategies and investment.

The Task Force recommendations build on these assumptions, and envision a simplification of the immigration system that is intended to make it fair and able to be governed by rules that are practical, enforceable, and in keeping with the nation's history, values, and interests. The Task Force hopes its analysis and recommendations serve as the foundation for a new discourse about immigration and immigration policy for the 21st century.

V. Attracting the Immigrants the United States Wants and Needs

RECOMMENDATION #1: The Task Force recommends the simplification and fundamental redesign of the immigration system of the United States. Immigration should take place through three new streams: temporary, provisional, and permanent. A redesigned system is the best way to meet the nation's current and future labor market needs.

Simplification

RECOMMENDATION #2: The Task Force recommends creating an independent federal agency to be called The Standing Commission on Immigration and Labor Markets. The Standing Commission would make regular recommendations to Congress for adjusting admissions levels in the temporary, provisional, and permanent immigration streams based on labor market needs, unemployment patterns, and changing economic and demographic trends.

Agency for levels

The deepening transformation of the US economy in an era of globalization demands a parallel transformation of the immigration selection system. The United States needs a system that accomplishes timely family unification and attracts the immigrant workers required for the United States to compete even more effectively in the 21st century.

NUMBERS AND CATEGORIES OF IMMIGRATION

Official data on net levels of immigration are misleading, and there is a profound mismatch between the supply and demand for permanent visas.

The existing system

Over the past five years, just under two-thirds of immigrants have been sponsored by US citizen family members, 17 percent have been employment-based, and 11 percent have been humanitarian admissions (refugees, asylees, etc.) The remainder fall into miscellaneous groups.[73] For those without family or employment ties, there are few means of legal entry (see Appendix II: Legal

Immigration Preference System, which outlines the family- and employment-based immigration preference categories and numerical limitations).

Official data report and define permanent immigration as the number of lawful permanent residents who are admitted each year. Based on that method of tallying, average annual immigration has been approximately 980,500 between FY 2001 and 2005.[74] As Figure 8 shows, overall admission numbers vary significantly from year to year (the number for FY 2005, for example, was 1.1 million) because of differences in the number of those adjusting from temporary to permanent status, changes in funding for and productivity by government agencies processing applications, and the availability of visa numbers. However, these numbers do not provide a full picture of actual net immigration into the United States in any one year.

The Task Force estimates that the actual net annual level of immigration averaged approximately 1.8 million between FY 2001 and 2005, almost double the numbers captured in official data of permanent immigration to the country (see Table 6). The numbers that comprise actual net annual immigration include not only new LPRs, but also some groups of temporary workers and their dependents, and unauthorized immigrants. The difference between the official and the actual numbers results primarily from two factors:

- illegal immigration is occurring at high levels; and

- where legal means are available, labor market demand is being met by large numbers of temporary work visa holders who often fill permanent jobs and are de facto immigrants.

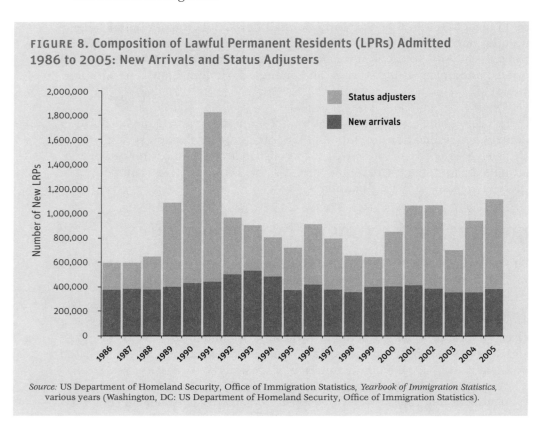

FIGURE 8. Composition of Lawful Permanent Residents (LPRs) Admitted 1986 to 2005: New Arrivals and Status Adjusters

Source: US Department of Homeland Security, Office of Immigration Statistics, *Yearbook of Immigration Statistics,* various years (Washington, DC: US Department of Homeland Security, Office of Immigration Statistics).

TABLE 6. Approximation of Actual Annual Immigration

	Average Number, FY 2001 to 2005
The Unauthorized (estimate by Jeffrey Passel)	500,000
All New Lawful Permanent Residents	980,478
Temporary Workers and Dependents*	324,586
H-1B	78,031
H-2B	43,611
O-1	3,836
Dependents of H-1B, H-2B, O	125,478
K, S, T, U	43,702
V	29,928
Total	1,805,064

* This is an estimate of the number of workers who entered each year on temporary visas intending to stay permanently, but obtained temporary visas rather than permanent visas because it was easier and faster to do so. We assume that 60 percent of H-1B, H-2B, and O-1 visa holders intend to remain in the country permanently, and that all K, S, T, U, and V visa holders will remain in the country permanently. We also assume that H-1B, H-2B, and O visa holders will bring an average of one dependent per principal.

Sources: Jeffrey S. Passel, "The Size and Characteristics of the Unauthorized" (Washington, DC: Pew Hispanic Center, March 2006); US Department of Homeland Security, *Yearbook of Immigration Statistics*: 2001–2005 (Washington, DC: US Department of Homeland Security Office of Immigration Statistics, 2006); US Department of State, Report of the Visa Office, 2005.

A core principle of the current system, which has been in place since 1952, has been separating temporary (non-immigrant) and permanent (immigrant) visas, as temporary visas were not intended to lead to permanent immigration. Yet through incremental changes in law and practice, many temporary visas are now temporary in name only. As stated earlier, over 60 percent of all LPRs between FY 2001 and 2005 were adjustments of status of people already in the country, rather than new arrivals.[75] In addition, those with temporary visas who are de facto immigrants are not counted in official estimates of permanent annual immigration until the year of their formal adjustment to permanent status.

As indicated in Table 7, 547,350 visas were issued in work-based temporary visa categories by consular officials in FY 2004.[76] The figure is roughly comparable to the estimated annual net increase in the unauthorized population, and is almost four times higher than the statutory cap on permanent employment-based visas.

Other significant characteristics of the immigration selection system include the following:

■ *Workers in the primary employment-based categories of the immigration system account for less than 8 percent of the annual LPR numbers.* This is particularly striking given the Task Force calculation that the US economy absorbs nearly one million immigrant workers each year.[77] Furthermore, although the law authorizes 140,000 permanent visas for employment each year, only about half that number of workers actually enters through that part of the admissions system each year. The reason is that dependents (spouses and children) are counted against the cap, and use half of the 140,000 visas. In contrast, approximately 70 percent of temporary work visas are issued to the principal applicant.[78]

TABLE 7. Temporary Work-Based Visa Issuances and Admissions, FY 2004

Visa Category	Admissions	Visas Issued	Ratio of Admissions to Visas Issued[2]
Treaty traders (E-1)	47,083	8,608	5.47
Treaty investors (E-2)	135,851	28,213	4.82
Specialty occupations (H-1B)	386,821	138,958	2.78
Registered Nurses (H-1A)	7,795	-	-
Chile/Singapore Free Trade Agreement (H-1B1)	326	79	4.13
Registered Nurses for Disadvantaged Areas (H-1C)	70	110	0.64
Agricultural workers (H-2A)	22,141	31,774	0.70
Nonagricultural workers (H-2B)	86,958	76,169	1.14
Industrial trainees (H-3)	2,226	1,410	1.58
Spouses and children of H1, H2, and H3 workers (H-4)	130,847	83,127	1.57
Intracompany transferees (L-1)	314,484	62,700	5.02
Spouses and children of intracompany transferees (L-2)	142,099	59,164	2.40
Workers with extraordinary ability/achievement (O-1)	27,127	6,437	4.21
Workers accompanying, assisting in performance of O1 workers (O-2)	6,332	2,611	2.43
Spouses and children of O1 and O2 workers (O-3)	3,719	1,679	2.22
Internationally recognized athletes or entertainers (P-1)	40,466	22,269	1.82
Artists or entertainers in reciprocal exchange programs (P-2)	3,810	211	18.06
Artists or entertainers in culturally unique programs (P-3)	10,038	8,689	1.16
Spouses and children of P1, P2, and P3 workers (P-4)	1,853	871	2.13
Workers in international cultural exchange programs (Q-1)	2,113	1,570	1.35
Workers in Irish Peace Process Cultural and Training Program (Q-2)	368	11	33.45
Spouses and children of Q2 workers (Q-3)	11	0	-
Workers in religious occupations (R-1)	21,571	8,806	2.45
Spouses and children of R1 workers (R-2)	6,443	2,976	2.16
Professional workers US-Canada Free-Trade Agreement (TC)	12	-	-
Spouses and children of Canada Free Trade workers (TB)	40	-	-
Professional workers NAFTA (TN)[1]	66,207	908	NA
Spouses and children of NAFTA workers (TD)	12,595	-	-
Total	**1,479,406**	**547,350**	**2.70**

Notes: The visas included here reflect our definition of "work-based" visas. While some J and F visa holders also work, no data is available on how many work and how many do not. Therefore, J and F visas were not included in this table. This definition of work-based visas differs from the definition used by the DHS Office of Immigration Statistics, which does not include E visas, for example. The E-3 visa for Australians was not created until 2004, so there were no E-3 visas issued or admissions in FY 2004.

[1] The number of TN visas (for NAFTA workers) issued reflects TN visas issued to Mexican workers but does not reflect the number of Canadian NAFTA workers entering the United States, as these individuals are not required to hold a visa. The number of TN admissions includes admissions of both Mexican and Canadian NAFTA workers.

[2] Data on admissions and visas issued provide two different measures of the level of immigration under a particular temporary visa type. Admissions count the number entries to the United States on a particular visa in a given year. If a single person enters the country twice in a year, that person will account for two admissions. Data on visas issued reflects the number of a particular type of visa issued in a given year. Not all visas issued are used in the year in which they are issued, and some are never used at all. However, given that admissions figures may count a single person multiple times, data on visas issued gives a better proxy for the number of people who enter on a given visa in a given year.

Sources: Deborah W. Meyers, "Temporary Worker Programs: A Patchwork Policy Response," Task Force Insight No. 12 (Washington, DC: Migration Policy Institute, January 2006). Based on US Department of State "Report of the Visa Office," 2004; US Department of Homeland Security, *Yearbook of Immigration Statistics,* 2004 (Washington, DC: US Department of Homeland Security Office of Immigration Statistics, 2006).

- *Statutory ceilings do not accurately represent the actual numbers of admissions in certain categories.* For instance, the H-1B temporary worker visa (skilled professionals) is currently capped at 65,000. However, an additional 20,000 visas are available for those who earned an advanced degree at a US university or work for educational institutions and employees of government or nonprofit research organizations are exempt from the cap.[79] As a result, the actual number of H-1B visas issued annually now exceeds 100,000. (There were 124,100 H-1B visas issued in FY 2005.) Similarly, the ceiling on family-based immigration is 480,000, but it can be pierced based on the number of immediate relatives of US citizens, who are numerically exempt. In practice, the levels have been running over 600,000 in recent years.[80]

- *Statutory ceilings also bear little relationship to the demand for immigrant workers.* While 5,000 permanent employment-based visas are available each year for unskilled workers, approximately 500,000 unauthorized immigrants are being added to the US population each year and an estimated 300,000 – 350,000 enter the US labor force.[81] The overwhelming majority work and find jobs in the low-skill, low-wage, low-value-added sectors of the economy. Similarly, although the H-2A program for temporary agricultural workers has no caps, the program is deeply underutilized. It is seen as overly bureaucratic and unresponsive to employers and it contains few commensurate gains for workers. With little enforcement against illegal hiring, there are few incentives to use the program. Only about 31,000 H-2A visas are issued annually when over half of the nation's agricultural work force of over 2 million is estimated to be unauthorized.[82]

- *The terms "non-immigrant" or "temporary" visas are often misleading.* Requirements for temporary visas vary widely regarding duration of stay (a few months to as long as an activity lasts), educational qualifications (none to advanced degrees), labor market tests, and eligibility to adjust to permanent status. In response to ad hoc changes in immigration law over time, temporary visas are often issued for unlimited tenure jobs, with adjustment to permanent status from temporary visas now permitted for half of all temporary worker admissions (H-1s, L-1s, and O-1s).[83]

The requirements for what are termed "temporary" and "permanent" visas have become excessively complex, improvised, and misleading. The chaotic nature of immigration rules represents a true public policy danger in that the system invites manipulation by potential workers and employers, ad hoc fixes by policymakers, and widespread loss of confidence from the public.

The immigration system should provide legal channels for effectively regulating employment-based immigration — regardless of skill levels — so that immigration can function as a strategic national resource. Sufficient opportunities for legal immigration to meet labor market needs will reduce pressures for illegal immigration, providing the opportunity for border enforcement and other controls to become more effective.

A proposal for a new system

The Task Force proposal sets immigration levels of approximately 1.5 million annually as a starting point. That number would be adjusted every two years on the basis of the analysis and recommendations of a new agency, The Standing

Commission on Immigration and Labor Markets, described below. The starting point of 1.5 million is about 300,000 less than the true annual levels of immigration, 1.8 million, that the United States is experiencing. The 1.5 million admissions number is a transparent and realistic benchmark from which to manage immigration as it is actually occurring. The proposed level is less than today's 1.8 million because some whom the system "locks in" can be expected to choose to travel to and from the country for work purposes if they can, rather than relocate residences with their dependents as happens today.

In addition, the proposal rationalizes an outdated selection system, provides legal channels of entry for immigration that is occurring illegally in response to legitimate labor market demands, and envisions regular numerical adjustments in response to changing economic and demographic conditions. Because family-based immigrants work and employment-based immigrants bring their families, family and employment-based immigration overlap. Nonetheless, the crisis in immigration policy turns on labor market issues. Thus, the policy focus of the proposal is primarily on employment-based immigration.

The Task Force proposal would accomplish the following:

- simplify the increasingly complex array of specialized visa categories and procedures so the system can better meet family unification of the closest family members and labor market goals in actual practice;

- establish legal channels to regulate and manage varying immigration flows that are responding to employer, worker, and family conditions in the United States and elsewhere;

- provide flexibility to adapt to rapid changes and adjust numerical levels of immigration based on systematic and ongoing review of the impacts of immigration on the country; and

- recognize that temporary and permanent immigration are often a continuum that is beneficial to the economy and society. The linkage between temporary and permanent immigration should be acknowledged in immigration policy because it is the way immigration really happens, and it contributes to the vibrancy of the economy and to successful immigrant integration.

The proposal has the following key features:

- It creates a new immigration stream called provisional visas. Provisional visas allow for lengthier stays than temporary visas and for the opportunity of bridging to permanent immigration after several years, based on meeting employment and other criteria.

- It provides opportunities for employment-based immigration of all skill types in the permanent stream.

- It provides a new type of visa — strategic growth visas — in the permanent stream to help the United States compete more effectively for international talent.

- It organizes employment-based immigration around streamlined employer recruitment procedures as the best way to allocate immigrant labor efficiently, consistent with appropriate rights and protections of all workers.

- It provides for biennial adjustments of immigration levels, based on ongoing analysis of the impact of immigration on labor markets and the economy.

Such a system would respond to a broad set of current and future labor market needs by providing for legal, regulated flows in a flexible, transparent fashion. It would eliminate the rationale for large, guest-worker programs from an earlier era that tie workers to a single employer with no opportunity to qualify for permanent immigration.

During World War II, the United States and Mexico established such a program — the bracero program — that lasted until 1964. The Task Force has concluded that bracero-like guest-worker programs do not match workers with employers in ways that uphold the nation's values and interests. Bracero-like guest-worker status circumscribes the labor and other rights of workers, which, in turn, undermines the interests of US workers.[84] Such programs also explicitly foreclose integration, even as the workers often remain in the country, leading to the likelihood of such workers and their families living for long periods at the margins of the economy and society.

The broad outlines of the proposal for a new system follow. The proposed system is described in full in Appendix III-a, Summary of a Proposed Simplified Temporary and Provisional Visa System, and III-b, Summary of Proposed Changes in Redesigned Permanent Immigrant System.

Temporary immigration

Temporary (non-immigrant) visas play an important role in a healthy immigration system that contributes to a dynamic and fluid economy. However, the temporary visa system has become exceedingly complex, sprawling, unnecessarily complicated, and is often used to meet ongoing labor market needs in permanent jobs.

There are 24 temporary visa categories delineated in the Immigration and Nationality Act (INA) by letters. Over 70 sub-categories (e.g., H-1A, H-1B, H-2A, H-2B, etc.), have been created to accommodate a widening menu of specialized purposes.[85] For example, there is now an H-1B1 visa for professionals who qualify under the Chile or Singapore Free Trade Agreement (see Appendix I: Temporary Visa Categories and Admission Numbers for Fiscal Year 2004, for the detailed listing).

The Task Force proposes a streamlining and reduction of the 24 principal categories to seven, and the 70 or more sub-categories to 25. Four of the seven new principal categories belong in a redefined temporary visa stream.

Temporary visas would include the following:

- *Visitor visas (V).* Approximately 90 percent of temporary admissions to the United States each year are short-term tourists and visitors for business.[86] These visitors would continue to be granted a visa of limited duration and would not be authorized to work or to bring family members who do not have their own visas.

- *Representatives of foreign governments, international organizations, and foreign media (R).* This category would combine four current categories and maintain their requirements.

- *Treaty and Reciprocal Exchange Visas (T).* This category would be comprised of treaty trader, treaty investor, trade agreement worker, and exchange visitor visas that are subject to reciprocal or other agreements with other nations. The category would combine such visas and maintain current requirements.

- *Student visas (S).* Students ranging from short-term trainees to graduate students would be admitted under one visa and their admission numbers would remain unlimited. In a key change serving US competitiveness and public diplomacy interests, graduate-degree students would no longer be required to return to their home countries automatically upon the completion of their studies and training programs, except those with certain scholarships that require it. Instead, and upon completion of their degrees, they would be eligible to seek and accept a job and then apply for provisional or permanent resident status, depending on the job. Students with degrees in mathematics, sciences, and informatics could receive preference under this system.

- *Seasonal and short-term workers (W).* Temporary visas for work would be for truly temporary needs, including seasonal and short-term workers at all skill levels. In circumstances where there is seasonal or intermittent work, temporary work visas provide a good way to augment the US work force. Because of the nature of the jobs, temporary stays can be reasonably well assured.

  W visa holders would be admitted for one year or less and be dependent on sponsorship by a US employer. W visa holders could freely travel back and forth to their home countries during the duration of their visa, but they would not be able to bring spouses or other family members. In this way, legal entry would be available to many who now come illegally for seasonal, limited, and intermittent duration jobs, and would accommodate many of the needs of employers with such jobs to offer. This approach is the best way to encourage circular migration for large numbers of workers from Mexico and other nearby countries who work in agriculture or limited duration occupations and assignments.

  The W visa would also apply to highly skilled workers, or persons with extraordinary abilities, who currently receive a three-year visa, but are needed for less than one year.

Provisional immigration

The new provisional visa bridges the false divide that now exists between certain forms of temporary and permanent immigration, creating an integrated system that organizes immigration around the ways in which immigration and labor markets work in practice.[87]

Provisional visas would allow employers to recruit workers for permanent jobs who may eventually be interested in permanent immigration and applying for a "green" card. Such visas provide both employers and workers the flexibility to exercise choices before committing to permanent immigration. The visas would act as a tool to attract the best and brightest at all skill levels, many of whom are shopping for the best offer in a competitive international marketplace.

Provisional visas would also be suitable for large numbers of workers who are not in temporary or seasonal jobs across the occupational spectrum. Such a program would meet employer needs for foreign-born workers in jobs that are more permanent than envisioned by the temporary immigration stream. In combination with temporary visas, the new provisional visa category ensures that sufficient opportunities would exist to meet the current and longer term needs of the economy in ways well-tailored to individuals and the labor market.

■ *Provisional visas (P).* This category provides for applicants of all skill levels who have employer sponsors. Provisional visa holders would be admitted for three-year periods, renewable once. Provisional visa holders would work in permanent or year-round jobs and transition into permanent residence after three years if they qualify and so choose. Provisional visas would be issued to workers with extraordinary ability, workers in jobs that require a BA or more, and workers in low- and semi-skilled jobs who currently have no real chance for legal immigration. Provisional visa holders would be able to bring dependent family members with them.

Employers of most provisional workers would be required to participate in an attestation process or become pre-certified as a licensed employer of foreign-born workers. The initial penalty for non-compliance would be to forfeit hiring foreign workers for a designated time period. Fees would be required, and the revenue generated from them would be used to meet a wide range of immigration capacity-building needs, including employer verification, workplace enforcement, and The Standing Commission described below. Those with provisional visas would be eligible to change employers after an initial period and would have the same labor protections as similarly employed US workers.

The number of provisional visas would initially be set to approximate current flows of such workers who enter both legally and illegally. The numbers would then be adjusted according to recommendations made by The Standing Commission.

In addition to an employment offer, qualifications for adjusting to permanent status would include evidence of continued employment in the occupation or field for which the applicant's educational or professional credentials served as the basis for the provisional visa, ability to speak English, and renewed clearance of a security and background check.

■ *Other provisional visas (O).* This category reflects those who are admitted to the United States on a provisional basis for reasons other than employment. It includes fiancées (who must marry within 90 days of their entry), victims of trafficking, and witnesses or informants who provide information valuable to the government regarding criminal activities.[88] Many eventually adjust to permanent status.

Permanent immigration

To achieve the goals of the immigration system, permanent immigration should be timely both for family unification and employer sponsors, while continuing to facilitate and expand the self-immigration of individuals who can readily contribute to economic growth and the advancement of knowledge.

The Task Force proposal substantially increases the numbers of permanent employment-based visas and provides for all skill ranges to be eligible to apply for permanent immigration after they have received a provisional visa. Some prospective immigrants would be able to apply, or be sponsored for, permanent immigration directly. They could also choose to enter on a provisional visa and then apply for permanent status at a future point. Thus, employment-based immigration would be a combination of those "graduating" from provisional status, and others applying directly for permanent immigration.

In addition, the proposal establishes new visa categories and changes others, as follows:

■ *Strategic growth visas.* This new visa creates an avenue for recruiting and retaining the world's best and brightest, including advanced degree foreign students — typically with a doctorate — in strategically important disciplines. Strategic growth visas would include individuals who currently qualify under the first preference employment-based category (those with extraordinary ability and outstanding professors and researchers) as well as investors and persons in critical industries. Examples might include biomedical research or energy independence projects. The visas would not be subject to numerical or per-country limits, or to a labor market test. Individuals could self-petition or be sponsored by an employer.

■ *Diversity visas.* This category of 50,000 visas annually operates by lottery, and was created in the 1990s to diversify the immigrant applicant pool by allowing countries and regions whose nationals were underrepresented in the United States to have access to US immigration.[89] The Task Force proposal eliminates this visa in favor of focusing more on family unification and employment-based immigration. Recent immigration from Africa, Eastern Europe, and South Asia has grown substantially under this visa, but now networks can be relied upon to continue the robust pace of immigration from these regions through the expanded number of worker and family visas. New provisional visas and expanded numbers and categories of permanent visas at all skill levels would be open to countries worldwide, resulting in increased diversity in the applicant pool by other means.

■ *Family reunification.* The Task Force proposal would speed dramatically the reunification of spouses and minor children of green card holders by exempting them from annual caps. This way, the integrity of close family relationships would be safeguarded in the most meaningful way. The proposal also would raise per-country limits to reduce excessively long waits for permanent immigrant visas for countries like Mexico, China, India, and the Philippines that account for the most demand for immigration, especially family-based immigration. Furthermore, the Task Force proposal urges Congress to set priorities for clearing the current backlogs in all family categories as part of a comprehensive immigration reform package, recognizing the special equities of people who have followed the rules of the current selection system and waited to join their families.

Family-based immigration is the dominant source of immigrants in the permanent system. Family unification not only serves an important value, it is also the fulcrum upon which successful integration rests. Family networks that support newcomers are uniquely important to the social and economic health of communities and the nation. However, these goals are frustrated when family unification does not happen in a timely manner.

Without systemic changes, backlogs will be chronic. Applicants will be spending productive years of their working lives waiting in long visa lines. For many in these family categories, family unification will remain elusive, and their immigration categories will be meaningless. In the face of visa demand that will exceed supply for the foreseeable future, the system cannot, by definition, be effective or credible in delivering timely family unification if all the current family preference categories are retained.

Therefore, difficult tradeoffs may have to be made. Task Force members did not all agree on changes in the family preference system, except on the proposal to exempt spouses and minor children of permanent residents from numerical limitations. Yet, the Task Force proposal suggests that it would be prudent to re-examine the continued viability of the current category of siblings of US citizens. In practice, many of those who qualify for this category may be able to immigrate faster to the United States through the new and expanded provisional and permanent employment-based categories. Since employment-based immigration is largely shaped by informal social networks, many employment-based immigrants through the provisional and permanent systems are likely to be family members of those already here.

Organizing employment-based immigration around greatly expanded opportunities for employer-sponsored immigration is a sound way to ensure efficient matching of immigrant workers with labor market needs. It also ensures that immigrants have jobs when they get here, a critical element of immigrant self-sufficiency and successful integration. The system the Task Force proposes provides employers and workers with multiple potential paths for legal entry, maximizing flexibility and the choices available to workers and to sponsors of potential immigrants.

FLEXIBILITY IN THE IMMIGRATION SYSTEM: THE STANDING COMMISSION ON IMMIGRATION AND LABOR MARKETS

To harness the benefits of immigration, policy must be responsive to changing economic, political, and social conditions instead of residing within a rigid framework that dates back to the 1950s.[90] As the current debate demonstrates, immigration policymaking often founders on the lack of consensus about a basic question: How many and what kinds of immigrants should the United States admit?

In some ways, the answers are subjective and not easily resolved. But many *can* be quantified. Systematically gathering and examining information on the costs, benefits, and impacts of immigration would establish a foundation for informed decision-making and public debate about immigration admission levels and policies. Immigration is a dynamic public policy issue that is of immense consequence to the nation now and for the future. Policymakers must have better information and mechanisms to manage immigration and adjust properly. Furthermore, the public needs dispassionate research and analysis to be fully informed.

Establishing appropriate immigration levels is a powerful policy tool that contains some of the characteristics of monetary policy.[91] Yet in contrast to setting interest rates, which are formally reviewed eight times a year on the basis of calculations by over 400 professional economists working for the Federal Reserve Board, immigration limits are locked into statutes that have been revisited, on average, less than once per decade.[92] When immigration levels are changed, they are the product of political compromises made during contentious legislative debates.

Managing immigration in the national interest requires a parallel institutional capacity to monitor and analyze information as the basis for making changes. This capacity does not exist. The Task Force proposes creating a new independent federal agency called The Standing Commission on Immigration and Labor Markets. The Standing Commission would be charged with making recommendations to the president and the Congress for adjustments to levels and categories of immigration. Its mandate would be to propose changes that support economic growth while maintaining low unemployment and preventing wage-depression. Baseline immigration levels would be set in the immigration statutes, with the requirement that The Standing Commission conduct ongoing analysis of labor market conditions and trends and propose adjustments to these levels.

The Standing Commission's analyses would also provide information needed by operational agencies, such as the Department of Labor, in carrying out their regulatory responsibilities. In this way, The Standing Commission's work would be analogous to that of the Census Bureau or the Bureau of Labor Statistics, which serve decision-makers and agencies charged with allocating social services program funds or economic policymaking, for example.

Adjusting immigration levels

The Standing Commission would be required to submit a report and recommendations every odd-numbered (non-election) year. After a specified period for Congressional consultation, unless Congress enacted legislation to maintain the statutory baseline levels, the president would issue a formal Determination of New Levels and other adjustments in immigration categories for the coming two years. A somewhat similar procedure has been successfully used in setting annual refugee admissions levels and has achieved timely changes with full involvement of both the executive and legislative branches. In addition to recommendations for adjustments in immigration levels, The Standing Commission would prepare an annual report for the president, Congress, and the public. It would also make its research reports and data publicly available.

Absent institutional changes like those the Task Force recommends, even the most carefully crafted legislation will be out of date quickly, leading to recurring cycles of misalignment between immigration law and practice, and to an ensuing corrosive breakdown of public trust.

Composition

The Standing Commission would be in the executive branch. It would be comprised of five voting members with recognized expertise in fields related to immigration and labor markets. The president would appoint the members with the advice and consent of the Senate to serve for five-year, staggered terms, with one renewal. The chair would have a two-year, renewable term. No more than three members could be from the same political party. The Secretaries of State, Homeland Security, Justice, Labor, Commerce, Health and Human Services, and Agriculture would be ex officio members. The statute would require full sharing of immigration information and cooperation by executive branch departments with The Standing Commission.

Staffing

The Standing Commission would be supported by a professional staff charged with ongoing analysis of data on the economic impacts of immigration, compilation and analysis of labor market data regarding immigrant and native-born workers, and review of relevant demographic shifts and trends in the global economy. A somewhat comparable body, the US Sentencing Commission, promulgates and regularly amends federal criminal sentencing guidelines and carries out research on sentencing issues, including comprehensive data analysis. That Commission has a staff of approximately 100 and an annual budget of $14 million.[93] The Standing Commission budget would be drawn from the fees collected for new provisional visa requirements as outlined above.

VI. Enforcing the Rules

RECOMMENDATION #3: The Task Force recommends that mandatory employer verification and workplace enforcement be at the center of more effective immigration enforcement reforms. DHS should create a Workplace Enforcement Advisory Board to help build support for new employer enforcement policies and monitor the progress of new measures.

RECOMMENDATION #4: The Task Force calls for a secure, biometric Social Security card and a plan for replacing existing cards. The secure Social Security card, "green" cards, and immigration work authorization cards should become the only documents that verify work eligibility.

People cross the border illegally or overstay their visas because of the availability of jobs in the United States. Yet the United States has largely maintained a laissez-faire approach at the workplace, concentrating immigration enforcement resources and efforts almost entirely upon border controls, especially at the US-Mexico border.

Between 1986 and 2002, about 60 percent of immigration enforcement appropriations were allocated for border control. Only about 10 percent were dedicated to interior enforcement, and workplace enforcement made up only a small part of interior enforcement efforts.[94] The message has been unmistakable: Crossing the border is difficult and dangerous but there are jobs for those who succeed. A flexible immigration system that can adapt to change and meet the nation's needs must also be grounded in tough-minded rules and resolute and effective enforcement.

EMPLOYER VERIFICATION

Employer verification of employees' eligibility to work and workplace enforcement must be at the center of reforms to combat illegal immigration. Without effective employer compliance and enforcement, other reforms — including border enforcement — cannot succeed. Only by reducing access to employment by unauthorized workers will pressures to evade border controls be reduced.

The IRCA experience

In 1952, Congress first passed legislation imposing sanctions on those harboring or abetting unauthorized immigrants. But an agreement known as the Texas Proviso exempted employment from being considered as "harboring." It took until 1986 and passage of the Immigration Reform and Control Act (IRCA) for hiring of unauthorized workers to be made illegal.[95] However, implementation of employer sanctions has been notoriously ineffective.

Under IRCA, employers are required to fill out and retain a form (the I-9) for every person who is hired. The I-9 attests that the employer has seen documents that establish the person's identity and legal status, but there is no requirement to verify their authenticity. Congress skirted requiring a system of verification of documents because it raised the possibility of a national ID system. Business objected to new burdens, civil liberties advocates warned against the dangers of a massive federal database, and ethnic minorities argued it would lead to discrimination because they would be asked to show identification when others would not.

As a result, more than two dozen different kinds of existing documents were allowed to demonstrate employment eligibility. Because most were easy to counterfeit, a fraudulent document industry flourished. Without verification, employers find it easy to comply with the letter of the law, unauthorized workers procure the documents they need to be hired, and the government's ability to show the "knowing" employment of unauthorized workers is difficult to prove. Thus, there is a high degree of compliance on paper alongside rampant levels of employment of unauthorized immigrants.

The low priority and ineffectiveness of meaningful employer enforcement is reflected in federal spending patterns. Immigration enforcement spending in general has increased fivefold since 1986, from $1 billion to almost $5 billion.[96] The southwest border has consistently received the largest share of that funding.[97] Less than 10 percent of enforcement spending has flowed to employer enforcement.[98] An average of 6,600 worksite enforcement cases per year were completed between 1991 and 1998, less than 10 percent of interior enforcement activity.[99] Between 2000 and 2003, the number of cases INS and ICE completed fell to fewer than 2,200 annually, less than three percent of its case activity[100] (see Figure 9). Only three notices of intent to fine were issued in FY 2004.[101]

For non-compliant employers, the cost savings from employing illegal labor can outweigh the possible cost of sanctions. Fines range from $100 to $1,000 per unauthorized immigrant for paperwork errors, and from $250 to $10,000 for substantive violations. The range has not changed since 1986.[102]

DHS has recently announced prosecutions of several high-profile workplace cases and says it will now pursue employer sanctions violations vigorously, bringing criminal charges against employers rather than administrative fines.[103] However, in similar past efforts, even where there has been evidence of employer complicity with migrant smugglers and fraudulent document vendors, the government has not had good success in prosecuting sanctions cases.

The case for optimism

Important changes in both the politics and technology of workplace enforcement make it reasonable to posit that a new initiative might have the chance to succeed.

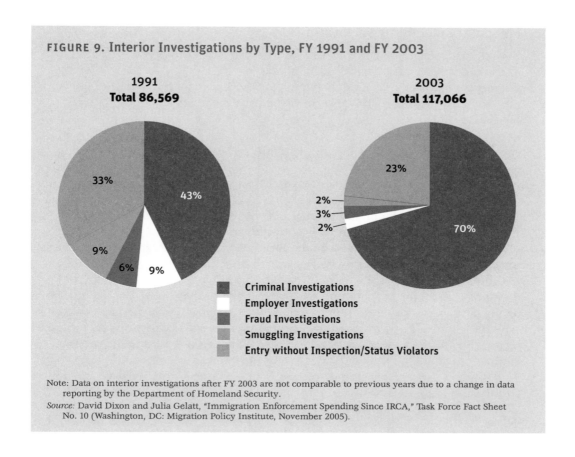

FIGURE 9. Interior Investigations by Type, FY 1991 and FY 2003

1991
Total 86,569

2003
Total 117,066

43%
33%
9%
6%
9%

23%
2%
3%
2%
70%

■ Criminal Investigations
□ Employer Investigations
■ Fraud Investigations
■ Smuggling Investigations
▨ Entry without Inspection/Status Violators

Note: Data on interior investigations after FY 2003 are not comparable to previous years due to a change in data reporting by the Department of Homeland Security.

Source: David Dixon and Julia Gelatt, "Immigration Enforcement Spending Since IRCA," Task Force Fact Sheet No. 10 (Washington, DC: Migration Policy Institute, November 2005).

The political changes are reflected in the legislation passed by both the House and Senate calling for mandatory employer electronic verification of new employees. The business community now supports employer compliance through verification. Employers seek predictability, access to a legal work force, and the ability to hire individuals whose status can be verified electronically in a simple, reliable way. The change in attitude is pivotal because compliance in hiring only authorized workers must become a new norm that replaces the widespread violations that have become acceptable business practices in some quarters today.

Technology changes since 1986 have also been a factor. People have become accustomed to using credit cards, magnetic strips, and computer chips for every-thing from online banking to airline boarding passes. The technologies required for verification are now experienced as conveniences, rather than as perils or intrusions. Concerns about privacy and linked government databases persist, but key constituencies are prepared to work with government agencies and Congress to build in proper safeguards instead of opposing verification measures altogether.

Finally, since 9/11, Americans and foreign governments have accepted the role of federal databases and reliable identification in a new security environ-ment, and government agencies have been able to win greater support for investments in modern information technology and data systems.

Mandatory electronic verification

Both the House and Senate bills call for expansion of a prototype system known as the Basic Pilot, which has been in operation since 1997. The Basic Pilot has demonstrated that as a technical matter, and with a small number of employers, electronic verification can work. However, the timetables laid out in current legislative proposals are too short. The House bill calls for employers to use an expanded Basic Pilot system to verify the work eligibility of all new hires within two years of the date of the bill's enactment, and to verify the eligibility of all existing workers within six years. The Senate bill calls for electronic verification of new hires no later than 18 months after an appropriation of $400 million to upgrade the Basic Pilot database.[104]

The overhaul of employment verification and workplace enforcement is a major undertaking. Only about 10,100 employers have registered to use the electronic verification provided by the Basic Pilot and the program is actively used by more than 5,000 employers — less than one-tenth of 1 percent of all US employers.[105] The scale-up that is required will have to reach more than 8 million employers and 144 million workers, and process more than 50 million hiring decisions each year.[106] Getting there will require intensive public education and new habits by employers and workers in every occupation and location. To be workable as a mandatory requirement, substantial investments in the completeness and quality of data will have to be made.

Database issues

The Basic Pilot searches both Social Security and immigration databases. The accuracy of the system must be dramatically improved if it is to be reliable. The problems that need to be corrected include delayed entry of data reflecting admission or status changes, data entry errors, the ability of individuals to view and correct their records, and alternate spellings or word order of foreign names. In order to achieve a more complete database, it may prove useful to integrate all visa issuance and admissions databases — including data from the US-VISIT program — into Basic Pilot and Social Security data systems. The most glaring deficiencies in the databases are all likely to affect non-citizens disproportionately, though inaccurate results impact US citizen workers and employers as well.

Further, the Verification Division within US Citizenship and Immigration Services (USCIS) at DHS that is charged with overseeing the reforms necessary to generate accurate and timely information needs to be fully staffed. Both USCIS and the Social Security Administration (SSA) must be given sufficient, sustained resource infusions and support to upgrade their databases, establish robust privacy and security safeguards, create effective methods to counteract and punish discrimination, and define procedures for individuals to review and correct their data, so that verification can be reliable and as routine as paying taxes or providing W-2 forms. Considering the potential for interfering with people's livelihoods, the standards for government performance on verification must be exacting, with clear and effective redress mechanisms.

Basic Pilot

Under current law, US employers must request from their new hires documents that establish identity and employment eligibility, and they are required to record that they have reviewed such documentation. However, employers are not required, nor have they had the tools, to verify the authenticity of such documentation or, therefore, to verify employees' authorization to work. The Basic Pilot program was one of three voluntary electronic verification pilot programs established in 1997. The other two — the Citizen Attestation Verification Pilot (CAVP) and the Machine-Readable Document Pilot (MRDP) — were allowed to expire in 2003, but Basic Pilot was continued and expanded nationwide in 2004.

Basic Pilot allows participating employers to submit identification and work authorization data via the Internet for verification of employment eligibility. The data are checked against the Social Security Administration (SSA) database and the US Citizenship and Immigration Service (USCIS) databases and employers are notified of the results. This system excels in detecting fake identity cards because they are not in the databases, but it fails to detect the fraudulent use of borrowed or stolen documents that are in the databases.

Equally important, the system generates an unacceptably high level of secondary verification responses. Twenty percent of noncitizens and 13 percent of US citizens are initially not confirmed and can only be confirmed if they contact SSA or USCIS to resolve discrepancies in their information, which must be done manually by USCIS. Ninety percent of these tentatively non-confirmed applicants fail to pursue their cases because employers mishandle their applications, workers find it easier to change employment than to correct their records, or they do not have legal status and are not authorized to work. In cases where unauthorized immigrants are deterred from seeking employment, the system is doing what it is intended to do. However, the time-consuming and costly delays for legitimately work-authorized individuals indicate that the accuracy of the system must be dramatically improved for it to be workable as a mandatory requirement. An independent assessment of the Basic Pilot program in 2002 found that less than one-tenth of 1 percent of all submissions were ultimately determined to be from persons unauthorized for employment, though it is unclear how many of those who failed to contest their tentative nonconfirmation findings may have also been unauthorized for employment.

The Basic Pilot Process: Step by Step

1) Employers submit a new employee's information via the Internet, based on the I-9 process. This information is electronically checked against the SSA's enumeration database. If the person has attested to being a US citizen, the employer then receives either a confirmation that the employee is authorized to work or receives a tentative nonconfirmation. Information for noncitizens whose information matches SSA's database is referred electronically for a check against a USCIS database.

2) Employees whose cases receive a tentative nonconfirmation must visit a local SSA office to correct their records to address any changes or errors in their personal information.

3) Information on noncitizen employees that does not match the USCIS database is forwarded for a manual check against other DHS databases, which takes one business day or less. If this check cannot confirm work authorization, the employee is issued a tentative nonconfirmation and is asked to call an Immigration Status Verifier (ISV), who then resolves the case using information from the phone call and immigration documents, if requested.

4) After a tentative nonconfirmation has been issued, employees have eight business days to visit an SSA office or call USCIS. SSA and USCIS have two additional business days to complete the verification and respond to the employer.

5) On the tenth day, or one day after an employee with an SSA tentative nonconfirmation notifies the employer that he or she has visited SSA, the employer reverifies the employee, and should receive verification of the employee's work eligibility.

6) If employees do not take steps to resolve the tentative nonconfirmation within the required time frame, employers must terminate employment.

Source: Kevin Jernegan, "Eligible to Work? Experiments in Verifying Work Authorization," Task Force Insight No. 8 (Washington, DC: Migration Policy Institute, November 2005); Information provided by the USCIS Office of Policy and Strategy.

Timeline

Legislation that requires universal participation in an electronic verification system without first addressing the flaws in the Basic Pilot program will fail. In particular, it will create unacceptable burdens for prospective workers and businesses alike, particularly small businesses, which constitute the largest overall number of employers in the country. Task Force discussions with knowledgeable government officials led to the conclusion that three years' preparation time should be provided for implementation of mandatory verification. It might be possible to pilot the program in industries of particular sensitivity to terrorism concerns, such as chemical plants or transportation facilities. However, without the time and resources to make changes properly, the rush to *appear* tough on workplace enforcement will harm innocent workers, disrupt hiring practices and productivity, encourage non-compliance, and further undermine the legitimacy of immigration enforcement.

Investing the time and money to build a durable system that can be phased in over time need not mean postponing improvements in employer enforcement. There are many measures that can be taken immediately to strengthen workplace rules. None of the pending legislative proposals provide a fully developed plan and timetable for employer verification. The Task Force has developed one as an example of a comprehensive agenda of actions and timelines that should be carried out in conjunction with building a mandatory verification system.

Workplace Enforcement Advisory Board

The Secretary of Homeland Security should create a new advisory body to assist in the political and policy challenges that accompany electronic verification and strengthened workplace enforcement. The advisory board should be comprised of representatives of the key constituencies whose cooperation, expertise, and support is vital for the initiative to succeed. Members should include business leaders and other representatives of employers, labor union and other worker organization representatives, immigrant rights advocates, and security and privacy experts. Given the history of workplace enforcement and the ambition of mandatory electronic verification, a smoothly operating system that achieves

Sample Agenda of Actions for Implementing Mandatory Electronic Verification by Employers

Upon enactment of legislation:

- Fully staff the Verification Division within USCIS and establish the interagency process, roles, and funding required to upgrade the Social Security Administration (SSA) and US Citizenship and Immigration Services (USCIS) databases. Database integration should also include appropriate visa issuance, admissions, and US-VISIT data; substantially increase the numbers of status verifiers; expand outreach and education efforts and regional call centers aimed at training employers; and designate staff for ongoing evaluation and oversight.

- Allocate funding for systems enhancements that create electronic linkages between CBP and SSA field officers and SSA and USCIS database managers.

- Publish final regulations that reduce the number of documents that may be used to establish identity and work eligibility from 27 to 7, i.e., lawful permanent resident ("green" cards) and employment authorization documents (EAD), US passports, driver's licenses and state-issued non-driver ID cards, Social Security cards, and birth certificates.

- Train employers to implement new document requirements.

- Establish a Workplace Enforcement Advisory Board to work closely with the secretary of DHS on implementation of new verification requirements. The Board's role would be to promote "buy in" by key stakeholders and advise DHS on the effectiveness of its implementation efforts. The Board should include representatives from business, labor, immigrant communities, state government, privacy interests, and relevant executive branch agencies.

Within one year:

- Publish final regulations regarding new fines for paperwork and substantive violations of existing eligibility verification requirements, discriminatory hiring practices, and violations of Basic Pilot rules designed to protect workers and job applicants. These rules include prohibitions against misuse of the system, such as submitting an applicant's name to the system prior to an offer of employment, submitting an employee's name to the system in response to a union organizing campaign or other labor demand, and terminating employment based on unresolved non-confirmations.

- Increase outreach, education, and enforcement of these provisions by the Office of Special Counsel for Immigration-Related Unfair Employment Practices.

- Create simple procedures for individuals to review their personal eligibility data and correct their records as needed. Corrections must be able to be processed immediately.

- Establish an office within ICE dedicated to worksite enforcement. The new office should pursue high-profile cases aimed at achieving deterrence.

- Submit a plan to Congress for producing a new secure Social Security card and a timetable for replacing existing cards. The card should include biometrics and proven anti-fraud technology akin to that used for "green" cards and employment authorization cards (EAD) now issued to non-citizens.

Within two years:

- Develop credit card-style readers that can read REAL ID driver's licenses, "green" cards, and employment authorization cards. Such readers would allow Basic Pilot participants to submit identity and eligibility data via a card swipe, rather than by Internet.

- Complete upgrades to the electronic verification databases. This will require close cooperation among the Verification Division, SSA, CBP, USCIS, and US-VISIT. All EAD data, Social Security name changes, and other changes in immigration, citizenship, or employment-authorized status must be automatically transmitted to the verification database in real time through enhanced system inter-connectivity.

Within three years:

- Require participation by groups of designated employers in an electronic verification system modeled on the existing Basic Pilot. The secretary of DHS, in consultation with the Advisory Board, should determine the scope of initial mandatory participation based on an analysis of error rates in the upgraded databases, the effectiveness of privacy protections, the burden imposed on work-authorized workers and employers, and the effectiveness of anti-discrimination mechanisms. Participation could be determined by industry, size of business, geography, and/or citizenship status of job applicants, for example, or begin in industries of particular sensitivity to terrorism concerns. Wider participation should be phased in gradually as the Secretary and the Board determine that mandatory participation has not imposed undue burdens on legal workers or employers, or led to employment discrimination.

- Begin replacement of existing Social Security cards with secure, biometric cards. Eventually only three types of documents should be used for employer verification: secure Social Security cards, "green" cards, and EADs.

employer compliance as a standard business practice must be treated as a long-term proposition. Employers wish to comply with verification requirements but must be given adequate support and compliance assistance in moving to such a comprehensive new system. An advisory body could help maintain momentum, and enhance both outreach to affected constituencies and feedback to DHS in this important task.

Secure documents

In addition to confirming that job applicants are eligible to work, an effective verification system must also assure that individuals have valid, secure identification documents that tie the cardholder to the information on the card. The Task Force believes that it is time to develop a secure, biometric, machine-readable Social Security card that allows citizens to easily establish both their identity and eligibility to work.[107] Currently, citizens have less secure documentation than non-citizens. Government agencies already issue such cards for non-citizens in the form of work authorization and "green" cards for LPRs. Citizens need analogous documents for a new system to work.

The objective of the REAL ID Act, scheduled for implementation by May 2008, is to create a secure identity document by mandating uniform federal standards and anti-fraud technology for state driver's licenses.[108] But it seems unlikely that the REAL ID provisions alone will solve the document problem for workplace enforcement purposes. Non-secure breeder documents, such as birth certificates or Social Security cards, are used to obtain drivers' licenses, thus making them subject to fraud.

The law shifts a federal responsibility to create a secure national document onto states and weakens document oversight. State Department of Motor Vehicle officials lack the training to adjudicate complex issues of immigration status, especially since it is unclear how any immigration document verification would function in practice. Adjudication errors are likely in the cases of greatest importance — those involving vulnerable humanitarian migrants and professional counterfeiters or terrorists. Officials who err on the side of caution are likely to discriminate against non-European ethnic groups. States see REAL ID as an unfunded mandate (cost estimates run to $13 billion), and privacy advocates are concerned about data misuse. REAL ID includes no particularized counterterrorism tools and, as written, may make it difficult for some non-US citizens with legal status to acquire drivers' licenses. A simpler, more complete, and more secure system is required.

The importance of reliable documents is broadly accepted as one aspect of a layered security system in the post-9/11 era. Standard, federally issued documents that prove identity and eligibility to work in the United States should be treated as an important layer of this new system. Secure documents are also the best antidote to the potential for discrimination based on ethnicity or national origin in hiring practices. Along with "green" cards and work authorization cards, they are existing documents already used to obtain work. Making the Social Security card secure upgrades and safeguards the reliability of a document whose purpose is directly tied to employment and work eligibility.

ENFORCEMENT AT US BORDERS

RECOMMENDATION #5: The Task Force recommends accelerated implementation of "smart border" measures that combine personnel, equipment, and technology to reduce illegal immigration and protect against terrorist entry. The Task Force calls upon the administration to submit an annual report to Congress and the American people that lays out measures of effectiveness for border enforcement and reports progress in meeting them.

RECOMMENDATION #6: The Task Force recommends strengthening immigration enforcement in other areas of border security, especially legal ports of entry (air, land, and sea) and overseas visa issuance. Visa and legal immigration admissions procedures must not be the "weak links" in border protection, and legitimate crossings must be facilitated to promote trade and travel.

RECOMMENDATION #7: The Task Force calls for systematic protection of the human and civil rights of immigrants and for including border community perspectives in border enforcement operations. Such efforts must include active steps by the government to disband vigilantism of any form along the border.

Border enforcement is an essential element of immigration policy. A core responsibility of any nation is to prevent access to its territory by people and materials that pose a threat. Americans across the political spectrum believe that the United States has lost control of its borders, and that border enforcement — especially at the US-Mexico border — must be strengthened.

Until recently, concern was confined to states on or near the southwestern border, but concern has spread so that citizens across the country feel a sense of crisis and are calling for more effective border enforcement.[109] Yet despite a decade of unprecedented resource growth for border enforcement, the numbers of illegal immigrants that cross the border or overstay their visas with impunity have led to a sense that no one is in charge, and that the federal government lacks the ability and will to address the problem.[110]

The overwhelming majority of unauthorized migrants enter the United States in search of work to provide better lives for their families. They do not represent an inherent threat to US security. But illegal entry and residence undermines the rule of law and the integrity of the nation's border security and immigration systems. In the wake of the 9/11 attacks, border security has become an issue of high priority to many Americans. Border enforcement must rest on layers of security that effectively deter illegal immigration and target catastrophic security, safety, and health threats. Better deterrence at the borders will also build public confidence in other aspects of the nation's immigration policies and system.

Border enforcement has four intertwined goals. Each require different methods and techniques, but should be understood as part of an integrated strategy. They are:

- security (protecting against terrorism and other threats);

- safety (protecting against criminals, violence, smuggling, drug trafficking, and threats to quality of life, including public health concerns);

- control (restricting the illegal entry of people and goods); and

- regulation (facilitating the flows of people and goods the United States wishes to admit).

Unsatisfactory results

When IRCA passed in 1986, border enforcement, employer sanctions, and legalization were the key elements of the "three-legged stool" that aimed to combat illegal immigration.[111] Although significant investments at the border and changes in border enforcement strategy did not begin in earnest until the mid-1990s, border enforcement still received 57 percent of the supplemental funds from IRCA, and resource infusions for border enforcement have increased by 500 percent since IRCA[112] (see Figures 10 and 11). Indeed, border enforcement has been the only component of immigration funding that consistently wins bipartisan political support, irrespective of outcomes.

Law enforcement has become an increasingly visible presence along the border, and many areas have been transformed by wall-like fencing, miles of new roads, helicopters, and stadium lighting. Despite a continuing hardening of the border and greater control in urban areas in California and Texas, there is little evidence that illegal immigration has been deterred or reduced. Instead, the flow

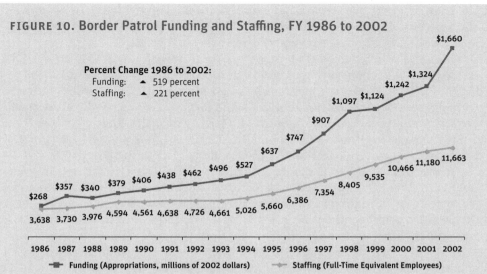

FIGURE 10. Border Patrol Funding and Staffing, FY 1986 to 2002

Percent Change 1986 to 2002:
Funding: ▲ 519 percent
Staffing: ▲ 221 percent

Funding values: $268, $357, $340, $379, $406, $438, $462, $496, $527, $637, $747, $907, $1,097, $1,124, $1,242, $1,324, $1,660

Staffing values: 3,638, 3,730, 3,976, 4,594, 4,561, 4,638, 4,726, 4,661, 5,026, 5,660, 6,386, 7,354, 8,405, 9,535, 10,466, 11,180, 11,663

Years: 1986 1987 1988 1989 1990 1991 1992 1993 1994 1995 1996 1997 1998 1999 2000 2001 2002

━■━ Funding (Appropriations, millions of 2002 dollars)   ━━ Staffing (Full-Time Equivalent Employees)

Note: Full-time equivalent employees (FTEs) for 1991 to 2002 include a proportional amount of FTEs assigned to Construction and to Data and Communications, activities that supported Border Patrol efforts. FTEs for 1986 to 1990 do not include these additional staff. Comparable recent data on immigration enforcement spending are not available after FY 2002. In FY 2003, the DHS took over most of the immigration enforcement duties of the INS. The organization of immigration and other enforcement duties under the DHS is very different from the organization under the INS.

Source: Deborah W. Meyers, "US Border Enforcement: From Horseback to High-Tech" (Washington, DC: Migration Policy Institute, November 2005), based on data from David Dixon and Julia Gelatt, "Immigration Enforcement Spending Since IRCA," Task Force Fact Sheet No. 10 (Washington, DC: Migration Policy Institute, November 2005).

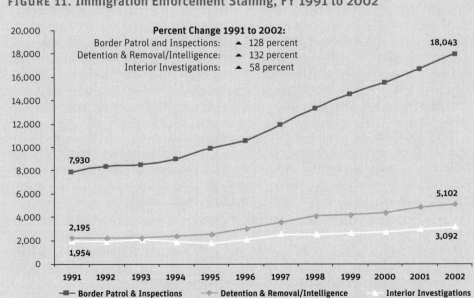

FIGURE 11. Immigration Enforcement Staffing, FY 1991 to 2002

Percent Change 1991 to 2002:
Border Patrol and Inspections: ▲ 128 percent
Detention & Removal/Intelligence: ▲ 132 percent
Interior Investigations: ▲ 58 percent

Border Patrol & Inspections: 7,930 ... 18,043
Detention & Removal/Intelligence: 2,195 ... 5,102
Interior Investigations: 1,954 ... 3,092

Years: 1991 1992 1993 1994 1995 1996 1997 1998 1999 2000 2001 2002

━■━ Border Patrol & Inspections   ━◆━ Detention & Removal/Intelligence   ━▲━ Interior Investigations

Note: Comparable recent data on immigration enforcement staffing are not available after FY 2002. In FY 2003, the DHS took over most of the immigration enforcement duties of the INS. The organization of immigration and other enforcement duties under the DHS is very different from the organization under the INS.

Source: David Dixon and Julia Gelatt, "Immigration Enforcement Spending Since IRCA," Task Force Fact Sheet No. 10 (Washington, DC: Migration Policy Institute, November 2005).

has been diverted, as migrants have turned to smugglers, fraudulent documents, and new entry routes through remote, dangerous areas.[113] Estimated costs of hiring a smuggler tripled between the early and late 1990s.[114]

The average length of stay by those who enter illegally increased as well. Two factors may be responsible. For some, enhanced border enforcement has led to the "locking-in" effect — decisions by migrants to bring their families to the United States rather than traveling back and forth to visit them.[115] For those who are known to the government — primarily visa overstayers — and have stayed in unlawful status for more than six months, statutory three- and ten-year prohibitions against lawful re-entry have also kept them "locked-in."

The unauthorized population is estimated to have grown from between 4 and 5 million in 1994, when major new border investments and strategies began, to an estimated 11.5-12 million in 2006.[116] Research shows that between 1997 and 2004, the probability of apprehension has fallen from 33 to 19 percent, and the estimated cost per border apprehension has risen fivefold from $300 in the early 1990s to $1,700 in 2002.[117] Non-fiscal costs have risen as well. These include the impact of border enforcement on communities on both sides of the border, as well as the human cost in deaths at the border, which reached a high of 473 in FY 2005.[118]

Annual report on effectiveness

The rising investment in border enforcement, combined with seemingly increasing unauthorized flows, suggest that the cost of doing "more of the same" must be re-examined to assess the dividends on the investment — whether more personnel, fences, and technology are achieving their goals.

To date, objective measures for evaluating the effectiveness of border enforcement have not been developed, despite multiple Government Accountability Office (GAO) reports calling for them.[119] Today's metrics are nearly meaningless. They center on data such as how many agents are on line-watch duty, or how many apprehensions of unauthorized border crossers have been made. Apprehensions are simply a compilation of the numbers of arrests that Border Patrol agents make. These data typically count the same person several times. The government still does not ask the question of how many *individuals* are being apprehended, even though it now has the technology to make reasonable estimates.

The Task Force recommends inclusion of the following as key data in the annual report: recidivism rates; smuggling fees; apprehensions (and locations) of human smugglers, criminals, and those with known or suspected terrorist connections; the likelihood of apprehension; and complaints received and outcomes of investigations. Additional analysis should focus on the share of resources allocated to border patrol activities and port-of-entry work; incidence of fraudulent documents; and the costs and benefits of infrastructure investments. These analyses should help Congress ensure that future appropriations are well spent and support the right goals.

Three specific areas that deserve greater focus are:

■ *Border Patrol staffing.* Appropriations requests and legislation have focused disproportionately on Border Patrol agents. An annual report by the administration on border immigration enforcement should include information on Border Patrol staffing levels; attrition rates of agents; agent productivity measured by surveillance and other technologies; costs/benefits of additional agents in terms of estimated annual flow/stock of the unauthorized population; and the support staff needs of agents for tasks such as transporting those arrested, building roads, and staffing surveillance cameras.

The president's National Guard initiative, which is placing up to 6,000 National Guard troops at the border over the next two years, is described as a force-multiplier until the Border Patrol is increased from 12,000-18,000 agents.[120] The initiative makes sense because only personnel with comprehensive training in immigration law, ethics, and civil rights should be enforcing US laws at the border. Moreover, the military has long provided support to the Border Patrol in building roads and providing other services. However, when new agents are hired to patrol the border, demand for support will rise proportionately. If there is the need for levels of support at that order of magnitude, it should be reflected in permanent, new staffing ratios and resource allocations.

It is important to be realistic about the ability of any agency to hire, train, and absorb such large numbers of new agents in such a relatively short time period. It takes 30 applicants to field one Border Patrol agent.[121] Border Patrol agents require a wide variety of skills and their work can be very physically demanding. They often operate in dangerous environments yet must also be able to interact appropriately with US citizens and border community residents. They must become proficient with an array of technologies. Job candidates must pass challenging background checks and entry and medical exams. It is the only federal law enforcement agency that has a foreign language requirement and language proficiency tests are mandatory elements of their training curriculum.

During earlier high-growth periods, the GAO found that agents with less than two years of experience tripled between 1994 and 1998, and the share of agents with more than five years' experience fell by two-thirds.[122] The GAO also found that there had been an increase in the ratio of non-supervisory to supervisory agents. Residents of border communities have expressed concerns about whether new agents have the requisite training (particularly in human and civil rights) to deal with the complex and often chaotic situations in which they often must work.

In July 2003, former Customs and Border Protection (CBP) Commissioner Robert Bonner acknowledged difficulties in retaining Border Patrol agents. Attrition rates doubled from 5 to 10 percent between the early and late 1990s and then spiked to 18 percent in 2002 before declining. Among the challenges the Border Patrol faces are low pay relative to other law enforcement jobs, lack of upward mobility, poor working conditions, and lack of job satisfaction.[123] Congress must be attentive to the importance of the longer-term vitality of the Border Patrol, and the pitfalls of crash hiring programs.

■ *Effectiveness of technology.* Technology is critical to enforcement, but technology initiatives have had a checkered history at the border. The DHS Inspector General (IG) reported in December 2005 that systems were not working as planned, that they were not linked, and that their benefits were unclear.[124]

Sensor technology, for example, has not been able to differentiate between cattle or people, and fails because of weather. Sixty percent of sensor alarms are not investigated, and when they are, officers are often dispatched on false alarms. Similarly, remote video surveillance efforts have yielded few apprehensions, control centers cannot talk to each other, and various components of surveillance and communications systems are not integrated. Half of the planned remote video surveillance sites were never even installed.[125] An unmanned aerial vehicle (UAV), another highly touted border control initiative, crashed in April, after approximately seven months in operation at a loss of millions of dollars.[126]

The Inspector General has challenged the Border Patrol to quantify the benefits of these programs. However, problems in data collection and cataloguing and the lack of performance measures have made that impossible. The IG further challenged the effectiveness of oversight on large contracts.[127] Both findings are troubling, particularly given the high costs of these programs.

DHS's Secure Border Initiative (SBI) is the most recent attempt to develop a comprehensive border security approach to reduce unauthorized migration. It openly acknowledges through solicitation of private industry assistance that DHS needs help in determining how to secure the border in an effective and integrated manner. Expanded use of technology, including an integrated network of sensors and cameras, is a key component of SBI, which is expected to rely both on contractors and technology with long track records in providing assistance to the Department of Defense. It is to cost about $2 billion.[128] SBI is a follow-up to two previously failed technology initiatives to integrate border technology and modernize equipment that nevertheless received $429 million in funding since FY 1997.[129]

Participants in those earlier initiatives believe that the current attempt can only succeed through better dialogue among the key parties, including the Border Patrol, the vendor community, and cross-border officials. The goal should be to clarify a strategy where all stakeholders — public and private — agree on the problem to be solved, the metrics that can measure progress and success, and the technology solutions most likely to achieve measurable results.[130]

It is critical that the promised integration and interoperability of technology projects involving databases, watch lists, and counterterrorism information systems come to fruition.[131] Inspectors, consular offices, and border patrol agents rely on accurate and timely information. They must be provided with the tools necessary to do their jobs. The United States must redouble efforts to resolve the outstanding technical and interagency information sharing issues to ensure that solid data are available to those who need them when they need them. Resolving information-sharing issues is also critically important for meeting post-9/11 national security needs.

■ *Protection of human and civil rights.* Border enforcement measures must also protect the basic human and civil rights of migrants. Unauthorized migrants are crossing the border in increasingly dangerous areas. Human rights groups estimate that over 4,000 migrants have died crossing the border since 1994, up from just ten per year during the 1980s.[132] Stepped-up enforcement has also fostered far more smuggling, exposing migrants to additional dangers. Authorities at all levels must take effective steps to minimize this unacceptable loss of life, and to protect migrants' rights by providing for orderly crossing of legal migrants, disbanding border vigilante groups, and disrupting smuggling networks.

Steps to enhance such accountability include:

■ strengthened civil rights training for all personnel engaged in border enforcement, including involvement of experienced human rights organization representatives in training curricula;

- development of an oversight mechanism for law enforcement misconduct, including a revised complaint process for those who believe their rights have been violated, posting information at primary ports of entry explaining how to file complaints, and requirements for public access to reports on the outcomes of investigations; and

- a clear, transparent, closely monitored policy to prevent racial and ethnic profiling in border communities.

Border fencing, high-tech equipment, and increased enforcement personnel contribute to environmental degradation and divided border communities. At the same time, the larger US border presence has played a role in border-area violence and strained US relations with Mexico and other regional allies. Border communities are often the ones most affected by checkpoints, raids, profiling, or targeted enforcement operations.

The safety and security of communities along the border should be incorporated into border enforcement discussions. New fencing projects should not move forward without independent analysis of their environmental, community, and diplomatic impacts. Implementation should include consultation with border communities and respect for the environment and the rights of indigenous people.

Enforcement policies need to promote US security and deter illegal activity. Smart enforcement needs to be grounded in cost-effective measures that reduce illegal flows and keep them at minimal levels. More broadly, ensuring that immigration policy strengthens national security requires not only controls but also healthy relations with stakeholders, including affected communities and regional allies.

Legal channels of entry

Border security also demands stepped up enforcement measures at legal ports of entry.

Some new estimates suggest that as much as 40 to 50 percent of the unauthorized population may have entered the United States through a port of entry where they passed through immigration inspection and then overstayed their visas. Several hundred thousand may have violated the terms of properly issued

TABLE 8. Inspections at US Ports of Entry, FY 1999 to 2004

	Number (in millions)					
	FY 1999	FY 2000	FY 2001	FY 2002	FY 2003	FY 2004
All ports of entry: air, land, and sea	525.2	534.2	510.6	444.7	427.7	428.9
Land ports of entry	435.3	437.9	414.4	358.4	338.6	333.3
Mexican border	319.5	324.0	314.3	274.4	259.4	254.7
Canadian border	115.9	113.9	100.0	84.0	79.2	78.5
	Percentage					
Land inspections as share of all inspections	82.9%	82.0%	81.2%	80.6%	79.2%	77.7%

Notes: Of those undergoing inspections at land ports of entry, 99.9 percent are granted admission into the United States. Data current as of August 30, 2005.

Source: DHS, Office of Immigration Statistics, Performance Analysis System (PAS) G-22.1.

border crossing cards.[133] As southwest border enforcement increases between ports of entry, incentives to use legal crossings and procedures improperly will also increase. Such procedures must be continuously monitored and strengthened to reduce their susceptibility to misuse. The challenge is especially difficult because legal ports of entry handle millions of crossings annually, and facilitation of commerce and legitimate travel is a critical goal for border enforcement agencies and for the nation (see Table 8).

Border enforcement must be understood to encompass a broad set of responsibilities that include not only the land borders but also legal ports of entry at both southern and northern land borders, airports, seaports, and overseas consulates. Despite the fact that all of the 9/11 hijackers came through legal ports of entry and used visas obtained at overseas consulates,[134] legal channels of entry are often overlooked in the public debate and in Congressional appropriations (see Figure 12). It is widely believed that terrorists are unlikely to risk their lives or operations by crossing through the desert or entrusting themselves to smugglers. They are far more likely to attempt to use legal channels, relying on high-quality fraudulent documents or fraudulently procured visas. This analysis does not, of course, ignore the possibility that terrorists could be generated within the Western Hemisphere.

One of the primary responses to 9/11 that has strengthened immigration controls has been the US-VISIT program, which requires biometric information and checks for everyone traveling to the United States.[135] Upon full implemen-

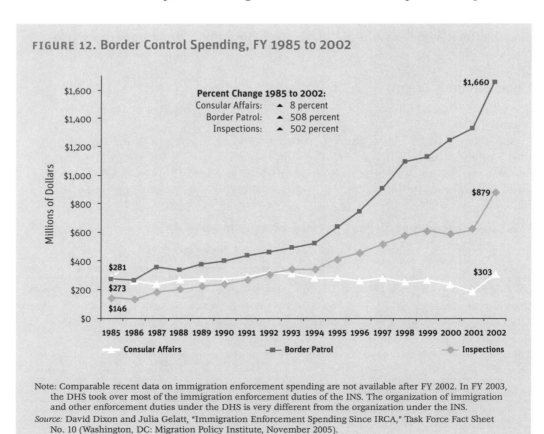

FIGURE 12. Border Control Spending, FY 1985 to 2002

Note: Comparable recent data on immigration enforcement spending are not available after FY 2002. In FY 2003, the DHS took over most of the immigration enforcement duties of the INS. The organization of immigration and other enforcement duties under the DHS is very different from the organization under the INS.

Source: David Dixon and Julia Gelatt, "Immigration Enforcement Spending Since IRCA," Task Force Fact Sheet No. 10 (Washington, DC: Migration Policy Institute, November 2005).

tation, the system is estimated to cost as much as $10 billion.[136] Though the program can play an important role in countering illegal overstays because it contains identifying information about individuals who are in the country for temporary periods, it tracks only entries, not exits, except at a few airport locations.[137]

Enforcement against visa overstays has been notably lacking and is difficult to pursue effectively. To realize the benefit of US-VISIT, exit information would have to be systematically gathered and an enforcement strategy developed to use the information to reduce the incidence of visa overstays. While not as politically popular as additional Border Patrol agents or certain technologies, improving the capabilities of ports of entry to enforce rules regarding illegal entrance and timely departure is essential to restoring integrity to the border and reducing the incidence of visa overstaying as a substantial aspect of the problem of illegal immigration.

Borders that work

The goal must be borders that are both secure and efficient.

The Homeland Security Act of 2002 states that in addition to DHS's mandate to prevent the entry of terrorists and terrorist weapons, DHS is also tasked with ensuring the "speedy, orderly, and efficient flow of lawful traffic and commerce."[138] In some locations, increased cross-border traffic along with heightened scrutiny of legal entrants has caused dramatic increases in the length of time that migrants, workers, visitors, and those engaging in commerce must wait to enter the United States. According to a recent study by the San Diego Association of Governments, over 3 million potential working hours in San Diego County are spent in delays at the border, resulting in $42 million in lost wages in that county alone.[139]

To address this issue, DHS must dedicate more attention to expanding and promoting existing programs that can speed border crossings for frequent crossers. At present the programs are underutilized, lack incentives to register, and have had a minimal impact on reducing congestion and waiting times. An example of a good initiative that smoothed the flow of commerce and people was piloted on the northern border at Detroit-Windsor in 2005. Called the "25% challenge," Customs and Border Protection (CBP) officials instituted new staffing measures for peak crossing times and established inspection booths that could be raised and lowered to clear either commercial truck or passenger vehicles quickly. With these relatively simple steps, the time required to cross the border was reduced by 25 percent. Many more such initiatives leading to permanent improvements in facilitating legitimate border crossings and commerce should be implemented.[140]

Infrastructure improvements at legal crossing points are needed almost everywhere. In consultation with local communities, business leaders, and other stakeholders, DHS should develop a long-term plan for port of entry infrastructure investments. Such investments constitute an expensive undertaking that will require coordination with other agencies, but will contribute greatly to promoting the secure and efficient borders that are essential to the nation's economic well-being.[141]

IMMIGRATION ENFORCEMENT AND NATIONAL SECURITY

RECOMMENDATION #8: The Task Force recommends that detecting, disrupting, and dismantling terrorist travel and its supporting infrastructure be treated with the same depth and urgency as efforts devoted to terrorist communications and finance.

Terrorism by a few and migration by many are characteristics of an era of rapid communication and cheap transportation. But each presents distinct challenges, and the government needs to do more to focus on the distinct challenge — and opportunity — presented by terrorist travel.

Migration measures to combat terrorism

Migration is a response to economic and social forces; terrorism is a criminal act undertaken for political purposes. Robust regulation of immigration is an important counterterrorism tool, but it is not effective by itself. While much of the contemporary debate about immigration and US security is premised on the assumption that large-scale unauthorized crossings of the US-Mexico border create unique opportunities for terrorist infiltration, it is widely believed that terrorists are more likely to take advantage of clandestine entry across the Canadian border or maritime crossings.[142] Terrorists also utilize travel facilitation services, fake documents that help them cross through legal ports of entry, and smuggling networks. So crime control focused on these areas is important. At the same time, enforcement officials could target their activities at security threats more efficiently if the crossings of those seeking to work in the United States were redirected from illegal flows to legal flows through ports of entry.

Nevertheless, significant strides have been made in migration-related measures in the last few years that can also help combat terrorism. With regard to visa policies, for instance, the US government now requires personal interviews of nearly all visa applicants, has enhanced security checks on visa applicants, has reviewed countries participating in the Visa Waiver Program, and has terminated two programs that allowed travel through the United States without visas.[143] In addition, the State Department's Consular Lookout and Support System (CLASS), which also includes a list of known and suspected terrorists, has been dramatically expanded with contributions from other agencies; visa applicants' electronic files from consular posts overseas are now shared with inspectors at US ports of entry; and provision of advance passenger information to DHS is mandatory.[144]

Document security also has been greatly enhanced through the use of machine-readable visas and passports, and the application of biometric identifiers embedded in travel and identification documents. Increasingly, biometrics are based on common standards and can be read by interoperable technology. Programs that track the entry, and, in some instances, the post-entry behavior of the foreign-born have been implemented, including the US-VISIT entry-exit program and the Student and Exchange Visitor Information System (SEVIS) program.[145] SEVIS now manages data for over 875,000 students and exchange visitors and their dependents, arresting 592 in 2005; the US-VISIT program has processed 60 million travelers, preventing 1,170 from entering since its inception.[146] As automated document screening tools are strengthened, it becomes increasingly important to focus on lost and stolen passports.

Additional hardening of the land border is largely an issue of migration management. The role of border enforcement in counterterrorism described in the 2002 National Strategy for Homeland Security seeks the optimal balance between the need for security and the need to facilitate commerce, travel, and the movement of people. The policy's main tools are significantly improved systems for screening travelers, and information-sharing within and between governments. The "smart borders" strategy best expresses the intersections between the immigration system and terrorism prevention and deterrence measures.[147]

Collaboration with other countries

As part of the efforts described above, the United States has deepened collaboration with Canada and Mexico. Bilateral enforcement teams and task forces focus on law enforcement issues of common concern, such as smuggling and the transit of third-country nationals, and the countries share information on visa policies and travelers, as well as collaborate on risk-based assessments.[148] Greater information sharing also has allowed development of programs for frequent travelers, such as NEXUS and SENTRI for passenger traffic and FAST for commercial traffic.[149]

Although cooperation at the working level between immigration, border, and law enforcement officials from neighboring countries is longstanding, US, Mexican, and Canadian officials across the board have intensified joint efforts, recognizing that a critical counterterrorism tool is sharing law enforcement and intelligence information. Security improvements are likely to continue, as the leaders of the three nations more fully institutionalize cooperation on security issues through adoption of the 2005 Security and Prosperity Partnership.[150]

Terrorist mobility

Mobility is an essential capability of terrorist organizations, often requiring terrorists to make contact with enforcement personnel at border crossings and other immigration processes. These points of contact represent vulnerabilities for the terrorists, and opportunities for counterterrorism officials. The ability to move operatives around the world is critical to terrorist organizations. Governments are directing substantial resources to combat terrorist communications, financing, recruiting, and training, but terrorist mobility is receiving less attention.

Constraining terrorists' mobility is a different task than managing immigration. Terrorist tracking requires a distinct mindset and resource allocations, and it is dependent on vastly strengthened intelligence collection and analysis; information-sharing between agencies; upgraded travel documents and systems; vigorous law enforcement; and cooperation with foreign law enforcement and intelligence officials.

Terrorist mobility must be studied and tracked in detail for counterterrorism officials to prevent and disrupt terrorist mobility. The United States spent tens of billions of dollars gathering intelligence on troop movements and weapon systems deployments during the Cold War. An effort that employs comparable techniques and receives priority attention by intelligence agencies — working closely with border enforcement and other law enforcement agencies — will be required to understand and act aggressively against terrorist travel.

A key task is distinguishing terrorists from other travelers who may or may not be violating immigration laws.[151] The ability to know who might be dangerous depends upon officials at the border having access to real-time information collected through intelligence and law enforcement operations. Here, watch lists of suspected terrorists are particularly important. However, a DHS official recently testified that officials at the border do not yet have ready access to all necessary information, and that a strategic plan for collecting, analyzing, and disseminating intelligence related to border security is still lacking.[152]

A new government-wide *National Strategy to Combat Terrorist Travel* has recently been published by the National Counterterrorism Center. In addition, the strategy's emphasis on preventing terrorists from crossing US borders highlights the need to work with other nations to prevent terrorists from crossing international borders; to build the capacity of partner nations to constrain terrorist mobility; to make systematic efforts to limit terrorists' access to the technical and other resources necessary to travel; and to promote increased information sharing on terrorist travel across the federal government and with state, local, and tribal law enforcement agencies.[153]

PROTECTING WORKERS

RECOMMENDATION #9: The Task Force recommends replacing the existing case-by-case labor certification system with one that provides for pre-certified employers, designates shortage occupations for blanket certifications, and uses a streamlined individual certification process for non-shortage occupations.

RECOMMENDATION #10: The Task Force recommends that temporary and provisional workers have the right to change employers without jeopardizing their immigration status and have worker protections that are comparable to those of similarly employed US workers.

A redesigned immigration system that better aligns immigration flows with US labor market needs must not diminish the employment opportunities, or undermine the wages or working conditions, of US workers. In part, mandatory worker verification, which assures that only work-authorized foreign-born workers are employed in the United States, speaks to that goal. However, protections must also encompass labor law enforcement more broadly.

Protection of US workers

Protecting the interests of US workers must remain an overarching priority of an immigration selection system.

At present, a labor certification process is intended to protect the wages, working conditions, and job opportunities of US workers from unfair competition from foreign workers. Well intended, the process has been criticized by employers, workers' advocates, and policy experts as cumbersome, ineffective in meeting the interests of US workers, and unresponsive to the legitimate needs of employers seeking to hire foreign workers. Various attempts to reform the system have been made. The most recent has been in place two years. It will take longer to determine the impact it may have.

Labor Certifications versus Attestations

Labor Certification

In the current Labor Certification process, an employer wishing to sponsor a foreign worker must establish—and the DOL must certify—that no US workers are willing, able, qualified, and available to perform the job in the time and place where it will be performed, and that the employment of the foreign worker will not adversely affect the wages or working conditions of similarly employed US workers. To establish this, the employer submits an individual application to the state employment security agency (SESA), which later sends the application to the certifying officer in the regional Department of Labor (DOL). The application describes the position being offered, its minimum requirements, and the education and job experience of the foreign worker. The regional officer may either approve the labor certification, or issue a Notice of Findings, citing possible deficiencies in the labor search or the job requirements. If an employer does not then successfully refute the Notice of Findings, the labor certification is denied. Employers may appeal denials to the DOL's Board of Alien Labor Certification Appeals, and if unsuccessful, in a federal district court.

PROS: The process gives the DOL control in determining whether qualified US workers are available to perform the job. Its cumbersome nature can act as a deterrent against non-meritorious applications.

CONS: It is bureaucratic, elevates form over substance, and is frequently unrelated to real world recruitment and hiring decisions. Further, the process is so time consuming as to make the connection between an available job and the hiring of a worker tenuous.

Attestation (Labor Condition Application)

In a labor attestation (Labor Condition Application (LCA)), an employer attests that 1) they are offering the foreign worker the higher of either the "actual wage" the employer pays to other similarly employed individuals or the "prevailing" wage for that type of position, 2) the working conditions of the foreign employee will not adversely affect the working conditions of other similarly-employed workers, 3) there is no strike or lockout at the place of employment, and 4) employees have been notified of the filing of the attestation by either posting the attestation at the workplace or by giving notice to a union representative. The LCA is filed at the regional DOL office. The DOL verifies the form's completeness, but does not have authority to evaluate the merits of the information provided on the form. An approved LCA is valid for three years.

PROS: The LCA process eliminates DOL processing delays and shifts the foreign labor oversight process from a "pre-admission" to a post-admission one. Employers can hire workers, and workers can obtain employment, within a reasonable period.

CONS: Unless post-admission oversight is robust enough to prevent abuse, the LCA process can become an avenue for bypassing the full worker protections the attestation is intended to guarantee.

Source: Demetrios G. Papademetriou and Stephen Yale-Loehr, *Balancing Interests: Rethinking U.S. Selection of Skilled Immigrants* (Washington, DC: Carnegie Endowment for International Peace, International Migration Policy Program, 1996), 48–49 and 83.

Pre-certified employers

With respect to temporary and provisional workers as described in Chapter V of the Task Force report, employers who regularly utilize these categories for large numbers of workers should have the opportunity to become pre-certified by the Department of Labor (DOL) to sponsor foreign workers. The pre-certifications would require employers to file labor condition attestations (LCAs) that the job is temporary (in the case of temporary workers), that no striking workers are being replaced, and that prevailing wages will be paid. Employers should be required to follow generally accepted recruitment and employment practices that include the routine advertising of jobs and ongoing recruitment of US workers. Additional criteria, such as an established practice of hiring only authorized workers, evidence of training programs in place for all workers, and compliance with established workplace rules, could also be reasonably required of employers for pre-certification. Pre-certifications could be granted on the basis of conditions that might vary over time, for example, for shortage occupations or industries in particular regions.

To provide incentives for these employers to hire US workers, substantial filing fees should be charged for sponsoring a foreign worker. Fee levels could vary depending on the size of the employer's workforce, the nature of the work, or the ratio of foreign workers to the overall workforce. As with other fees discussed in this report, the revenues should be designated for capacity-building to implement new immigration mandates.

Employer attestation

Employers without pre-certification would be required to file and obtain individually approved attestations from the Department of Labor (DOL). The attestation process would require a recruitment effort by the employer, including consultation with the relevant worker representative; posting of the job offer in appropriate electronic job registries; and a statement on the outcomes of all US worker referrals.

Labor certification

In the case of direct employment-based permanent immigration, employers would be required to obtain labor certification from DOL. The only exception would be for workers in strategic growth categories. Blanket certifications could be issued for occupations designated by DOL as shortage occupations, based on analyses provided by The Standing Commission. The designated list would reflect market conditions and be subject to ongoing review. If the occupation did not meet the requirements for blanket certification, an employer would go through a streamlined version of the current labor certification process, relying principally on DOL's electronic registries for posting the job, and recruiting US workers.

Protections of all workers — US and foreign-born

Large numbers of immigrant workers with varying immigration statuses pose challenges for protecting the workplace rights of both foreign- and native-born workers.[154] The issue deserves more attention than it has received in the current legislative debate for these reasons:

- Violations of rights and protections of foreign workers affect all workers — native and foreign-born.

- Foreign workers are particularly vulnerable to exploitation due to limited English-language skills, lack of knowledge regarding legal protections, and dependence on employer sponsorships.

- Workplace enforcement has proven inadequate in some areas and needs to be improved, especially in the low-wage sector.[155]

- Some forms of temporary worker programs have had a troubling legacy of abuse and exploitation.[156]

New and expanded forms of non-permanent, employment-based immigration must start with a set of premises different from past bracero-like guest-worker and temporary worker programs. Key requirements must include:

- *Changing employers.* To reduce the potential for exploitation, workers must be able to change employers after an initial period of several months, as long as the new employer is pre-certified and is within the industry or occupation for which the worker was originally sponsored. For valid cause, workers would be allowed to change employers earlier. Currently, under most temporary worker programs, the foreign worker is tied to an employer, establishing an inherently unequal relationship.[157]

- *Rights on par with US workers.* Temporary and provisional workers should have the same labor rights and protections as similarly employed US workers.[158] This includes access to and protection of US courts. Under existing temporary worker programs, workers' exclusive remedies are complaints to regulatory bodies that lack adequate resources and appropriate remedies.

The law must also reduce disincentives for reporting violations. In some instances, unscrupulous employers have used immigration status to retaliate against workers who assert their rights. A whistleblower provision should protect workers (both US and foreign) against employer retaliation.

OTHER ENFORCEMENT

RECOMMENDATION #11: The Task Force recommends that the role of state and local police in immigration enforcement be limited to identifying, holding, and transporting removable aliens who are legitimately arrested for involvement in non-immigration offenses during normal police work. State and local police should be able to submit ID information to DHS officials qualified to make an independent determination regarding a person's legal status and any potential terrorist connections.

Beyond border control and workplace enforcement, there are many important enforcement issues that should be part of any comprehensive package of legislative and administrative reforms. The Task Force believes that state and local enforcement of immigration laws raises questions of particular urgency for new policymaking.

State and local enforcement

In the long run, successful enforcement of immigration law requires that immigration policy be widely accepted, and regarded as worthy of the same kind of law enforcement cooperation that prevails in other areas of public policy. However, in the near term, cooperation should take only measured steps that do not undermine trust between police officials and immigrant communities in reporting crime, nor contribute to broad misuses of authority without adequate preparation, training, or supervision.[159]

The most promising avenue is cooperation in select communities allowing for assistance in identifying, holding, and transporting removable aliens found among those already legitimately arrested for non-immigration offenses. Where criminal aliens are incarcerated, coordinated efforts between state and local officials and ICE/DHS should better ensure that criminal aliens are identified and returned to their home countries upon completing their sentences in the United States. Approaches of this type should occur only after a formal agreement is signed between specific local or state agencies and DHS.[160] Agreements should spell out adequate training requirements carried out by federal officials and ongoing federal supervision.

Removal proceedings and appeals

The Task Force discussed a wide range of other interior enforcement issues including backlogs in the immigration and federal court systems, and challenges to due process for immigrants in removal proceedings. The Task Force believes these issues are important in developing a comprehensive approach to US immigration reform that enforces immigration laws while maintaining a strong commitment to individual rights.

The term "aggravated felony" — requiring deportation in immigration law after the person has served his or her sentence — was originally restricted to a few serious crimes like murder, rape, and drug trafficking. Reforms in 1990, 1996, and 2005 expanded the definition to cover over 50 classes of crimes, including numerous minor offenses like shoplifting, and many offenses defined as misdemeanors in criminal law.[161] Congressional actions have also limited judicial review in many immigration proceedings. The REAL ID Act suspended immigrants' access to district courts for writs of habeas corpus. That law also allows deportation of immigrants while their appeals in federal courts are pending.

Increases in the number of offenses deemed "aggravated felonies," coupled with increases in the number of unauthorized immigrants in the country, have led to a surge in cases before the Board of Immigration Appeals (BIA). Faced with a growing backlog of cases, the Department of Justice initiated a series of reforms in 1999, and again in 2002, aimed at "streamlining" BIA review of immigration appeals. Under the streamlined rules, some cases before the BIA could be reviewed by only one BIA member rather than the normal three-member panel, and in many cases the BIA could issue judgments without opinion ("summary affirmances").[162] The reforms also halved the number of BIA members from 23 to 11.[163]

The streamlining led to a steep rise in the percentage of cases appealed to the federal courts, from historic levels of 10 percent to 25 percent of BIA rulings recently[164] (see Figure 13). The immigration caseload has grown especially

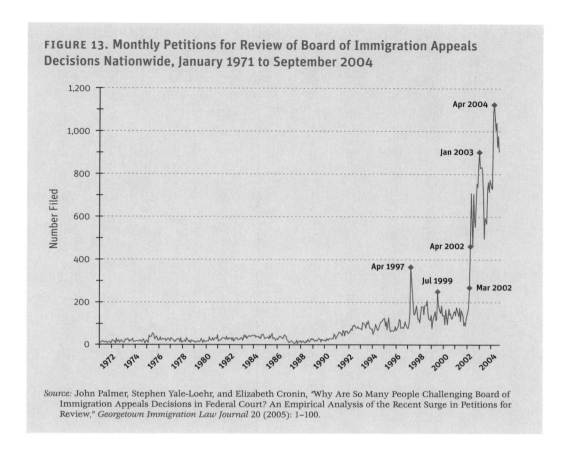

FIGURE 13. Monthly Petitions for Review of Board of Immigration Appeals Decisions Nationwide, January 1971 to September 2004

Source: John Palmer, Stephen Yale-Loehr, and Elizabeth Cronin, "Why Are So Many People Challenging Board of Immigration Appeals Decisions in Federal Court? An Empirical Analysis of the Recent Surge in Petitions for Review," *Georgetown Immigration Law Journal* 20 (2005): 1–100.

rapidly in the 9th Circuit Court of Appeals, increasing from 8 to 48 percent of all cases between 2001 and 2004.[165] Federal judges have issued harsh criticisms of the trend, and of the quality of immigration and BIA judges' decision-making.[166]

The consequences of removal from the United States are significant, not only for the immigrants, but also for their US-born family members. Individuals in removal proceedings do not have the right to appointed counsel. By statute, they can be represented but "at no expense to the Government."[167] As the right to appeal has diminished and the number of crimes catalogued as aggravated felonies has risen, absconder rates have soared. The estimated population of absconders now grows by about 40,000 persons per year.[168]

A variety of short- and long-term reforms could address appeals backlogs and strengthen immigrants' legal rights. Consideration should be given to restoring discretionary relief from removal in cases involving extraordinary circumstances. Appropriate judicial review must be assured. And a promising new idea would be a re-examination of the BIA and consideration of replacing the BIA with an Article I court for immigration. Elevating the BIA from an executive agency to a legislative court might attract a higher caliber of judges and produce higher quality reviews of immigration judges' decisions. Further, an Article I immigration court could capture the benefits of specialized courts and expertise, as well as intercircuit dialogue and generalist review.

In addition, Congress could authorize a pilot project for government appointed counsel in removal cases, or expand an existing program (the Legal Orientation

Program) to educate immigrants about their rights, help identify immigrants who may be eligible for relief, and provide support for those representing themselves. Increased education and representation for those in removal proceedings would benefit both immigrants and the government by promoting better-prepared cases, efficient proceedings, shorter detention periods, and better legal decisions, which, in turn, could reduce the number of appeals.

VII. Immigrant Integration

RECOMMENDATION #12: The Task Force recommends the creation of a National Office on Immigrant Integration to provide leadership, visibility, and a focal point at the federal level for integration policy as a critical national challenge.

RECOMMENDATION #13: The Task Force recommends an earned path to permanent legal status for unauthorized immigrants currently in the United States as an essential element of policies to address current illegal immigration.

as soon as publiaed

RECOMMENDATION #14: The Task Force recommends that a policy for earning legal status include a state impact aid program administered by the federal government. Impact aid should be allotted as a block grant with strict accountability for state spending.

block grant

Immigration ultimately succeeds through effective integration. Although immigration policy is set by the federal government, historically the integration of newcomers into communities and the life of the nation has been carried out locally by families, employers, schools, churches, and nongovernmental organizations — largely in the absence of substantial governmental support.

Whatever the imagery — melting pot, salad bowl, or mosaic — immigrant integration, or "assimilation," to use the terminology of an earlier peak immigration era, has been highly successful throughout American history. Successful integration of newcomers builds communities that are stronger economically and more inclusive socially and culturally. The process is a two-way street that involves change by immigrants as well as by receiving communities.

INTEGRATION POLICY CHALLENGES

Research indicates that integration is still proceeding across immigrant groups and across most indicators of social and economic mobility: educational attainment, labor force participation, income, and job quality.

Progress is particularly notable across generations. For example, second-generation immigrant youth from Asia, and particularly Latin America, have higher rates of school enrollment than the first generation. There has been a sharp rise in the share of Mexican teens aged 16 to 20 enrolled in school full-time, from 35 percent in the first generation to 57 percent in the second generation (see Figure 14). Second-generation Mexican school enrollment rates now approach those of both white and African-American children of US natives. The shares of second-generation students from Asia, Europe, and other Latin American countries actually exceed those of the children of natives.[169] These data are notable because the second generation is the crucible of integration success.

However, there are legitimate concerns that integration among new immigrants will not continue as it has in the past. Reasons for concern include the following:

- High and changing immigration flows since the 1990s that are unprecedented pose challenges for communities and all levels of government.

- The unauthorized constitute one-third of the total foreign-born population, compared to 15 percent only a decade ago.[170]

- The share of low-income children who are children of immigrants has been on the rise, increasing from 22 to 26 percent between 1999 and 2002.[171]

- The limited English proficient student population almost doubled in size between the 1993 and 2003 school years, with especially rapid proportional growth in new gateway states like North Carolina (500 percent growth) and Nebraska (340 percent growth).[172]

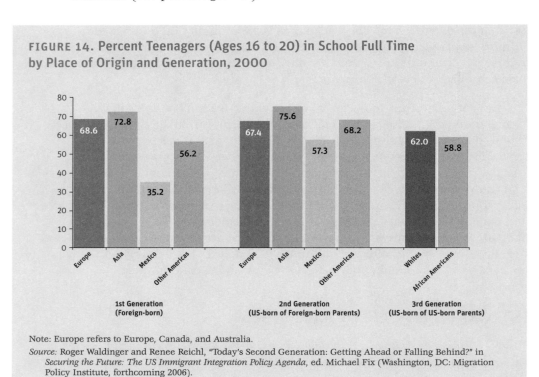

FIGURE 14. Percent Teenagers (Ages 16 to 20) in School Full Time by Place of Origin and Generation, 2000

1st Generation (Foreign-born): Europe 68.6, Asia 72.8, Mexico 35.2, Other Americas 56.2
2nd Generation (US-born of Foreign-born Parents): Europe 67.4, Asia 75.6, Mexico 57.3, Other Americas 68.2
3rd Generation (US-born of US-born Parents): Whites 62.0, African Americans 58.8

Note: Europe refers to Europe, Canada, and Australia.

Source: Roger Waldinger and Renee Reichl, "Today's Second Generation: Getting Ahead or Falling Behind?" in *Securing the Future: The US Immigrant Integration Policy Agenda*, ed. Michael Fix (Washington, DC: Migration Policy Institute, forthcoming 2006).

- While immigrant workers have high labor force participation rates, they are concentrated in low-paying jobs, accounting for one of every five low-wage workers.[173]

- Adults in low-income immigrant working families are almost twice as likely to be without health insurance as their counterparts in native-born families, 56 versus 29 percent respectively.[174]

These trends are troubling and represent significant local and national challenges. The failure of the federal government to address the problem of a growing unauthorized population has practical consequences, such as increasing demand for schools and emergency medical care. In addition, institutions that promoted immigrant integration in the past — such as unions, manufacturing firms, urban schools, and local political party machines — have weakened. Immigration has also rapidly extended to areas without a recent history of immigration and the infrastructure needed to promote integration. States like Nevada and North Carolina have seen their foreign-born populations rise by more than 100 percent since 1990.[175] Many migrants to these new growth states are more likely to be unauthorized, poor, and less educated than immigrants to more traditional locales.

Clearly there is a need for focused integration efforts to ensure the success of new Americans, mitigate fiscal impacts, promote intergovernmental cooperation, and allocate the costs of and services provided by integration programs. But while US immigration policies are specified in great detail in US laws, immigrant integration policies are skeletal, ad hoc, and under-funded.

Recent legislative efforts at all levels of government have varied widely in the extent to which they encourage, inhibit, or ignore altogether the goal of immigrant integration. There are many issues to consider in establishing an immigrant integration agenda. The Task Force has selected only the two it considers of primary importance and in need of urgent attention: 1) development of a national policy office that will serve as a focal point for policy in general, and English-language acquisition in particular, and 2) health care.

State Leadership on Integration: A Case Study of Illinois

In 2005, Illinois Governor Rod Blagojevich, announced his "New Americans Initiative," an executive order aimed to help 60,000 Illinois immigrants learn English and pass the naturalization exam by 2008. There are 1.6 million foreign-born people living in Illinois: less than 40 percent are currently US citizens, and about 348,000 have not naturalized even though they are eligible to do so.

The $3 million per year initiative is supported by several large foundations and national organizations focused on immigrant issues. The project brings the government in partnership with the Illinois Coalition for Immigrant and Refugee Rights to provide funding to community organizations for outreach, civics and English classes, and some legal counseling. It targets suburban Chicago and communities in Southern Illinois where social service agencies currently lack the infrastructure needed to deal with large inflows of immigrants.

Source: Illinois Coalition for Immigrant and Refugee Rights (ICIRR), New Americans Initiative, http://www.newamericans-il.org/.

A National Office of Immigrant Integration

There is no national policy or organizational entity to promote immigrant integration. (The Office of Refugee Resettlement monitors the integration of refugees and asylees, who compose a small share — about 10 percent — of annual immigration flows.) Similar to the role that the Small Business Administration plays for small businesses in the country, a national Office for Immigrant Integration would provide a focal point for immigrant integration activities and programs. The office would have a mandate to:

- establish national goals and indicators for immigrant integration and measure the degree to which they are met;

- assess and coordinate federal policies;

- provide technical assistance as agencies shape policies and programs that bear on integration;

- coordinate federal action and serve as an intermediary with state and local governments in meeting integration goals; and

- systematically examine current and future supply and demand for English acquisition services among migrant families, and authorize means for meeting that demand.

In setting national goals for immigrant integration, one model might be the United Nations' Millennium Development Goals, which established a blueprint for meeting the needs of the world's poor.[176] In the case of immigrant integration,

National Goals for Immigrant Integration

The National Office on Immigrant Integration could set integration goals in a number of areas, such as health care access, education, and civic engagement. These goals would aim to reduce differences between the foreign-born and native populations or promote immigrant integration gains over time or across generations.

National immigrant integration goals might address:
- High school and college enrollment rates
- High school and college completion rates
- Child academic achievements in reading and math
- English proficiency gains among children of immigrants
- Labor force participation
- Earnings
- Poverty rates
- Rates of occupational downgrading among workers
- Health insurance coverage rates
- Receipt of pension benefits
- Naturalization rates
- Electoral participation among eligible immigrants
- English proficiency levels of immigrant adults

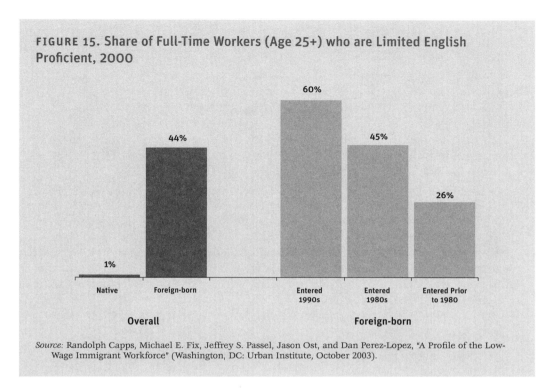

FIGURE 15. Share of Full-Time Workers (Age 25+) who are Limited English Proficient, 2000

Source: Randolph Capps, Michael E. Fix, Jeffrey S. Passel, Jason Ost, and Dan Perez-Lopez, "A Profile of the Low-Wage Immigrant Workforce" (Washington, DC: Urban Institute, October 2003).

the results should be detailed in an annual report to the president that is available as a public resource.

The office proposed in this report could build on the Bush Administration's recently announced Task Force on Immigrant Integration, established by an executive order issued in June 2006, convening cabinet-level agencies under the direction of DHS. The core mission outlined for the initiative is to "provide direction to executive departments and agencies concerning the integration into American society of America's legal immigrants, particularly through instruction in English, civics, and history." As of this writing, the scope of the Task Force's staffing, funding, and policy reach remain in the formative stages.

English-language acquisition

English is the language of opportunity for today's immigrants. Learning to speak, read, and write in English is arguably the most important integration challenge facing immigrants. It opens the door to jobs that can pay family-sustaining wages; it allows immigrants to communicate with their neighbors, children's teachers, health care providers, landlords, and law enforcement officials; and it is required for the US citizenship exam and full civic engagement, including the ability to vote in elections.

The need is pressing. The Limited English proficient (LEP) population has increased dramatically, accounting for more than 8 percent of the *total* US population in 2000. The number of individuals who reported that they spoke English less than very well grew 52 percent from 14 million in the 1990 Census to 23 million in 2000.[177] Almost half of all immigrant workers are LEP (see Figure 15).

Immigrant education policy is in flux with the enactment, implementation, and pending 2007 reauthorization of the No Child Left Behind Act (NCLB).[178]

Despite the controversies it has generated, the NCLB is perhaps the most important piece of integration legislation enacted in a decade, as it requires that schools identify and teach LEP and low-income immigrant children, and it holds schools accountable for their performance. Nevertheless, NCLB is an exception within the broader field of immigrant integration.

Despite the centrality of English to immigrant well-being and national productivity, language policies are scattered. Policies for LEP adults are particularly disjointed since they are not driven by any national body, such as the US Department of Education's Office of English Language Acquisition that oversees LEP students in the K-12 education system.

Federal workforce development programs and English-language programs remain uncoordinated, despite the large population of immigrant workers that needs to acquire both job training and English skills to advance economically. The principal national program for adult English-language learning has faced budget cuts in recent years, even amid widespread over-subscription for English classes.[179] And while employers have a stake in an English-proficient workforce, little has been done to leverage that interest to expand English-language offerings originating in the private sector.

To support the goal of enhanced English language acquisition, the National Office for Immigrant Integration should:

- develop policies that expand the reach of adult language and literacy instruction;

- coordinate English instruction with national workforce development policies; and

- connect demand for immigrant workers with employer-sponsored English instruction.

A more coherent set of language acquisition policies would require a systematic examination of patterns of demand for English acquisition; government and private spending; intergovernmental and private sector roles; and the expanding role and potential of technology as an alternative to traditional classroom instruction for teaching English.

Health care

The US health care system is built on a voluntary, employer-based insurance model that is supplemented by a social safety net — federally financed programs like Medicaid, Medicare, and the State Child Health Insurance Program. More than 44 percent of non-citizen immigrants do not have health insurance, in large part because they work in low-wage jobs with few benefits, and because the high price of purchasing individual or family policies is prohibitive[180] (see Table 9).

While many low-income citizens can still turn to the safety net for insurance, most legal immigrants entering the United States after 1996 are effectively barred from federal health insurance programs for at least five years.[181] The resulting high rates of un-insurance translate into lower rates of health care use and, perhaps, to poorer health outcomes for immigrants.[182] They have also frequently translated into high levels of uncompensated care provided by public hospitals, clinics, and charitable organizations. These burdens are regularly cited by local

TABLE 9. Health Insurance Coverage of the US Population, by Immigration Status, 2004

	Uninsured	Employer-Sponsored Insurance	Medicaid/ SCHIP	Non-group & Other Private	Medicare & Other Public	Total
US-Born Citizens	13.3%	59.1%	13.0%	5.5%	9.1%	100.0%
Naturalized Citizens	17.2%	54.9%	10.3%	5.4%	12.2%	100.0%
Non-Citizen Immigrants	44.1%	36.5%	12.6%	4.0%	2.9%	100.0%

Source: Leighton Ku and Demetrios G. Papademetriou, "Access to Health Care and Health Insurance: Immigrants and Immigration Reform," in *Securing the Future: The US Immigrant Integration Policy Agenda*, ed. Michael Fix (Washington, DC: Migration Policy Institute, forthcoming 2006).

officials and citizens as an important source of the tensions associated with immigration.

Comprehensive immigration reform that raises the number of immigrant admissions should shield providers, states, localities, and taxpayers from added fiscal burdens. Since even US citizens do not have universal access to health insurance, the government cannot selectively extend coverage to immigrants.

The Task Force urges innovative, market-based approaches that consider:

- requiring contributions from immigrants or sponsoring employers to finance insurance plans;

- focusing on more cost-effective preventive care to new immigrants;

- enabling businesses to join together to purchase health plans, pooling risks and extending coverage to US native and immigrant workers alike; and

- negotiating bilateral agreements with sending countries to support public health clinics in areas where their nationals reside (see Appendix IV: Innovative Approaches to Promoting Health Coverage for New Immigrants).

Future — like past — integration must involve a commitment by immigrants themselves, receiving communities, the private and nonprofit sectors, and governmental actors at all levels. Yet the laissez-faire approach to integration of the past leaves too much to chance for today's immigrants and the critical economic and social role they will play in America's future.

THE UNAUTHORIZED POPULATION

What to do about the estimated 11 million or more unauthorized immigrants living in the United States is the most contentious issue in the current legislative debate (see Figure 16). The issue of the unauthorized population is also the most urgent integration challenge the country faces. Among the legislative alternatives that have been proposed, the Task Force supports the opportunity for legal status, including an eventual path to citizenship, as an essential element in comprehensively addressing illegal immigration.

The United States lacks the capacity to enforce the departure of a significant percentage of the millions of unauthorized immigrants, many of whom have lived and worked in the United States for years and have US citizen children.[183]

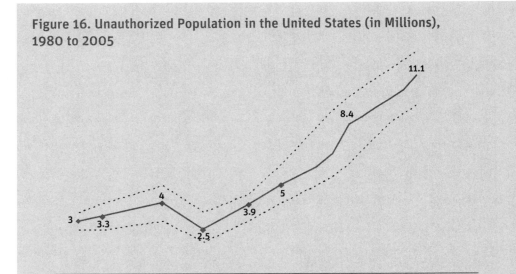

Figure 16. Unauthorized Population in the United States (in Millions), 1980 to 2005

11.1

8.4

4

3.9

5

3

3.3

2.5

1980 1982   1986   1989   1992 1996   2000   2005

Note: While the unauthorized population was estimated at 11.1 million in 2005, the estimate for 2006 is 11.5 to 12 million, which is the number used elsewhere in this report. The dashed lines represent the lower and upper bounds of the estimated size of the unauthorized population.

Source: Jeffrey S. Passel, "The Size and Characteristics of the Unauthorized Migrant Population in the U.S." (Washington, DC: Pew Hispanic Center, March 2006).

The Task Force also does not believe a policy of attrition through substantial re-movals can work. The costs in dollars; economic, family, and community disruption; and foreign relations would prove unacceptable to the American people.

Providing a path to legal status for the unauthorized is in the national interest for several reasons:

- The unauthorized population in the United States is making important economic contributions to the nation's productivity, competitiveness, and fiscal health. Contributions to tax revenues — for example through payroll taxes to the federal government and sales taxes at local and state levels — will increase substantially because of increased earning power from legal status.[184]

- Unauthorized immigration is made possible in part by a web of false documents and international smuggling networks that can constitute national security vulnerabilities. Conferring legal status should reduce the incentives driving these markets.

- Individuals who do not have legal status have minimal legal rights and are, therefore, subject to many forms of exploitation. The potential for widespread abuses of basic rights undermines the rule of law and the well-being of communities in many important areas, for example housing, employment standards, and public health.

- The existence of a sizeable unauthorized population dilutes progress toward immigrant integration, which is contingent on an immigrant's opportunity to "belong" in American society and fully participate in its civic and public life. The unauthorized have no legal claim to be or stay in the United States, are ineligible for most government benefits and services, and have very limited rights. The potential for an increasingly stratified society along lines of legal status is dangerous social policy.

The lessons of IRCA suggest that the legalization process should be simple, with an eligibility date that is as recent as possible. Requiring applicants to provide elaborate documentation of their history in the United States invites misrepresentation. Rather, the ideal process would involve registration for work eligibility in the United States, accompanied by a background security check and payment of a substantial fine for illegally entering the United States.

During subsequent years, legalizing immigrants would be required to demonstrate a knowledge of English, steady employment, payment of taxes, and good moral character in order to earn lawful permanent residence and, ultimately, citizenship. Those applying for legal status should be permitted to travel to and from the United States. Some proportion is likely to decide to return permanently to their countries of origin.

Most importantly, a legal status program will only succeed if it is undertaken as part of a package of reforms that also achieves effective enforcement and creates expanded opportunities for legal migration.

State impact aid

States should not bear a disproportionate burden arising from the consequences of federal immigration policy. Therefore, as it did in 1986, the federal government should administer a state impact aid program in conjunction with a legalization scheme. The aid program should provide states with more flexibility to find solutions that fit their different needs, populations, and funding mechanisms than was the case with IRCA.

As part of the 1986 IRCA, a $4 billion State Legalization Impact Assistance Grant (SLIAG) was created to help defray anticipated costs that states would incur in terms of health care, public assistance, and English/civics classes for newly authorized immigrants. SLIAG's administrative requirements for establishing reimbursement claims proved to be confusing and cumbersome. The grant program narrowly defined reimbursable costs, and reimbursements were delayed. As a result, available funds were raided for other uses, which penalized states waiting to be reimbursed for expenditures.[185]

Based on lessons learned from SLIAG and the contrasting 1996 welfare reform block grant model, it is more effective to cover the costs arising from a new legalization program through a block grant, rather than a reimbursement scheme.[186] A block grant encourages states to be innovative and allows them to target urgent needs. Such flexibility would have to be accompanied by clear guidelines for accountability against which states would plan expenditures and measure results.

VIII. Strengthening Institutional Capacity

RECOMMENDATION #15: The Task Force recommends that the president: 1) name a White House coordinator for immigration policy; 2) issue an executive order establishing an interagency cabinet committee for immigration policy; and 3) strengthen the capacity of executive branch agencies to implement major new immigration mandates.

The three other traditional countries of immigration — Australia, Canada, and New Zealand — all have cabinet-level immigration ministries dedicated to administering the immigration policies of their nations, as do several European Union member states. With the creation of the Department of Homeland Security (DHS), the United States has gone in the opposite direction, dividing the immigration functions that had been administered by INS into separate new bureaus within DHS[187] (see Appendix VI: Who Does What in US Immigration). One result has been fragmentation of responsibility and weak, largely ineffective immigration policy development and coordination by the executive branch.

POLICY PROCESSES AND INTERAGENCY COORDINATION

The restructuring of immigration agencies after 9/11 has resulted in immigration being treated almost solely as a security issue. Another massive reorganization would be counterproductive at this time. However, the Task Force believes there is an urgent need to mobilize government resources and authorities more effectively, develop and implement new policy agendas, and strengthen accountability in carrying out immigration mandates. All are tasks that require cross-agency action, which large, autonomous government agencies are not well-suited to do.

Many of the reform ideas under consideration in Congress — for example, mandatory employer verification, granting legal status to millions of unauthorized immigrants, quadrupling employment-based visas — are more ambitious than anything that has been attempted before in the immigration arena. Mandatory employer verification alone involves at least three separate organizational entities within DHS and three non-DHS federal agencies.[188] Much of the legislation being debated has government-wide implementation implications and requirements.

Federal Agencies with Immigration and Integration Responsibilities

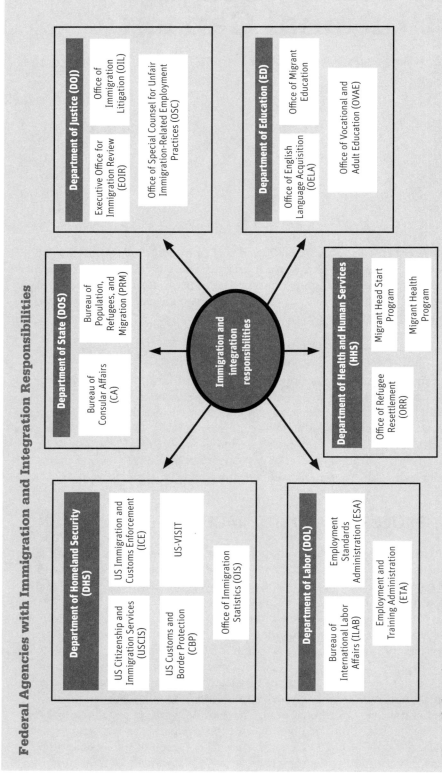

Department of Justice (DOJ)

Executive Office for Immigration Review (EOIR)

Office of Immigration Litigation (OIL)

Office of Special Counsel for Unfair Immigration-Related Employment Practices (OSC)

Department of Education (ED)

Office of English Language Acquisition (OELA)

Office of Migrant Education

Office of Vocational and Adult Education (OVAE)

Department of State (DOS)

Bureau of Consular Affairs (CA)

Bureau of Population, Refugees, and Migration (PRM)

Immigration and integration responsibilities

Department of Health and Human Services (HHS)

Office of Refugee Resettlement (ORR)

Migrant Head Start Program

Migrant Health Program

Department of Homeland Security (DHS)

US Citizenship and Immigration Services (USCIS)

US Immigration and Customs Enforcement (ICE)

US Customs and Border Protection (CBP)

US-VISIT

Office of Immigration Statistics (OIS)

Department of Labor (DOL)

Bureau of International Labor Affairs (ILAB)

Employment Standards Administration (ESA)

Employment and Training Administration (ETA)

Note: For further explanation, see Appendix VI.

Source: Adapted from Megan Davy, Deborah W. Meyers, and Jeanne Batalova, "Who Does What in US Immigration," *The Migration Information Source,* December 1, 2005.

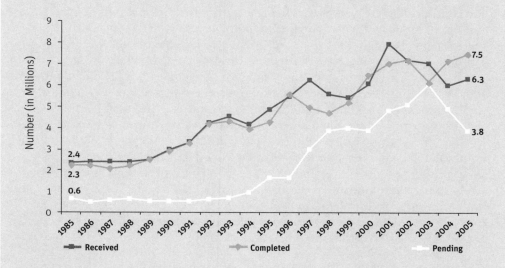

FIGURE 17. Immigration and Naturalization Applications Received, Completed, and Pending at USCIS, FY 1985 to 2005

Notes: Number completed is sum of approved and denied. Data are current as of June 29, 2005. Note that counts for the last few years are provisional, and may be revised.

Sources: Kevin Jernegan, "Backlogs in Immigration Processing Persist" (Washington, DC: Migration Policy Institute, June 2005). Updated using DHS, Office of Immigration Statistics, G-22.2 Adjudication Summary Report and G-22.3 Naturalization Summary Report.

Should such proposals become law, sizeable resource infusions and rapid institutional capacity-building would be required. In addition, both a DHS and interagency policy superstructure would be required to handle the myriad decisions and coordination tasks required. Neither exists at present.

Even without legislation, policy development, coordination, and oversight must be strengthened.

The existing agencies are handling massive workloads, often with insufficient resources or information systems infrastructure. Many aspects of the immigration system — for example, border control, detention and removal, and backlog reduction — present formidable management challenges. Immigration agencies need more support and engagement by senior-level officials to deliver the results Congress and the public expect.

The Task Force urges the president to name a high-level White House official to coordinate immigration policy. Similar appointments have worked successfully in areas such as HIV/AIDS policy. An interagency committee would establish a mechanism through which this official could provide leadership, and a focal point in the government for immigration matters. By using an executive order to convene the committee, the president would signal the importance of the issues and the need to work together across organizational lines. At a minimum, members should include the secretaries of Homeland Security, State, Labor, Agriculture, Commerce, Health and Human Services, Education, and the Attorney General.

POLICY INFORMATION

The answers to basic questions about immigration are also necessary to inform responsible decision-making and oversight. How many individuals try to enter the country illegally? Is the number rising or falling? Who are immigrants and non-immigrants and what happens to them once they arrive in the United States? How many leave the country within the required time? Which categories of non-immigrants apply for permanent residence and at what rates?

Currently, the government cannot answer such questions. The data immigration agencies gather track workload information — numbers of applications or enforcement actions — not individuals. As a result, it is impossible to know, for example, how many people (as opposed to visa issuances) are actually in the country working on temporary visas. Until data gathering improves, it will continue to be very difficult to determine the effectiveness of current policies, programs, or resource investments. The significance of the role immigration is likely to play in the future of the nation demands far higher standards of quality and investment in immigration data collection. Immigration information and analysis should be on a par with the work produced by agencies such as the Bureau of Labor Statistics and the Census Bureau.

IMPLEMENTING NEW MANDATES

The challenges of employer and workplace enforcement provide an example of the institutional capacity, coordination, and robust programs that would be required to effectively implement the proposals the Task Force is making or the legislation currently under consideration. The vast majority of employers are law-abiding. But they want laws to be realistic with simple, reliable compliance procedures. In this regard, employers' interests align with those of the government and the larger society because deterrence against hiring unauthorized workers will result only from broad employer compliance, which requires workable verification combined with diligent enforcement that holds employers accountable and prosecutes violators.

Yet, to date, no government agency or office has had workplace enforcement of immigration requirements as its priority mission. After a modest initial investment following IRCA, attention to workplace enforcement waned during the 1990s.[189] It reached a new low after 9/11 as the anti-terrorism mission was given to ICE, which also inherited the employer and other interior enforcement control responsibilities of the INS. The number of employers prosecuted for employing unauthorized immigrants fell from 182 in 1999 to four in 2003, while fines collected fell from $3.6 million to $212,000.[190] Following 9/11, employer enforcement took place almost solely as a function of oversight on critical infrastructure (e.g., airports, nuclear facilities) rather than on a cross-section of industries that typically employ unauthorized workers.[191]

Employer enforcement would be substantially improved if it received dedicated resources directed to a specific office within ICE or another organizational focal point with sole responsibility for employer enforcement of immigration requirements. Although the administration has recently turned its attention to high-profile prosecutions of such cases, absent greater institutionalization, workplace enforcement is likely to be overshadowed by other urgent demands again, as has repeatedly occurred in the past.[192] The mission of a new entity or office should be employer education and liaison to encourage compliance, compliance monitoring, and enforcement actions when employers fail to meet verification and other immigration law requirements.

Similarly, responsibilities that have traditionally been part of the mission of the Department of Labor would need to be strengthened. The Task Force proposals for pre-certifying employers to hire foreign workers and procedures for attestation that the employer is engaged in verifiable and ongoing efforts to recruit US workers, for example, are designed to make the immigration system more responsive to legitimate employer needs for legal foreign workers and to reduce meaningless bureaucratic practices that have become outdated. At the same time, streamlined procedures call for systematic oversight so they are not abused. Providing for effective oversight needs to become a priority because important government agencies responsible for enforcing labor protection laws have experienced steady reductions in resources.[193] As a result, government agencies have become less prepared to regulate more than eight million employers.

Such oversight can be accomplished in a variety of ways. Audits of pre-certified employers should be conducted periodically; to the greatest extent possible, such audits should be carried out electronically, using modern tracking and information systems for new employer compliance programs that government agencies need to create. In addition, both complaint-driven and random compliance audits should become a new norm for all employers who participate in the temporary and provisional immigration systems, with sectors employing large numbers of foreign workers receiving additional attention. Graduated penalties should be established to deter habitual violators or unscrupulous employers from violating the terms and conditions of the program in which they are participating. Bars from continuing access to such programs should also be considered for repeat-violators.

Large-scale immigration and streamlined procedures for hiring foreign workers can also result in discrimination and other violations of rights of US workers. Thus, complaint procedures and government programs and law enforcement agencies that combat discrimination and other violations of labor standards and working conditions would also require adequate resources and support if new immigration policies are to succeed and win public confidence.

Meaningful enforcement is essential to protecting US workers and assuring the integrity of a new immigration selection system. The issues and capacity needs outlined here regarding employer and workplace enforcement are but one set of challenges inherent in implementing sweeping immigration policy mandates. Experience has shown that unless government agencies are strengthened and, when necessary, new structures created, implementation weaknesses will hinder the achievement of important national policy goals.

IX. The Regional Context of Immigration

RECOMMENDATION #16: The Task Force recommends that the United States engage Mexico and Canada in longer-term initiatives directed at management of labor flows in the context of regional economic interdependence, growth, and security.

Illegal migration is a regional issue. Nearly 80 percent of the unauthorized population in the United States is from Latin America, primarily from Mexico and Central America[194] (see Figure 18). These nations are tied to the United States by social and historical connections, and increasingly by trade agreements and other economic connections that have contributed to the emergence of regional labor markets that often function outside of political boundaries.

The US immigration policy debate is overwhelmingly a domestic conversation, but its consequences have profound regional implications and consequences for neighboring nations.[195] Governments in the region are deeply concerned about how US policy changes will affect them. Key issues include the potential for large-scale removals of unauthorized immigrants in the United States, a legal status guest-worker program, hardening border enforcement, and changes in current patterns of legal and illegal immigration to the United States.

The flow of remittance earnings from migrants in the United States to families and communities in their home countries is a particularly pressing concern. Remittances have reached record amounts and represent a major source of income to millions of individuals and communities. Estimates are that more than $20 billion of remittances flowed to Mexico in 2005, representing its second highest source of foreign earnings, next to oil.[196] For smaller nations, such as El Salvador, the impact of remittances on the economic viability of the nation may be even greater. Roughly one in eight Salvadorans is estimated to live in the United States and remittances accounted for 17 percent of El Salvador's Gross Domestic Product (GDP) in 2005.[197] Changes in these income streams have the potential to be highly destabilizing.

In the longer term, the United States prospers when its neighbors prosper. US interests call for working even more cooperatively throughout the region to resolve the problems of illegal migration, and to harness the benefits of migration. Highly

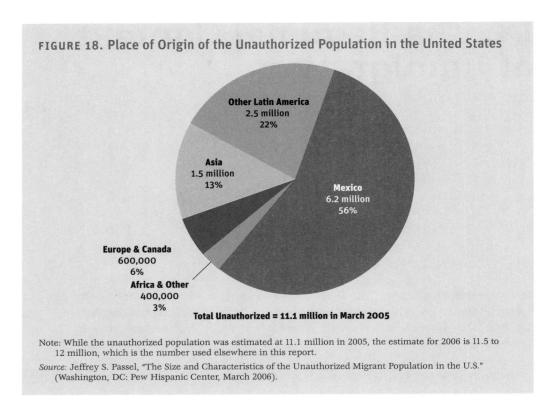

FIGURE 18. Place of Origin of the Unauthorized Population in the United States

Other Latin America
2.5 million
22%

Asia
1.5 million
13%

Mexico
6.2 million
56%

Europe & Canada
600,000
6%

Africa & Other
400,000
3%

Total Unauthorized = 11.1 million in March 2005

Note: While the unauthorized population was estimated at 11.1 million in 2005, the estimate for 2006 is 11.5 to 12 million, which is the number used elsewhere in this report.

Source: Jeffrey S. Passel, "The Size and Characteristics of the Unauthorized Migrant Population in the U.S." (Washington, DC: Pew Hispanic Center, March 2006).

developed regional social and economic ties represent an important opportunity to ground migration policy within a foreign policy framework (see Table 10). The goal should be to shift economic integration into a healthier pattern, moving away from the mutually reinforcing dependencies on remittances and cheap labor to a system of regulated labor flows and economic interdependence that results in viable economies and higher standards of living throughout the region.

ECONOMIC DEVELOPMENT

Remittances to migrant countries of origin, emigration, or current foreign assistance programs are not likely to sufficiently develop regional economies to have the necessary broad-based impact to mitigate the root causes of migration.[198] Large portions of sending country populations live below the poverty line of their nations: 36 percent in El Salvador, 53 percent in Honduras, and 75 percent in Guatemala.[199] Ten percent of Mexico's total population and 15 percent of its working-age population resides in the United States.[200] Experiences in countries such as Ireland, South Korea, Malaysia, and Taiwan have demonstrated that only sustained economic growth and social development can transform traditional countries of emigration into immigrant destinations.[201]

Fifteen years ago, many experts believed that expanded trade with and investment in migrant countries of origin were a key to reducing unauthorized migration.[202] While there is no doubt that NAFTA spurred economic growth in Mexico, a decade later it is also clear that NAFTA was no panacea for solving illegal immigration: Enduring social networks and historical experiences, as

	Visas issued for temporary workers, transferees, or exchange visitors, FY 2005	Permanent migration to United States, FY 2005	US foreign-born population, by nationality, 2005	Estimated unauthorized population in the United States, by nationality, 2000[4]	Country's total population, 2006	Value of remittances to country in 2005[2] (millions of US dollars)	Share of country's imports coming from the United States, 2004	Share of country's exports going to the United States, 2004
Canada[1]	64,266	21,878	674,000	122,000	33,098,932	-	58.7%	84.5%
Costa Rica	1,998	2,278	52,000	NA	4,075,261	$362	44.9%	44.4%
Dominican Republic	4,197	27,504	695,000	89,000	9,183,984	$2,682	44.8%	40.2%
El Salvador	802	21,359	1,121,000	404,000	6,822,378	$2,830	31.2%	23.1%
Guatemala	4,535	16,825	546,000	NA	12,293,545	$2,993	40.9%	29.4%
Honduras	1,273	7,012	379,000	NA	7,326,496	$1,763	40.0%	41.9%
Mexico	114,880	161,445	10,805,000	4,784,000	107,449,525	$20,034	56.6%	88.6%
Nicaragua	713	3,305	181,000	NA	5,570,129	$850	22.3%	36.1%

Notes: 1. Canada's unauthorized estimate refers to Canada plus other North American countries (excluding Mexico), and Canada's permanent migration figure includes Newfoundland. 2. Remittances include remittances from all countries, not only the United States. 3. Temporary visa numbers include the following visas: H, J, L, O, P, Q, R, and TN (NAFTA). For Canada, the numbers also include the 63,847 admissions of NAFTA workers, who do not require visas for entry. 4. More recent data on the countries of origin of the unauthorized population are not available. Therefore, these numbers do not match data on the unauthorized cited in other parts of this report, which describe the unauthorized population in 2005 and 2006.

Sources: US Census Bureau, Current Population Survey, March 2005; US Department of State, "Report of the Visa Office 2005"; World Trade Organization, Statistics Database, http://stat.wto.org/.; Jeffrey S. Passel, Jennifer Van Hook, Frank D. Bean, "Estimates of the Legal and Unauthorized Foreign-born Population for the United States and Selected States," Based on Census 2000 (Warminster, PA: Sabre Systems, June 1, 2004); Inter-American Development Bank, "Remittances to Selected Latin American Countries in 2005"; US Central Intelligence Agency, *The World Factbook,* July 2006.

well as demand in the United States for workers and a substantial supply of underemployed people in Mexico, remain at the root of illegal immigration. NAFTA was not able to create sufficient and sustained increases in net employment, nor could it overcome external factors such as the 1994 peso crisis. Freer trade and a more open economy are only components of the broader and longer-term effort necessary to enhance the economic prospects of Mexico and its residents.[203]

Development is ultimately the responsibility of migrant countries of origin. These countries must continue efforts to create domestic environments that attract investors, such as stable and transparent economic and political systems, and sustain those efforts over decades. Domestic policy programs like electrification or road construction in rural areas; enhancements in the primary and secondary education system; job creation targeted to reducing income inequality; and access to loans and other programs that support small business are also necessary.

In Mexico, the new president must focus on generating formal sector jobs, increasing the global competitiveness of the economy, implementing fiscal and labor law reforms, and enhancing efficiency in energy production, while also maintaining the progress toward financial stability and political accountability made in recent years.[204]

The development of Mexico and Central America is also in the interest of the United States. The United States can:

- continue contributions to international financial institutions;

- support teacher-training to improve the education and skills of the labor force;

- encourage privatization of particular industries and investment in infrastructure; and

- and help mitigate the negative impacts of structural changes, such as freer trade, by allowing the importation of competitive goods.

At the same time, the United States must know when to show patience and refrain from interference.[205]

Development is a generations-long project requiring sustained economic growth, job creation, greater income equality across the region, and changing perceptions that better opportunities can be found by going North. Any potential reduction in migration flows due to development is likely to be experienced only in the long term, and only if complementary measures are in place to reduce demand for foreign labor in the United States, improve the legal immigration framework, and better enforce immigration and labor laws. Since development generally spurs migration in the near to medium term, emigration from Mexico and Central America is likely to continue at high levels, either through legal or illegal channels, for the foreseeable future.

MIGRATION MANAGEMENT

Until development can reduce migration, regulation and management of migration flows is necessary. Mexico, in particular, has been seeking to manage migration as a shared responsibility with the United States.[206] In February 2006, Mexican leaders publicly outlined a statement of principles and responsibilities in a document adopted unanimously by members of both the Mexican Senate and Chamber of Deputies.[207] Mexico has also initiated an effort with Central and South American countries to develop a regional strategy for addressing immigration and border security issues.[208]

Cooperation at the US-Mexico Border

Since the second half of the 1990s, Mexico and the United States have worked together closely on issues of border safety and security. The declarations and agreements that came out of this period (including the 1997 Joint Declaration on Migration by the two presidents, the 1998 Memorandum of Understanding between Mexico's National Population Council (CONAPO) and the US Immigration and Naturalization Service (INS), and the 1999 Memorandum of Understanding on Cooperation Against Border Violence) laid the foundation for the formation of subsequent agreements and partnerships. Cooperation deepened after the 2000 election of current President Vicente Fox, who committed himself to working with the United States on immigration policy. After the terrorist attacks of 9/11, Mexico increased security and surveillance in the border region and improved information sharing with Interpol and with the United States.

In the past five years, Mexico has launched several initiatives both independently and bilaterally with the United States that addressed cross-border issues such as security, organized crime, drug trafficking, and human smuggling. A Federal Investigation Agency focused on fighting organized crime and corruption was created in 2001, and Mexico and the United States signed the US Mexico Border Partnership and Action Plan in March 2002. This 22-point Smart Border agreement was designed to ensure the secure flow of people and goods and protect the border infrastructure. Its action steps include harmonizing point-of-entry operations, cross border cooperation, facilitating NAFTA travel, combating alien smuggling, improving screening of third country nationals, electronic exchange of information, and contraband interdiction. In 2003, Mexico launched Operation Centinela in an effort to strengthen detention operations of certain undocumented immigrants, improve measures to target organized crime and human trafficking, and better protect strategic sites against potential terrorist attacks.

By February 2004, the United States and Mexico had signed a Memorandum of Understanding regarding a Safe, Orderly, Dignified, and Humane Repatriation of Mexican Nationals that aimed to strengthen the ability of both governments to manage migration flows while protecting the human rights of immigrants. It also established an Interior Repatriation program that has now been operating successfully for two years. The Security and Prosperity Partnership of North America (SPP) is a strategy that was launched by President Bush, President Fox, and Prime Minister Martin in 2005 to enhance security throughout North America while promoting economic and social prosperity and facilitating the legitimate movement of people and goods in the region. Thus far, principal actions of the Partnership include implementation of common border security protection strategies and increased information sharing and collaboration. Also in 2005, Mexico launched an effort against human smuggling, called OASSIS — Operation Against Smugglers (and Traffickers) Initiative on Safety and Security.

Sources: Embassy of Mexico, "Law Enforcement, Fight against Organized Crime and Border Security Fact Sheet," 2005; Deborah W. Meyers, "Does 'Smarter' Lead to Safer? An Assessment of the Border Accords with Canada and Mexico" (Washington, DC: Migration Policy Institute, June 2003); National Memorial Institute for the Prevention of Terrorism, Terrorism Knowledge Base, "Country Profile: Mexico," www.tkb.org.

Three discrete areas are ripe for fuller collaboration with Mexico and other primary sending nations in the region. They include:

- the continued targeting and dismantling of smuggling organizations;
- deportations; and
- regulating significant labor flows and other potential new US immigration policies.

Smuggling

The United States, Mexico, and Central American countries have a common interest in reducing smuggling. Smuggling undermines the rule of law, breeds corruption, spawns violence in border communities, and unnecessarily endangers the lives of migrants.

Working domestically and with foreign partners, the US government has begun placing greater emphasis on disruption of human smuggling and trafficking networks, including those with a nexus to terrorism, through the efforts of the Human Smuggling and Trafficking Center. The United States and Mexico should work together to strengthen enforcement efforts against people smugglers and other criminals who take advantage of vulnerable immigrants, and coordinate efforts to educate would-be migrants about the dangers associated with crossing the border outside normal ports of entry.

Deportation

Cooperation on deportation is essential, particularly as deportations are rising. Total annual deportations of Central Americans tripled since the mid-1990s, increasing from 8,057 in 1996 to 24,285 in 2004.[209] Deportation of migrants back to their country of origin can be facilitated through cooperation in verifying identity, reviewing criminal records, and promptly issuing travel documents. Rising deportations have had major impacts on hometown communities.[210] The United States could also help countries strengthen their systems for receiving deportees and reintegrating them into society, for example, by encouraging countries to reduce barriers to employment for returning deportees.

Bilateral management of new programs

New immigration policies and programs will benefit from bilateral cooperation with migrant countries of origin. Sending countries could play a role in screening potential workers for criminal records, verifying identity, evaluating credentials and relevant experience (including earlier stays in the United States), ensuring equal access to prevent corruption in the recruitment process, and educating migrants about labor rights. They could also play a role in developing guidelines for a licensed and regulated process in which the private sector might play a role in implementing a large new program. Similarly, sending country consulates in the United States could have access to worksites where immigrants are employed, and act as liaisons to US employers and government officials when there are charges of wage or working condition violations.

Security

Security concerns also demand regional cooperation. The United States cannot secure its borders alone, and the national security of the United States and its neighbors are deeply intertwined. The power of this new reality has been illustrated recently with the recent arrests of 17 highly armed terrorist suspects in Canada.[211] In an era where stateless terrorists and weapons flow across international borders, collaboration with Mexico and Canada is essential.

Significant progress has been made on a number of security fronts, particularly since 9/11, including increasing information sharing, interdicting smugglers and other criminals, and managing ports of entry to speed entry and control illicit activities. A great deal of the progress has been accomplished within the context of the post-9/11 Smart Border Accords, which codified working-level cooperation between the governments that dates back well over a decade.[212]

However, broader efforts to institutionalize these policies may be required in the United States, Mexico, and Canada. These efforts may include changes to laws governing information sharing, common document standards, and technological capabilities that allow for data sharing. It also may include funding and training of personnel, infrastructure improvements, and fuller partnerships with private sector stakeholders. The Security and Prosperity Partnership launched in March 2005 provides a framework for such progress.[213]

The value of North American security cooperation needs to be explained to segments of the public and politicians in each country. It is the basis for building broader cooperation that provides the only enduring answers to the challenges of illegal migration within the region. Progress toward longer term goals is deeply compromised by debates within the United States that focus, for example, on proposals to build walls the full length of the border. We need to emphasize the vital and constructive role our neighbors can play in border security.

The long-term challenge

If the current migration equation is to change, regional cooperation must produce greater parity in opportunities and standards of living among populations of all nations of the region. Altering the dynamics of illegal migration requires a broad, intensified, long-term commitment to regional integration at many levels. Such transformation can only evolve from aggressively building on existing security, private sector, and transnational social networks. All are critical building blocks toward full regional economic development. In the end, success will mean that migration becomes a matter of choice rather than of survival.

NOTES

1   About 9.8 million immigrants gained lawful permanent resident (LPR) status in the United States between 1990 and 1999, while an estimated 4.9 million immigrants entered and remained in the country without authorization. However, immigrants made up a larger share of the total US population at the turn of the century — about 15 percent, compared to only 12 percent currently. US Department of Homeland Security, *Yearbook of Immigration Statistics: 2004,* Table 1 (Washington, DC: US Department of Homeland Security Office of Immigration Statistics, 2006); Jeffrey S. Passel, "The Size and Characteristics of the Unauthorized Migrant Population in the U.S." (Washington, DC: Pew Hispanic Center, March 2006), http://pewhispanic.org/files/reports/61.pdf; and Tabulations from the Current Population Survey, March 2005.

2   For one recent poll of US opinions on immigration, see Pew Research Center for the People and the Press and Pew Hispanic Center, "America's Immigration Quandary: No Consensus on Immigration Problem or Proposed Fixes" (Washington, DC: Pew, March 2006), http://pewhispanic.org/reports/report.php?ReportID = 63.

3   Andrew Sum, Neeta Fog, Paul Harrington, et al., "Immigrant Workers and the Great American Job Machine: The Contributions of New Foreign Immigrants to National and Regional Labor Force Growth in the 1990s" (Boston, MA: Northeastern University Center for Labor Market Studies, August 2002), 16–17.

4   The Council of Graduate Schools found that 50 percent of students enrolled in graduate degree programs in engineering were foreign-born temporary US residents, while 41 percent of students enrolled in graduate degree programs in the physical sciences were foreign-born temporary residents. Heath A. Brown, "Graduate Enrollment and Degrees: 1986 to 2004" (Washington, DC: Council of Graduate Schools, Office of Research and Information Services, 2004).

5   About 10.4 percent of foreign-born workers are self-employed, compared to 9.4 percent of native workers. Jeanne Batalova and David Dixon, "Foreign-Born Self-Employed in the United States," *Migration Information Source* April 1, 2005, http://www.migrationinformation.org/USFocus/display.cfm?ID = 301.

6   US Census Bureau, "Growth of Hispanic-Owned Businesses Triples the National Average," Press Release (Washington, DC: US Census Bureau, March 21, 2006), http://www.census.gov/Press-Release/www/releases/archives/business_ownership/006577.html.

7   A study by the University of California, San Diego, found that one-quarter of Silicon Valley start-ups were established by Chinese and Indian immigrants during the 1990s. See AnnaLee Saxenian, "Silicon Valley's New Immigrant Entrepreneurs" (University of California, San Diego, The Center for Comparative Immigration Studies, May 2000).

8   Passel, "The Size and Characteristics of the Unauthorized" (see n. 1).

9   To access MPI's publications prepared for the Independent Task Force on Immigration and America's Future, see http://www.migrationpolicy.org/ITFIAF/publications.php.

10 See n. 1.

11 US Census Bureau, "Hispanic Population Reaches All-Time High of 38.8 Million, New Census Bureau Estimates Show," Press Release, June 18, 2003, http://www.census.gov/Press-Release/www/releases/archives/hispanic_origin_population/001130.html.

12 Ben J. Wattenberg, *First Universal Nation* (New York: Touchstone, 1992).

13 David Ellwood, "How We Got Here," In *Grow Faster Together. Or Grow Slowly Apart.* (Washington, DC: The Aspen Institute Domestic Strategy Group, 2002).

14 Andrew Sum, et al., "New Foreign Immigrants and the Labor Market in the US" (Boston, MA: Center for Labor Market Studies, Northeastern University, January 2005).

15 Ellwood, "How We Got Here" (see n. 13).

16 B. Lindsay Lowell, Julia Gelatt, and Jeanne Batalova, "Immigrants and Labor Force Trends: The Future, Past, and Present," Task Force Insight No. 17 (Washington, DC: Migration Policy Institute, July 2006), 3.

17 Richard Jackson, "The Global Retirement Crisis" (Washington, DC: Center for Strategic and International Studies, April 2002).

18 Ellwood, "How We Got Here" (see n. 13).

19 Lowell, Gelatt, Batalova, "Immigrants and Labor Force Trends" (see n. 16).

20 Ibid., 15–17.

21 The White House, "The President's Small Business Agenda: Helping Entrepreneurs Prosper," Fact Sheet (Washington, DC: The White House, April 2006), http://www.whitehouse.gov/infocus/smallbusiness/.

22 Batalova and Dixon, "Foreign-Born Self-Employed in the United States" (see n. 5).

23 See Maria Minniti, William D. Bygrave, and Erkko Autio, "Global Entrepreneurship Monitor 2005 Executive Report" (London School of Business, 2006).

24 US Census Bureau, "Growth of Hispanic-Owned Businesses Triples the National Average" (see n. 6); US Census Bureau, "Revenues for Asian-Owned Firms Surpass $326 Billion, Number of Businesses Up 24 Percent," Press Release (Washington, DC: US Census Bureau, May 16, 2006), http://www.census.gov/Press-Release/www/releases/archives/business_ownership/006814.html.

25 Saxenian, "Silicon Valley's New Immigrant Entrepreneurs" (see n. 7).

26 A Shanghai university ranks the world's universities based on the number of alumni and staff winning Nobel Prizes and Fields Medals, highly cited researchers, articles published in *Nature* and *Science,* articles in the Science Citation Index-expanded and the Social Science Citation Index, and academic performance with respect to the size of an institution. Institute of Higher Education, Shanghai Jiao Tong University, "Academic Ranking of World Universities 2005," http://ed.sjtu.edu.cn/ranking.htm.

27 National Science Board, "Science and Engineering Indicators 2006" (Arlington, VA: National Science Foundation, 2006), http://www.nsf.gov/statistics/seind06/pdf/volume1.pdf. This report cites the foreign-born share of science and engineering occupations based on both US Census American Community Survey data, and on the National Science Foundation 2003 Scientists and Engineers Statistical Data System. The higher percentages come from the ACS, while the lower percentages come from the NSF data.

28 Brown, "Graduate Enrollment and Degrees: 1986 to 2004" (see n. 4).

29 Gary Gereffi and Vivek Wadhwa, "Framing the Engineering Outsourcing Debate: Placing the United States on a Level Playing Field with China and India" (Durham, NC: Duke School of Engineering, December 2005).

30 NAFSA: Association of International Educators, "Restoring U.S. Competitiveness for International Students and Scholars" (Washington, DC: NAFSA, June 6, 2006), http://www.nafsa.org/public_policy.sec/public_policy_document/international_student_5/restoring_u.s._competitiveness.

31 The president's budget calls for $5.9 billion to fund this initiative in Fiscal Year (FY) 2007 and the president has urged Congress to appropriate more than $136 billion over the next ten years to "increase investments in research and development (R&D), strengthen education, and encourage entrepreneurship and innovation." President George W. Bush, "The State of the Union," http://www.whitehouse.gov/news/releases/2006/01/20060131-10.html.

32 For example, a recent poll by the Pew Research center found that 52 percent of Americans answered that "immigrants today are a burden on our country because they take our jobs, housing, and health care," while 41 percent said "immigrants today strengthen our country because of their hard work and talents." Pew, "America's Immigration Quandary" (see n. 2).

33 A National Academies Report showed that immigration lowers the wages of earlier immigrant cohorts, while research by economist George Borjas reports that Mexican immigrant flows from 1980 to 2000 lowered the wages of high school dropouts by 8 percent, and the wages of African-American workers by 4.5 percent. See James P. Smith and Barry Edmonston, eds., *The New Americans: Economic, Demographic, and Fiscal Effects of Immigration* (Washington, DC: The National Academy Press, 1997); George J. Borjas and Lawrence F. Katz, "The Evolution of the Mexican-Born Workforce in the United States," NBER Working Paper 11281 (Cambridge, MA: National Bureau of Economic Research, 2005); George Borjas, "Increasing the Supply of Labor through Immigration: Measuring the Impact on Native-born Workers," Center for Immigration Studies Backgrounder (Washington, DC: Center for Immigration Studies, May 2004). For a more complete discussion on the labor force impacts of immigration on US workers, see Julie Murray, Jeanne Batalova, and Michael Fix, "The Impact of Immigration on Native Workers: A Fresh Look at the Evidence," Task Force Insight No. 18 (Washington, DC: Migration Policy Institute, July 2006).

34 Harry J. Holzer, "Economic Impacts of Immigration," Testimony before the House Committee on Education and the Workforce, "U.S. Immigration Policy and its Impact on the American Economy," 109th Cong., 1st sess., November 16, 2005; Smith and Edmonston *The New Americans* (see n. 33).

35 Ellwood, "How We Got Here" (see n. 13).

36 Randy Capps, Michael Fix, Jeffrey S. Passel, Jason Ost, and Dan Perez-Lopez, "A Profile of the Low-Wage Immigrant Workforce," Immigrant Families and Workers, No. 4 (Washington, DC: Urban Institute, November 2003).

37 For example, the number of US Department of Labor Wage and Hour Division investigators has fallen from 921 nationwide in FY 1975 to 788 in FY 2004 and to 773 in FY 2005. These investigators are responsible for enforcing labor laws including minimum wage, overtime pay, limitations on child labor, and other workplace protections. The number of compliance actions taken by the Wage and Hour Division fell 36 percent between FY 1975 and FY 2004, from 58,758 to 37,872. Meanwhile, the number of US firms covered by wage and hour laws grew an estimated 55 percent, and the number of workplaces covered grew an estimated 112 percent. Annette Bernhardt and Siobhan McGrath, "Trends in Wage and Hour Enforcement by the U.S. Department of Labor, 1975-2004," Economic Policy Brief No. 3 (New York: Brennan Center for Justice at NYU School of Law, September 2005); and MPI Conversation with David Minsky, Chief of Staff, US Department of Labor, Employment Standards Administration, Wage and Hour Division, August 8, 2006. See also Katherine Lotspeich and Michael E. Fix, "The Department of Labor's Web-Based Compliance Assistance Resources" (Washington, DC: Urban Institute, August 2003).

38 Fenggang Yang and Helen Rose Ebaugh, "Transformations in New Immigrant Religions and Their Global Implications," *American Sociological Review* 66, no. 2 (April 2001): 269–288.

39 Janet Murguía and Cecilia Muñoz, "From Immigrant to Citizen," *The American Prospect,* November 10, 2005.

40 Lowell, Gelatt, and Batalova, "Immigrants and Labor Force Trends" (see n. 16), based on tabulations of data from the 2000 Census.

41 Just over 56 percent of all immigrant heads of household own their own homes. However, home ownership rates of immigrants vary among different immigrant groups. About 47 percent of heads of household who are immigrants from Latin America own their homes, compared to 64 percent of Asian immigrants and 72 percent of European immigrants. US Census Bureau, "Foreign-Born Population of the United States, Current Population Survey—March 2003 Detailed Tables (PPL-174)," Table 3.13, http://www.census.gov/population/socdemo/ foreign/ppl-174/tab03-13.xls.

42 While about 3 percent of whites and 7 percent of blacks in the United States marry outside of their race, between 10 and 20 percent of foreign-born Hispanics, and about 30 percent of US-born Hispanics marry non-Hispanics. Between 14 and 22 percent of Asian-born women intermarry, while between 5 and 7 percent of Asian-born men intermarry. Sharon M. Lee and Barry Edmonston, "New Marriages, New Families: U.S. Racial and Hispanic Intermarriage," *Population Bulletin* 60, no. 2 (Washington, DC: US Population Bureau, June 2005).

43 Median earnings increase from first-generation immigrants to their second-generation children for immigrants from all world regions. Further, by the second generation Mexican immigrants are less likely to work in the lowest paid jobs and more likely to hold jobs that offer health and pensions benefits. Roger Waldinger and Renee Reichl, "Today's Second Generation: Getting Ahead of Falling Behind?" in *Securing the Future: The US Immigrant Integration Policy Agenda,* ed. Michael Fix (Washington, DC Migration Policy Institute, forthcoming 2006). A large portion of immigrants pay payroll income and Social Security taxes, as well as sales taxes and property taxes—either directly, or as part of rental payments. A study of the Washington, DC, metropolitan area found that immigrant households pay nearly the same share of their income in taxes as native-born households. See Randolph Capps, Everett Henderson, Jeffrey S. Passel, and Michael E. Fix, "Civic Contributions: Taxes Paid by Immigrants in the Washington, DC, Metropolitan Area" (Washington, DC: Urban Institute, June 2006), http://www.urban.org/url.cfm?ID = 411338. About 92 percent of second-generation Hispanics and 96 percent of second generation Asians speak English "well" or "very well." Richard Alba, "Bilingualism Persists, But English Still Dominates," *The Migration Information Source,* February 1, 2005, http://www.migrationinformation.org/Feature/display.cfm?id = 282.

44 See Audrey Singer, "The Rise of New Immigrant Gateways" (Washington, DC: Brookings Institution, February 2004), http://www.brookings.edu/urban/pubs/20040301_gateways.pdf.

45 NAFSA, "Restoring U.S. Competitiveness" (see n. 30).

46 Admissions of nonimmigrants (those visiting the United States on a temporary basis) fell from almost 33 million in 2001 to about 28 million in 2002 and 2003, before recovering slightly to about 31 million in 2004. DHS, *Yearbook* (see n. 1).

47 The number of people traveling to the United States on temporary visas decreased substantially from all regions of the world following 9/11. However, while these numbers rebounded strongly between FY 2002 and 2004 for Europe and Eastern and South-Central Asia, temporary visits from Southeastern Asia and the Middle East remained at their post-9/11 lows. DHS, Yearbook (see n. 1). See also Stephen Yale-Loehr, Demetrios Papademetriou, and Betsy Cooper, *Secure Borders, Open Doors: Visa Procedures in the Post-September 11 Era* (Washington, DC: Migration Policy Institute, August 2005), http://www.migrationpolicy.org/pubs/ Secure_Borders_Report0905.pdf.

48 Michael Chertoff and Condoleezza Rice, "Remarks on Secure Borders and Open Doors in the Information Age" (US Department of State Event, Washington, DC, January 17, 2006).

49 Passel, "The Size and Characteristics of the Unauthorized" (see n. 1).

50 A report by the Pew Hispanic Center estimates that annual new arrivals of unauthorized immigrants exceeded the number of new arrivals of lawful permanent immigrants in 1998, 2000, 2003, and 2004. Jeffrey S. Passel and Roberto Suro, "Rise, Peak, and Decline: Trends in U.S. Immigration 1992-2004" (Washington, DC: Pew Hispanic Center, September 2005), http://pewhispanic.org/files/reports/53.pdf; Pew Hispanic Center, "Estimates of the Unauthorized Migrant Population for States based on the March 2005 CPS" (Washington, DC: Pew Hispanic Center, April 2006), http://pewhispanic.org/files/factsheets/17.pdf.

51 Passel, "The Size and Characteristics of the Unauthorized" (see n. 1).

52 Ibid.

53 David Dixon and Julia Gelatt, "Immigration Enforcement Spending Since IRCA," Task Force Fact Sheet No. 10 (Washington, DC: Migration Policy Institute, November 2005), http://www.migrationpolicy.org/ITFIAF/ FactSheet_Spending.pdf.

54 The temporary visa program does meet some demand for low-skill immigration as well. The number of H-2B visas issued to foreign workers (for temporary work in other than agricultural services) increased by 29,000 (50 percent) between FY 2001 and 2005.

55 US Department of State, "Report of the Visa Office 2005," Table XVIB, http://travel.state.gov/visa/frvi/ statistics/statistics_2787.html; US Department of State, Report of the Visa Office, Multiple Year Reports (1992– 2004), http://travel.state.gov/visa/frvi/statistics/statistics_2541.html. Note that not every visa issued is used in the year it was issued, and some are never used at all. However, looking at visas issued, while imperfect, is a better proxy for the number of people who enter on a given visa each year than the number of admissions, which counts a single person multiple times if they enter the country from abroad more than once in a given year.

56 The cap for FY 2007 was met three months before the new fiscal year began. This is the eighth time in the last ten years that the cap has been reached before the fiscal year began. US Citizenship and Immigration Services, "USCIS Reaches H-1B Cap," Press Release, June 1, 2006, http://www.uscis.gov/graphics/publicaffairs/news-rels/FY07H1Bcap_060106PR.pdf; Roy Mark, "Poof! H-1B Visas Gone," *Internet News.com,* June 5, 2005, http:// www.internetnews.com/ent-news/article.php/3611276.

57 Deborah W. Meyers, "Temporary Worker Programs: A Patchwork Policy Response," Task Force Insight No.12 (Washington, DC: Migration Policy Institute, January 2006), http://www.migrationpolicy.org/ITFIAF-12_Meyers.pdf. Employment-based immigration is capped at 140,000 entrants each year, though under the American Competitiveness in the 21st Century Act of 2000, unused visa numbers from previous years may be recaptured and used once this cap has been reached (for both employment and family-sponsored immigration). *Immigration and Nationality Act* § 201, 8 USC 1151; *American Competitiveness in the 21st Century Act of 2000,* Public Law 106-313.

58 DHS, *Yearbook* (see n. 1), Table 5.

59 Marc R. Rosenblum, "'Comprehensive' Legislation vs. Fundamental Reform: the Limits of Current Immigration Proposals," Task Force Policy Brief No. 13 (Washington, DC: Migration Policy Institute, January 2006), http://www.migrationpolicy.org/pubs/PolicyBrief13_Jan06_13.pdf.

60 US Department of State, "Visa Bulletin for July 2006," http://travel.state.gov/visa/frvi/bulletin/bulletin_2943.html.

61 Although the Immigration and Nationality Act (INA) provides 10,000 visas for low-skilled workers, this number has been temporarily reduced to 5,000 to make visas available under the Nicaraguan and Central American Relief Act of 1997 (NACARA). The reduction will last as long as is necessary to offset adjustments under the NACARA program. DOS, "Visa Bulletin" (see n. 60).

62 Daniel González, "States Fight Illegal Migration," *The Arizona Republic,* August 2, 2006, based on information provided by the National Conference of State Legislatures.

63 National Conference of State Legislatures, "Overview of State Legislation Related to Immigrants Introduced Jan–April 2006" (Washington, DC: NCSL, May 2006), http://www.ncsl.org/programs/immig/statelegislationoverview0506.htm; National Conference of State Legislatures, "Immigration Policy: News from the States 2005" (Washington DC: NCSL, August 2005), http://www.ncsl.org/programs/immig/immigstatelegis080105.htm. (Note that an Illinois bill on foreign medical practitioners was signed into law following the publication of this second document).

64 NCSL, "State Legislation 2006" (see n. 63).

65 "The Wrong Side of History," *The Economist,* July 13, 2006.

66 Ralph Blumenthal, "Citing Border Violence, 2 States Declare a Crisis," *The New York Times,* August 17, 2005.

67 National Conference of State Legislatures, "In-State Tuition and Unauthorized Immigrant Students" (Washington, DC: NCSL, April 2006), http://www.ncsl.org/programs/immig/tuitionandimmigrants.htm.

68 *REAL ID Act of 2005,* Public Law 109-13.

69 New Hampshire lawmakers debated, but ultimately defeated, legislation to bar the state's compliance with the REAL ID Act. The state of Washington has considered resolutions calling for the repeal of the REAL ID Act. Melissa Savage, "Real ID Update" (Washington, DC: National Conference of State Legislators, April 2006); Meg Heckman, "REAL ID Ban Dead" *Concord Monitor,* May 12, 2006.

70 Randy Capps and Jeffrey S. Passel, "Describing Immigrant Communities" (Washington, DC: Urban Institute Immigration Studies Program, December 2004), http://ffcd.org/uploadDocs/DescribingImmigrantCommunitites.pdf; Randolph Capps, Michael E. Fix, and Jeffrey S. Passel, "The Dispersal of Immigrants in the 1990s," Immigrant Families and Workers Brief No. 2 (Washington, DC: Urban Institute, November 2002); Chicago Council on Foreign Relations, "Keeping the Promise: Immigration Proposals from the Heartland," Report of an Independent Task Force (Chicago: CCFR, 2004).

71 Deborah L. Garvey, "Designing an Impact Aid Program for Immigrant Settlement," in *Securing the Future: The Immigrant Integration Policy Agenda,* ed. Michael Fix (Washington, DC: Migration Policy Institute, forthcoming 2006).

72 Humanitarian protection, including refugee resettlement and asylum, is beyond the scope of this report and the purview of the discussions of the Task Force.

73 DHS, *Yearbook* (see n. 1).

74 Ibid.

75 Ibid.

76 Meyers, "Temporary Worker Programs" (see n. 57).

77 We estimate this based on several assumptions. First, estimates show that roughly 60 percent of unauthorized workers are in the labor force. Given that the net increase in the unauthorized population is 500,000 a year, it is likely that 300,000 of these unauthorized immigrants work. According to tabulations of data from the March 2005 Current Population Survey, 63 percent of foreign-born persons aged 15 plus who had entered the country between 2002 and 2005 were in the labor force. Data from the DHS Office of Immigration Statistics show that roughly 16 percent of new LPRs have been younger than 15 over the recent years. Therefore, of an estimated 823,602 new LPRs aged 15 plus, it is likely that about 518,900 entered the US labor force. Finally, of the temporary workers and dependents we assume entered intending to stay permanently, about 125,500 were the workers. Further, adults entering on K and V visas likely resemble new LPRs in their labor force characteristics. This would mean that about 16,800 workers came each year on K visas, and about 5,800 came on V visas. In total, we estimate that 967,000 immigrant workers are absorbed into the US labor force each year.

78 Meyers, "Temporary Worker Programs" (see n. 57).

79 Of the 65,000 capped H-1B visas, 6,800 are set aside for the H-1B1 program, under the US-Chile and US-Singapore Free Trade Agreements. The American Competitiveness in the Twenty-First Century Act of 2000 (AC21) (Public Law 106-313) raised the numerical cap to 195,000 for FY 2001-2003. The cap returned to 65,000 in FY 2004. However, AC21 also exempted workers at nonprofit and governmental research organizations and

institutes of higher education from numerical limit. The H-1B Visa Reform Act of 2004 (Public Law 108-447) made 20,000 additional H-1B visas available for foreign workers who completed a graduate program in US universities, effective May 2005.

80   DHS, *Yearbook* (see n. 1).

81   See n. 61. DOS, "Visa Bulletin" (see n. 60). Passel, "The Size and Characteristics of the Unauthorized" (see n. 1).

82   DOS, "Report of the Visa Office" (see n. 54); Philip Martin, Michael Fix, and J. Edward Taylor, *The New Rural Poverty* (Washington, DC: The Urban Institute Press, 2006), 81 (Table 7.2).

83   Meyers, "Temporary Worker Programs" (see n. 57).

84   Tyche Hendricks, "Ex-braceros leery of guest worker plan," *The San Francisco Chronicle,* May 30, 2006.

85   Immigration and Nationality Act (INA) § 101 (US Code 8 § 1101).

86   DHS, *Yearbook* (see n. 1).

87   For discussion on the benefits of visas that allow a transition from temporary to permanent status, see Rosenblum, "'Comprehensive' Legislation vs. Fundamental Reform" (see n. 59).

88   For current requirements of various nonimmigrant visas, see Immigration and Nationality Act (INA) § 101 (US Code 8 § 1101).

89   While the INA allows for 55,000 visas, this number has been temporarily reduced to 50,000 under the Nicaraguan and Central American Relief Act of 1997 (NACARA). The reduction will last as long as is necessary to offset adjustments under the NACARA program. DOS, "Visa Bulletin" (see n. 60). For more on the diversity visa program, see US Department of State, "2007 DV Lottery Instructions," http://travel.state.gov/visa/immigrants/types/types_1318.html.

90   The McCarran-Walter Act of 1952 (Public Law No. 82-414) consolidated existing immigration law in one act known as the Immigration and Nationality Act (INA). Since 1952, changes in immigration policy have been affected through amendments to the INA. However, the basic architecture of US immigration law has remained in place since 1952. US Citizenship and Immigration Services (USCIS), "Immigration and Nationality Act," http://www.uscis.gov/graphics/lawsregs/INA.htm.

91   Rosenblum, "'Comprehensive' Legislation vs. Fundamental Reform" (see n. 59). On the setting of interest rates, see Federal Reserve Board, "Monetary Policymaking: Federal Open Markets Committee," http://www.federalreserve.gov/fomc/.

92   Major amendments to the INA include the Hart-Cellar Act of 1965, the Immigration Reform and Control Act (IRCA) of 1986, the Immigration Act of 1990, and the Illegal Immigration Reform and Immigrant Responsibility Act (IIRIRA) of 1996. However, only the 1965 and 1990 laws substantially changed the allocation of permanent immigrant visas.

93   Although members of the US Sentencing Commissions serve part-time, those serving on The Standing Commission on Immigration and Labor Markets would serve full-time. US Sentencing Commission, "An Overview of the US Sentencing Commission," http://www.ussc.gov/general/USSCoverview_2005.pdf; US Office of Management and Budget, *Budget of the United States Government, Fiscal Year 2007—Appendix,* Judicial Branch, http://www.whitehouse.gov/omb/budget/fy2007/pdf/appendix/jud.pdf.

94   Dixon and Gelatt, "Enforcement Spending Since IRCA" (see n. 53).

95   Tamar Jacoby, "An Idea Whose Time Has Finally Come? The Case for Employment Verification," Task Force Policy Brief No. 9 (Washington, DC: Migration Policy Institute, November 2005).

96   Dixon and Gelatt, "Enforcement Spending Since IRCA" (see n. 53).

97   Since 1975, at least 80 percent of border patrol agents have been stationed along the southwest border. Transactional Records Access Clearinghouse, Syracuse University, "Border Patrol Agents: Southern Versus Northern Border," TRAC Immigration, http://www.trac.syr.edu/immigration/reports/143/include/rep143table2.html.

98   Marc R. Rosenblum, "Immigration Enforcement at the Worksite: Making it Work," Task Force Policy Brief No. 6 (Washington, DC: Migration Policy Institute, November 2005), http://www.migrationpolicy.org/ITFIAF/PolicyBrief-6-Rosenblum.pdf.

99   US Department of Justice, *Statistical Yearbook of the Immigration and Naturalization Service, 1991–1998* (Washington, DC: Department of Justice Immigration and Naturalization Service, 1993-2000).

100 DHS, *Yearbook* (see n. 1).

101 US Government Accountability Office, *Immigration Enforcement: Weaknesses Hinder Employment Verification and Worksite Enforcement Efforts* GAO-05-813 (August 2005), http://www.gao.gov/new.items/d05813.pdf.

102 Rosenblum, "Immigration Enforcement at the Worksite" (see n. 98).

103 US Department of Homeland Security, "Department of Homeland Security Unveils Comprehensive Immigration Enforcement Strategy for the Nation's Interior," Press Release, April 20, 2006.

104 However, under the Senate bill, DHS could require critical infrastructure employers or those suspected of past hiring crimes to verify the employment eligibility of all employees before the 18 months have passed.

105 Numbers of employers registered and actively using Basic Pilot provided by the Office of Policy and Strategy of US Citizenship and Immigration Services, July 21, 2006.

106 Kevin Jernegan, "Eligible to Work? Experiments in Verifying Work Authorization," Task Force Insight No. 8 (Washington, DC: Migration Policy Institute, November 2005), http://www.migrationpolicy.org/ITFIAF/Insight-8-Jernegan.pdf; US Department of Labor, Bureau of Labor Statistics, Job Openings and Labor Turnover Survey (JOLTS), http://www.bls.gov/jlt/home.htm#overview; US Department of Labor, Bureau of Labor Statistics, "Employment Situation Summary," May 2006, http://www.bls.gov/news.release/empsit.nr0.htm.

107 The Government Accountability Office estimates the current cost of issuing a Social Security Card at $25 per person. Costs of issuing new, secure cards would vary depending on the exact security features, and on whether new cards would be issued to the approximately 300 million current card holders at once, through a graduated program, or only to new workers. In addition to increased costs for plastic cards with magnetic strips or barcodes, photographs, or other security features, the GAO estimates that the processing time involved in adding a picture and biometric identifier to the cards would add a cost of $3.50 per card, in addition to the cost of the new equipment required and costs associated with the periodic issuance of new cards to maintain current photographs. US Government Accountability Office, *Social Security Administration: Improved Agency Coordination Needed for Social Security Card Enhancement Efforts* GAO-06-303 (March 2006), http://www.gao.gov/new.items/d06303.pdf.

108 REAL ID Act of 2005, Public Law 109-13.

109 A few have taken matters into their own hands, calling themselves the Minuteman Project, to spotlight the issue.

110 Federal spending on border control efforts grew by $2.1 billion, or 306 percent, between FY 1985 and 2002. Spending on the Border Patrol specifically grew by $1.4 billion, or over 500 percent over this same period. While the merger of Customs and Border Patrol duties under Customs and Border Protection (CBP) makes it difficult to determine the exact current level of spending on immigration enforcement at the border, the combined budgets of CBP (excluding headquarters management and administration, reimbursable programs, automation modernization, and construction), ICE (excluding reimbursable programs), and the migrant interdiction activities of the Coast Guard were $5.6 billion in FY 2005. Dixon and Gelatt, "Enforcement Spending Since IRCA" (see n. 53); US Office of Management and Budget, *Budget of the United States Government, Fiscal Year 2007—Appendix,* Department of Homeland Security, http://www.whitehouse.gov/omb/budget/fy2007/pdf/appendix/dhs.pdf.

111 Demetrios G. Papademetriou, "Reflections on Restoring Integrity to the United States Immigration System: A Personal Vision," Task Force Insight No. 5 (Washington, DC: Migration Policy Institute, September 2005), http://www.migrationpolicy.org/pubs/Insight_Sept05_5.pdf; Betsy Cooper and Kevin O'Neil, "Lessons from the Immigration Reform and Control Act of 1986," Task Force Policy Brief No. 3 (Washington, DC: Migration Policy Institute, August 2005), http://www.migrationpolicy.org/pubs/PolicyBrief_No3_Aug05.pdf.

112 Dixon and Gelatt, "Enforcement Spending Since IRCA" (see n. 53).

113 Border Patrol apprehensions in the San Diego, California Border Patrol sector decreased from 565,581 in Fiscal Year (FY) 1992 to 138,608 in FY 2004, and fell from 248,642 to 104,399 in the El Paso, Texas, sector over this period. Meanwhile, apprehensions in the Tucson, Arizona, sector rose from 71,036 to 491,771. DHS *Yearbook* (see n. 1).

114 Douglas S. Massey, "Beyond the Border Buildup: Towards a New Approach to Mexico-U.S. Migration," *Immigration Policy in Focus* 4, no. 7 (Washington, DC: American Immigration Law Foundation, September 2005), http://www.ailf.org/ipc/infocus/2005_beyondborder.pdf.

115 Papademetriou, "Reflections on Restoring Integrity" (see n. 111); Michael Fix, Doris Meissner, and Demetrios Papademetriou, "Independent Task Force on Immigration and America's Future: The Roadmap," Task Force Policy Brief No. 1 (Washington, DC: Migration Policy Institute, June 2005), http://www.migrationpolicy.org/pubs/MPI_policyBrief_rdmp.pdf; Douglas S. Massey, "Backfire at the Border: Why Enforcement Without Legalization Cannot Stop Illegal Immigration" (Washington, DC: Cato Institute, June 13, 2005), http://www.freetrade.org/pubs/pas/tpa-029es.html.

116 Jeffrey S. Passel, "The Size and Characteristics of the Unauthorized" (see n. 1).

117 Massey, "Backfire at the Border" (see n. 115).

118 Karen Yourish, "Corridors and Barriers," *The Washington Post,* May 21, 2006.

119 See, for example, US Government Accountability Office, *Border Security: Key Unresolved Issues Justify Reevaluation of Border Surveillance Technology Program,* GAO-06-295 (February 2006), http://www.gao.gov/new.items/d06295.pdf; US Government Accountability Office, *Homeland Security: Recommendations to Improve Management of Key Border Security Program Need to be Implemented,* GAO-06-296 (February 2006), http://www.gao.gov/new.items/d06296.pdf; US Government Accountability Office, *Homeland Security: Visitor and Immigrant Status Program Operating, but Management Improvements are Still Needed,* GAO-06-318T (January 2006), http://www.gao.gov/new.items/d06318t.pdf.

120 President George W. Bush, Presidential Address on Immigration Reform, May 15, 2006, http://www.whitehouse.gov/news/releases/2006/05/20060515-8.html.

121 Johanna Neuman, "Nation Ahead of Congress on Immigration, Bush Says," *Los Angeles Times,* June 6, 2006.

122 US General Accounting Office, *Border Patrol Hiring: Despite Recent Initiatives, Fiscal Year 1999 Hiring Goal Was Not Met,* GAO/GGD-00-39 (December 1999), http://www.gao.gov/new.items/gg00039.pdf.

123 Robert Bonner, Director of US Customs and Border Protection, Testimony before Senate Committee on Appropriations, Subcommittee on Homeland Appropriations, 108th Cong., 1st sess., May 13, 2003.

124 US Department of Homeland Security, Inspector General, *A Review of Remote Surveillance Technology Along U.S. Land Borders,* OIG-06-15 (Washington, DC: DHS Office of the Inspector General, December 2005).

125 Ibid.

126 US Congressional Research Service, "Homeland Security: Unmanned Aerial Vehicles and Border Surveillance," CRS Report for Congress (February 2005), http://www.fas.org/sgp/crs/homesec/RS21698.pdf; Graham Warwick, "General Atomics Predator B UAV Crashes on Mexican Border on Customs and Immigration Patrol," *Flight International,* April 27, 2006.

127 DHS Inspector General, *A Review of Remote Surveillance Technology* (see n. 124).

128 US Department of Homeland Security, "DHS Announces Long-Term Border and Immigration Strategy," Press Release, November 2005, http://www.dhs.gov/dhspublic/interapp/press_release/ press_release_0795.xml; Customs and Border Protection, "U.S. Customs and Border Protection Publishes Secure Border Initiative (SBInet) Request for Proposal," Press Release, April 11, 2006, http://www.cbp.gov/xp/cgov/ newsroom/news_releases/042006/04112006.xml.

129 SBI replaces the America's Shield Initiative (ASI), which in turn had replaced the Integrated Intelligence Surveillance System (ISIS). ISIS, deployed in 1997, was a system of cameras, sensors, and databases intended to detect and prevent unauthorized migration. ASI was implemented in September 2004, and subsumed ISIS. ASI was intended to address the former program's shortcomings, and boost counterterrorism efforts. GAO *Key Unresolved Issues Justify Reevaluation* (see n. 119); Richard L. Skinner, US Department of Homeland Security Inspector General, Testimony before the House Committee on Homeland Security, Subcommittee on Management, Integration, and Oversight, 109th Cong., 1st sess., December 16, 2005.

130 Memorandum from the US Chamber of Commerce, July 26, 2006.

131 Multiple reports have discussed the need for better integration of terrorism watchlists. See, for example, Yale-Loehr, Papademetriou, and Cooper, *Secure Borders* (see n. 47); Government Accountability Office, *High Risk Series: An Update*, GAO-05-307, January 2005; Department of Justice Inspector General, *Follow-up Review of the Status of IDENT/IAFIS Integration*, Report Number 1-2005-001 (December 2004): i-x.

132 See, for example, the Web site of the Border Angels Network, a nonprofit agency founded in order to prevent migrant deaths along the border: http://www.borderangels.org/portal/index.php?option = com_ content&task = view&id = 17&Itemid = 30. This figure is generally in line with the official data from the Border Patrol, which reports death totals in the 300s to 400s in recent years. For information on border deaths in the 1980s, see Meyers, "US Border Enforcement" and Wayne A. Cornelius, "Death at the Border: Efficacy and Unintended Consequences of US Immigration Control Policy," *Population and Development Review* 27, no. 4 (December 2001): 661-685.

133 Many unauthorized immigrants from outside the Western Hemisphere are likely visa overstayers, while a smaller portion of immigrants from Mexico and other parts of Latin America initially entered the country legally. Jeffery Passel, "Modes of Entry for the Unauthorized Migration Population" (Washington, DC: Pew Hispanic Center, May 2006), http://pewhispanic.org/factsheets/factsheet.php?FactsheetID = 19.

134 The National Commission on Terrorist Attacks, *The 9/11 Commission Report* (New York: W.W. Norton & Company, Inc., 2004).

135 Rey Koslowski, *Real Challenges for Virtual Borders: The Implementation of US-VISIT* (Washington, DC: Migration Policy Institute, June 2005), http://www.migrationpolicy.org/pubs/Koslowski_Report.pdf.

136 Robert O'Harrow, Jr., and Scott Higham, "U.S. Border Security at Crossroads," *The Washington Post,* May 23, 2005.

137 Koslowski, *Real Challenges* (see n. 135); DHS Office of Inspector General, *Implementation of the United States Visitor and Immigrant Status Indicator Technology Program at Land Border Ports of Entry* OIG-05-11 (February 2005), http://www.dhs.gov/interweb/assetlibrary/OIG_05-11_Feb05.pdf. US-VISIT is testing its exit tracking processes at the following airports: Baltimore/Washington International, Chicago O'Hare International, Dallas/Fort Worth International, Denver International, Detroit Metropolitan Wayne County International, Fort Lauderdale-Hollywood International, Hartsfield-Jackson Atlanta International, Luis Muñoz Marin International in San Juan, Puerto Rico, Newark Liberty International, Philadelphia International, San Francisco International, and Seattle-Tacoma International, and at two seaports: Miami International Cruise Line Terminal and Long Beach and San Pedro seaports near Los Angeles. Department of Homeland Security, "US-VISIT: How It Works," http://www.dhs.gov/dhspublic/interapp/editorial/editorial_0525.xml.

138 *Homeland Security Act of 2002,* US Code 6 § 101.

139 San Diego Association of Governments, "Economic Impacts of Wait Times at the San Diego-Baja California Border" (California Department of Transportation, District 11, January 19, 2006), http://www.sandag.org/ programs/borders/binational/projects/2006_border_wait_impacts_report.pdf.

140 Memorandum from the U.S. Chamber of Commerce, July 26, 2006. Douglas Doan, "The 25% Challenge: Speeding Cross-Border Traffic in Southeastern Michigan," *Journal of Homeland Security* (Washington, DC: US Department of Homeland Security, April 2006), http://www.homelandsecurity.org/newjournal/Articles/ displayArticle2.asp?article = 142.

141 For more on this, see Deborah W. Meyers, *One Face at the Border: Behind the Slogan* (Washington, DC: Migration Policy Institute, June 2005), http://www.migrationpolicy.org/pubs/Meyers_Report.pdf; and Yale-Loehr, Papademetriou, and Cooper, *Secure Borders* (see n. 47).

142 Canada has recently experienced terrorist threats in its territory, such as the 17 highly armed would-be terrorists arrested in June 2006. Anthony DePalma, "Canada Saw Plot to Seize Officials," *The New York Times,* June 7, 2006.

143 Yale-Loehr, Papademetriou, and Cooper, *Secure Borders* (see n. 47).

144 Ibid.

145 Ibid. For further discussion on US-VISIT, see Koslowski, *Real Challenges for Virtual Borders* (see n. 135).

146 "SEVP Releases Four Fact Sheets," *Interpreter Releases* 83, no. 23 (June 12, 2006), 1141-1145; US Department of Homeland Security, "US-VISIT Update," June 23, 2006.

147 See Meyers, "US Border Enforcement" (see n. 110); The White House, *National Strategy for Homeland Security,* July 2002, http://www.whitehouse.gov/homeland/book/.

148 Yale-Loehr, Papademetriou, and Cooper, *Secure Borders* (see n. 47). See also Deborah W. Meyers, "Does Smarter Lead to Safer?: An Assessment of the Border Accords with Canada and Mexico," MPI Insight No. 2 (Washington, DC: Migration Policy Institute, June 2003), http://www.migrationpolicy.org/pubs/6-13-0 ~ 1.pdf.

149 Meyers, "Does Smarter Lead to Safer?" (see n. 148).

150 For more on the Security and Prosperity Partnership (SPP), launched by the presidents of the United States and Mexico and the prime minister of Canada in March 2005, see the SPP website: http://www.spp.gov/.

151 Susan Ginsburg, *Countering Terrorist Mobility: Shaping an Operational Strategy* (Washington, DC: Migration Policy Institute, January 2006), http://www.migrationpolicy.org/pubs/MPI_TaskForce_Ginsburg.pdf.

152 Charles E. Allen, DHS Assistant Secretary for Intelligence and Analysis (Chief Intelligence Officer), "DHS Intelligence and Border Security: Developing Operational Intelligence," Testimony before the House Committee on Homeland Security, Subcommittee on Intelligence, Information Sharing, and Terrorism Risk Assessment, 109th Cong., 2nd sess., June 28, 2006.

153 National Counterterrorism Center, "National Strategy to Combat Terrorist Travel," May 2, 2006, http://www.nctc.gov/images/u_terrorist_travel_book.jpg.

154 Rosenblum, "'Comprehensive' Legislation vs. Fundamental Reform" (see n. 59), 13.

155 See n. 37. Strong labor enforcement is especially important in industries employing low-wage workers, which have particularly poor records of compliance with wage and hour standards. Government studies have found that 100 percent of poultry industry employers, 60 percent of nursing homes, and between 26 to 65 percent of garment industry employers (depending on the location) were in violation of basic minimum wage and overtime protections. US Department of Labor, Employment Standards Administration, "FY 2000 Annual Performance Report Summary," March 31, 2001, http://www.dol.gov/esa/aboutesa/str-plan/ esa00rpt.pdf#search=%22ESA%20FY%202000%20performance%20report%22; US Department of Labor, Employment Standards Administration, Wage and Hour Division, "Nursing Home 2000 Compliance Survey Fact Sheet," http://www.dol.gov/esa/healthcare/surveys/nursing2000.htm; US Department of Labor, Wage and Hour Division, Garment Compliance Surveys for New York City, Los Angeles, and San Francisco, various years.

156 One of the most widely analyzed examples was the Bracero program that brought temporary Mexican workers to the United States between 1942 and 1964 to fill labor shortages brought about by World War II. Many Bracero workers were provided inadequate housing, including being housed in camps formerly occupied by prisoners of war; were paid wages below those paid to US-born workers; and were not provided the health and safety protections granted to US-born agricultural workers. See Meyers, "Temporary Worker Programs" (see n. 76). Among other examples, allegations of abuse have more recently been reported among some H-2B workers in New Orleans. These relate to violations of pay, exploitative recruitment fees, and false promises of minimum guarantees of work. Under current law, workers on H-2B visas are not able to work for anyone except the employer who sponsored their visa. See Leslie Eton, "Immigrants Hired After Storm Sue New Orleans Hotel Executive," *The New York Times,* August 17, 2006; Julia Cass, "Guest Workers Sue New Orleans Hotel Chain," The Washington Post, August 17, 2006.

157 Susan Martin, "US Employment-Based Admissions: Permanent and Temporary," Task Force Policy Brief No. 15 (Washington, DC: Migration Policy Institute, January 2006).

158 Temporary workers in the proposed selection system are expected to depart after their seasonal or short-term employment. Given the special nature of their employment, they may need a different set of protections. These might include guaranteed minimum employment, housing or housing allowances, insurance benefits — including workers' compensation — and transportation benefits. Further, consular representatives from countries of origin could be invited to survey worksites in immigrant-dependent regions and sectors and to assist their nationals when violations are detected.

159 Compounding the challenges of local immigration law enforcement, a database used by state and local police to check the criminal history of apprehended individuals often falsely indicates a past immigration violation. A study of the use of the National Crime Information Center (NCIC) database found that 42 percent of all immigration hits in response to a police query were "false hits" where DHS was unable to confirm that the individual was an actual immigration violator. Hannah Gladstein, Annie Lai, Jennifer Wagner, and Michael Wishnie, *Blurring the Lines: A Profile of State and Local Police Enforcement of Immigration Law Using the National Crime Information Center Database, 2002–2004* (New York: Migration Policy Institute at New York University School of Law, December 2005). For more on local immigration enforcement, see also Major Cities Chiefs Immigration Committee, "M.C.C. Immigration Committee Recommendations For Enforcement Of Immigration Laws By Local Police Agencies," 4–5, June 2006, http://www.houstontx.gov/police/pdfs/mcc_position.pdf; Ned Glascock, "Questioning Started in N.C.," *Raleigh News and Observer,* November 29, 2001; Scott Learn, "Cities React, Portland Catches the Heat," *The Oregonian,* December 17, 2001; Gretchen Schuldt, "Attorney General's Office Questions INS Plan," *Milwaukee Journal Sentinel,* December 7, 2001; "Portland Police Decline to Question Immigrants," *The Advocate* (Baton Rouge, LA), November 22, 2001; "Third City in Oregon Balks at Assisting Federal Interviews," *The New York Times,* November 30, 2001; Frank Rich, "Wait Until Dark," *The New York Times,* November 24, 2001.

160 Section 133 of the Illegal Immigration Reform and Immigrant Responsibility Act of 1996 (IIRIRA), which amended INA §287 (8 U.S.C. §1357(g)), authorized the Attorney General (now the Secretary of DHS) to enter into a written agreement with a state or locality so that qualified officers can be trained and given authority to perform specific immigration enforcement functions including investigation, apprehension, or detention of immigrants in the United States. The written agreement must articulate the specific powers and duties that may be performed by the state or local officer, and the duration of the agreement. Currently, Florida, Alabama, Arizona, California, and North Carolina have signed memorandums of understanding (MOUs) with DHS for local immigration enforcement. Lisa Seghetti, Stephen R. Viña, and Karma Ester, "Enforcing Immigration Law: The Role of State and Local Law Enforcement," Congressional Research Service Report to Congress, October 13, 2005, http://www.ilw.com/immigdaily/news/2005,1026-crs.pdf; US Immigration and Customs Enforcement, "Partners," http://www.ice.gov/partners/287g/Section287_g.htm.

161 The current definition of "aggravated felony" for immigration law is located in Section 101(a)(43) of the Immigration and Nationality Act (INA), and spans 21 paragraphs. The term was first used in 1988 to cover a few very serious crimes like murder, rape, and drug trafficking. Since then, Congress has expanded the definition by the

Immigration Act of 1990, The Antiterrorism and Effective Death Penalty Act of 1996 (AEDPA), Public Law 104-132, US Statues at Large 110 (1996): 1214; *The Illegal Immigration Reform and Immigrant Responsibility Act of 1996,* Public Law 104-302; and the *Real ID Act of 2005,* Public Law 109-13.

162 In 2002, 10 percent of BIA decisions were made with summary affirmances, but that number has since risen to 50 percent. Doris Meissner, Muzaffar Chishti, and Michael J. Wishnie, Statement for the Senate Judiciary Committee, *Immigration Litigation Reduction: Hearing before the Committee on the Judiciary.* 109th Cong., 2nd sess., April 3, 2006.

163 US Department of Justice, "Fact Sheet: Board of Immigration Appeals, Final Rule," Press Release, August 23, 2002, http://www.usdoj.gov/eoir/press/02/BIARulefactsheet.pdf.

164 David A. Martin, Testimony before the Senate Judiciary Committee, *Immigration Litigation Reduction: Hearing before the Committee on the Judiciary.* 109th Cong., 2nd sess., April 3, 2006.

165 The immigration caseload in the 9th Circuit Court of Appeals increased from 965 (8 percent of all cases) in the year ending June 30, 2001, to 4,835 cases in the year ending in June 2004 (48 percent of all cases). Meissner, Chishti, and Wishnie, Statement for the Senate Judiciary Committee (see n. 162).

166 In January 2006, Attorney General Alberto Gonzalez expressed concern over some immigration judges' "intemperate or even abusive" conduct toward asylum seekers, and ordered a thorough review of immigration courts. Mark Sherman, "Attorney General Chides Immigration Judges," *Associated Press,* January 10, 2006. Solomon Moore and Ann M. Simmons, "As Caseloads Skyrocket, Judges Blame the Work Done by the Board of Immigration Appeals," *Los Angeles Times,* May 2, 2005.

167 See Donald Kerwin, "Revisiting the Need for Appointed Counsel," MPI Insight No. 4 (Washington, DC: Migration Policy Institute), http://www.migrationpolicy.org/insight/Insight_Kerwin.pdf.

168 US Department of Homeland Security, "Fact Sheet: Secure Border Initiative," Press Release, November 2, 2005, http://www.dhs.gov/dhspublic/interapp/press_release/press_release_0794.xml.

169 Waldinger and Reichl, "Today's Second Generation" (see n. 43).

170 Passel, "Size and Characteristics of the Unauthorized" (see n. 1).

171 Randolph Capps, Michael Fix, and Jane Reardon-Anderson, "Children of Immigrants Show Slight Reductions in Poverty, Hardship" (Washington, DC: Urban Institute, 2003), http://www.urban.org/UploadedPDF/310887_snapshots3_no13.pdf.

172 Randolph Capps, Michael Fix, Julie Murray, Jason Ost, Jeffrey S. Passel, and Shinta Herwantoro, "The New Demography of America's Schools: Immigration and the No Child Left Behind Act" (Washington, DC: Urban Institute, 2005).

173 Randolph Capps, Michael Fix, Everett Henderson, and Jane Reardon-Anderson, "A Profile of Low-Income Working Immigrant Families" (Washington, DC: Urban Institute, 2005), http://www.urban.org/UploadedPDF/311206_B-67.pdf.

174 Ibid.

175 Michael E. Fix and Jeffrey S. Passel, "U.S. Immigration—Trends and Implications for Schools" (Washington, DC: Urban Institute, 2003), http://www.urban.org/url.cfm?ID=401654.

176 For more on the UN Millennium Development Goals, see http://www.un.org/millenniumgoals/.

177 US Census Bureau, Census 2000, Summary File 3, Tables P19, PCT13, and PCT14.

178 *The No Child Left Behind Act of 2001,* Public Law 107-120, US Statutes at Large 115 (2002): 1425.

179 Appropriations for Adult Education have fallen from $602 million in FY 2004, to $570 million in FY 2005, and $563 million in FY 2006. US Office of Management and Budget, *Budget of the United States Government, Fiscal Year 2006 and 2007—Appendix,* Department of Education.

180 Leighton Ku and Demetrios Papademetriou, "Access to Health Care and Health Insurance: Immigrants and Immigration Reform," in *Securing the Future: The US Immigrant Integration Policy Agenda,* ed. Michael Fix (Washington, DC: Migration Policy Institute, forthcoming 2006).

181 *The Personal Responsibility and Work Opportunity Reconciliation Act of 1996* (PRWORA) Public Law 104-193, US Statutes at Large 110 (1996): 2105.

182 On health outcomes, see Jane Reardon-Anderson, Randy Capps, and Michael Fix, "The Health and Well Being of Children in Immigrant Families," Assessing the New Federalism Policy Brief B-52 (Washington DC: Urban Institute, 2002).

183 Of the 11 million unauthorized immigrants estimated to have been in the country in 2005, an estimated 6.7 million had been in the country for five years or more. About 2.8 million had been in the country between two and five years, and only 1.6 million had been in the country for less than two years. About two-thirds (or 3.3 million) of the estimated 5 million children living with unauthorized immigrant parents in the United States are themselves US citizens. Jeffrey S. Passel, Pew Hispanic Center estimates based on the March 2005 Current Population Survey; Urban Institute, "Children of Immigrants: Facts and Figures" (Washington, DC: Urban Institute, May 2006), http://www.urban.org/UploadedPDF/900955_children_of_immigrants.pdf.

184 The Immigration and Naturalization Service (INS) and the Department of Labor conducted two surveys of immigrants participating in the legalization program under the Immigration Reform and Control Act of 1986. Analysis from these surveys has revealed that legal status brought better jobs and higher wages. To view data from the Legalized Population Surveys, see http://www.pop.psu.edu/data-archive/daman/lps.htm. For analysis of the data, see, for example, Mary G. Powers, Ellen Percy Kraly, and William Seltzer, "IRCA: Lessons of the Last US Legalization Program," *Migration Information Source,* July 1, 2004, http://www.migrationinformation.org/USFocus/display.cfm?ID=233; George J. Borjas and Marta Tienda, "The Employment and Wages of Legalized Immigrants," *International Migration Review* 27, No. 4 (Winter 1993): 712-747; Sherrie A. Kossoudji and Deborah

A. Cobb-Clark, "Coming Out of the Shadows: Learning about Legal Status and Wages from the Legalized Population," *Journal of Labor Economics* 20, no. 3 (July 2002): 598-628. For an example of the tax contributions made by immigrants, see Randolph Capps, Everett Henderson, Jeffrey S. Passel, and Michael E. Fix, "Civic Contributions: Taxes Paid by Immigrants in the Washington, DC, Metropolitan Area" (Washington, DC: Urban Institute, June 2006), http://www.urban.org/url.cfm?ID=411338.

185   Deborah L. Garvey, "Designing an Impact Aid Program" (see n. 71).

186   Under SLIAG, state and local governments were reimbursed — after the fact — for documented expenditures on services for the unauthorized immigrants who obtained legal status under IRCA's legalization program. Under *The Personal Responsibility and Work Opportunity Reconciliation Act of 1996* (PRWORA) Public Law 104-193, states are provided with block grants, and can allocate the funds as needed.

187   While border and interior immigration enforcement efforts and the adjudications of applications for temporary and permanent immigration were all contained within the former Immigration and Naturalization Service, under the DHS, Customs and Border Protection (CBP) is responsible for border enforcement, Immigration and Customs Enforcement (ICE) is responsible for interior enforcement, and US Citizenship and Immigration Services (USCIS) is responsible for adjudicating applications for immigration benefits.

188   Verification includes planning by the DHS Policy Directorate, verification and processing by USCIS, and enforcement by ICE. Outside of DHS, it involves the Internal Revenue Service, which collects payroll taxes and tax forms, the Social Security Administration, which verifies a match between a name and Social Security number, and the Department of Labor which cooperates with ICE in enforcing laws prohibiting the employment of unauthorized workers.

189   Employer investigations fell from 9 percent to only 2 percent of cases completed by INS Interior Investigations between 1991 and 2000. Dixon and Gelatt, "Enforcement Spending Since IRCA" (see n. 53).

190   Spencer S. Hsu and Kari Lydersen, "Illegal Hiring is Rarely Penalized," *The Washington Post,* June 19, 2006; DHS *Yearbook* (see n. 1). The number of full-time equivalent employees (FTEs) devoted to worksite enforcement fell from 240 in fiscal year (FY) 1999 to 90 in FY 2003 to roughly 65 in FY 2004. US Government Accountability Office, *Immigration Enforcement: Preliminary Observations on Employment Verification and Worksite Enforcement Efforts* GAO-05-822T (June 2005), http://www.gao.gov/new.items/d05822t.pdf.

191   GAO, *Weaknesses Hinder Employment Verification* (see n. 101).

192   Initiatives during the late 1990s and early 2000s to counter the presence of immigrants with criminal records, and counterterrorism efforts following 9/11, have diverted immigration enforcement efforts away from the workplace. GAO, *Preliminary Observations* (see n. 189).

193   See n. 37.

194   Passel, "The Size and Characteristics of the Unauthorized" (see n. 1).

195   Marc R. Rosenblum, *The Transnational Politics of U.S. Immigration Policy* (La Jolla, CA: University of California, San Diego Center for Comparative Immigration Studies, 2004).

196   Inter-American Development Bank Multilateral Investment Fund, "Remittances 2005: Promoting Financial Democracy" (Washington, DC: IADB, March 2006), http://idbdocs.iadb.org/wsdocs/getdocument. aspx?docnum=697487.

197   In comparison, remittances made up only 2.8 percent of Mexico's GDP in 2005. IADB, "Remittances 2005" (see n. 195). As of March 2005, there were about 1.1 million persons born in El Salvador living in the United States, while El Salvador itself has a population of about 6.8 million. Tabulations from the US Census Bureau, Current Population Survey, March Supplement, 2005; US Central Intelligence Agency, "El Salvador," *The World Factbook,* http://www.cia.gov/cia/publications/factbook/geos/es.html#Intro.

198   Mexico received nearly $74 million in foreign assistance in FY 2005, over half of which was dedicated to narcotics control and law enforcement activities. The next largest recipient of foreign assistance in Central America was Honduras. Nearly 40 percent of its $55 million was dedicated to development assistance, with another quarter each allocated to child survival and health and food aid. Connie Veillette, Clare Ribando, and Mark Sullivan, "US Foreign Assistance to Latin America and the Caribbean," Congressional Research Service report to Congress, March 30, 2005.

199   Ibid.

200   Carolyn Lochhead, "Give and Take Across the Border: 1 in 7 Mexican Workers Migrates — Most Send Money Home," *The San Francisco Chronicle,* May 21, 2006.

201   For more on these examples, see Devesh Kapur and John McHale, *Give Us Your Best and Brightest: The Global Hunt for Talent and Its Impact on the Developing World* (Washington, DC: Center for Global Development, Brookings Institution Press, 2005).

202   Commission for the Study of International Migration and Cooperative Economic Development, *Unauthorized Migration: An Economic Development Response for the Study of International Migration and Cooperative Economic Development* (Washington, DC: The Commission, 1990).

203   Demetrios Papademetriou, John Audley, Sandra Polaski, and Scott Vaughan, *NAFTA's Promise and Reality: Lessons from Mexico for the Hemisphere* (Washington, DC: Carnegie Endowment for International Peace, November 2003).

204   Commission, *An Economic Development Response* (see n. 201); Pamela K. Starr, "Challenges for a Postelection Mexico: Issues for US Policy," CSR No. 17 (Washington, DC: Council on Foreign Relations, June 2006).

205   Ibid.

206   Marc R. Rosenblum, "Beyond the Policy of No Policy: Emigration from Mexico and Central America," *Latin American Politics and Society* 4, no. 1 (2004): 91-125.

207 Mexican Secretary of Foreign Relations, "Mexico and the Migration Phenomenon" (February 2006), http://www.sre.gob.mx/eventos/fenomenomigratorio/docs/mexmigrationpheno.pdf.

208 Luis Ernesto Derbez, Foreign Minister of Mexico, comments at "Latin America's Response to the US Immigration Debate," public event convened by the Migration Policy Institute, *Foreign Affairs En Español,* and the Inter-American Dialogue (The Library of Congress, Washington, DC, May 2, 2006).

209 Mary Helen Johnson, "National Policies and the Rise of Transnational Gangs," *Migration Information Source,* April 1, 2006, http://www.migrationinformation.com/Feature/display.cfm?id=394.

210 Ibid.

211 In response to the recent arrests of 17 highly armed terrorist suspects in Canada, the Canadian government has announced the investment of hundreds of millions of dollars in transportation security, including air passenger screening. DePalma, "Canada Saw Plot to Seize Officials" (see n. 142); Office of the Prime Minister of Canada, "Prime Minister announces new measures to enhance the safety of Canadians," Press Release, June 16, 2006, http://pm.gc.ca/eng/media.asp?id=1207.

212 Meyers, "Does Smarter Lead to Safer?" (see n. 148).

213 See n. 150.

TASK FORCE MEMBER BIOGRAPHIES

Co-Chairs

SPENCER ABRAHAM is the Chairman and CEO of the Abraham Group, LLC. From 2001 to 2005, he served as the tenth Secretary of Energy. Prior to becoming Secretary of Energy, Mr. Abraham represented Michigan in the US Senate from 1995 to 2001. He served on the Budget, Commerce, Science and Transportation, Judiciary, and Small Business Committees. Secretary Abraham was a key Senate leader on such issues as technology, manufacturing, and immigration, having served as Chairman of the Senate Judiciary Subcommittee on Immigration as well as Chairman of the Senate Commerce Subcommittee on Manufacturing and Competitiveness. As a US Senator, Mr. Abraham was a forceful voice for the business community and free enterprise. Mr. Abraham endorsed policies and practices that promoted and enhanced America's competitiveness and global leadership. Among other things, Mr. Abraham led the support on free trade, legal and regulatory reform, and tax reform in the Senate.

Before his election to the Senate, Mr. Abraham served as Co-Chairman of the National Republican Congressional Committee from 1991 to 1993. He was also Chairman of the Michigan Republican Party from 1983 to 1990 and Deputy Chief of Staff to Vice President Dan Quayle from 1990 to 1991.

Mr. Abraham is a FOX News analyst and a periodic contributor of op-ed articles to the *Financial Times, The Weekly Standard*, and other publications. He is on the Board of Directors of Occidental Petroleum and also serves as a Distinguished Visiting Fellow at the Hoover Institution. Mr. Abraham holds a law degree from Harvard University and is a native of East Lansing, Michigan.

LEE H. HAMILTON is President and Director of the Woodrow Wilson International Center for Scholars, and Director of The Center on Congress at Indiana University. Mr. Hamilton served for 34 years in Congress representing Indiana's Ninth District. During his tenure, he served as Chairman and ranking member of the House Committee on Foreign Affairs (now the Committee on International Relations), chaired the Subcommittee on Europe and the Middle East, the Permanent Select Committee on Intelligence, and the Select Committee to Investigate Covert Arms Transactions with Iran. Mr. Hamilton also served as Chair of the Joint Economic Committee, working to promote long-term economic growth and development. As Chairman of the Joint Committee on the Organization of Congress and as a member of the House Standards of Official Conduct Committee, Mr. Hamilton was a primary draftsman of several House ethics reforms.

Since leaving the House, Mr. Hamilton has served as a Commissioner on the US Commission on National Security in the 21st Century (the Hart-Rudman Commission), and was Co-Chair with former Senator Howard Baker of the Baker-Hamilton Commission to Investigate Certain Security Issues at Los Alamos. Recently, Mr. Hamilton served as Vice Chair of the National Commission on Terrorist Attacks Upon the United States (the 9/11 Commission) and he co-chaired, with Governor Tom Kean, the 9/11 Public Discourse Project, which monitored implementation of the 9/11 Commission's recommendations. Mr. Hamilton was also recently a member of the Carter-Baker Commission on Federal Election Reform.

Mr. Hamilton is currently a member of the President's Foreign Intelligence Advisory Board, the President's Homeland Security Advisory Council, the Director of the Federal Bureau of Investigation's Advisory Board, the Director of Central Intelligence's Economic Intelligence Advisory Panel, the Secretary of Defense's National Security Study Group, and the US Department of Homeland Security Task Force on Preventing the Entry of Weapons of Mass Effect on American Soil. Mr. Hamilton is a graduate of DePauw University and Indiana University law school, as well as the recipient of numerous honorary degrees and national awards for public service. Before his election to Congress, he practiced law in Chicago and Columbus, Indiana.

Director

DORIS M. MEISSNER, former Commissioner of the US Immigration and Naturalization Service (INS), is a Senior Fellow at the Migration Policy Institute (MPI), where her work focuses on US immigration policy, immigration and national security, the politics of immigration, administering immigration systems and government agencies, and cooperation with other countries.

In 1993, President Clinton tapped her to serve as Commissioner of the INS, then a bureau in the US Department of Justice. She held the post through 2000. Her accomplishments included reforming the nation's asylum system; creating new strategies for managing US borders; improving naturalization and other services for immigrants; shaping new responses to migration and humanitarian emergencies; strengthening cooperation and joint initiatives with Mexico, Canada, and other countries; and managing growth that doubled the agency's personnel and tripled its budget. Prior to serving as Commissioner of the INS, Ms. Meissner served as a special assistant to the Attorney General; assistant director of the Office of Policy and Planning; executive director of the Cabinet Committee on Illegal Aliens; deputy associate attorney general, and executive associate commissioner of the INS; and a senior associate at the Carnegie Endowment for International Peace. Ms. Meissner created the Endowment's Immigration Policy Project, which evolved into the Migration Policy Institute in 2001.

Ms. Meissner's board memberships include CARE-USA, the Association of International Educators, the US-New Zealand Council, and the University of

Wisconsin-Madison Memorial Union. She is a member of the Council on Foreign Relations, the Inter-American Dialogue, the Pacific Council on International Diplomacy and the National Academy of Public Administration. Ms. Meissner earned her BA and MA degrees from the University of Wisconsin-Madison.

Members

T. ALEXANDER ALEINIKOFF is the Dean of the Law Center and the Executive Vice President for Law Center Affairs at Georgetown University. He has been a Senior Associate at the Migration Policy Institute and the International Migration Policy Program at the Carnegie Endowment for International Peace. From 1994-1997, Mr. Aleinikoff served as the General Counsel and then Executive Associate Commissioner for Programs of the Immigration and Naturalization Service (INS). Prior to joining the Clinton Administration, he was a full Professor of Law at the University of Michigan Law School. He has published numerous articles in the areas of immigration, race, statutory interpretation, and constitutional law, and he is also the author of the principal text and casebooks on US immigration, refugee, and citizenship law.

Congressman **HOWARD BERMAN** is a senior member of the International Relations Committee and the Judiciary Committee. He has gained increasing influence on such issues as foreign aid, arms control, antiterrorism, human rights, technology policy, trade legislation, copyright legislation, and immigration reform. As Ranking Member of the House Judiciary Subcommittee on Courts, the Internet and Intellectual Property, Mr. Berman plays a key role in shaping the copyright, trademark, and patent laws that are of vital importance to the entertainment, biotechnology, broadcasting, pharmaceutical, telecommunication, consumer electronics, and information technology industries. Prior to his election to the US Congress in 1982, Mr. Berman served in the California State Assembly where he was named Assembly Majority leader and served as Chair of the Assembly Democratic Caucus and the Policy Research Management Committee.

OSCAR A. CHACÓN has been Director of Enlaces América, a project of the Chicago-based Heartland Alliance for Human Needs and Human Rights, since August 2001. Enlaces América is dedicated to the empowerment of Latino immigrant organizations in the United States and is committed to fostering a just, dignified, and sustainable way of life for their communities in the United States and in their countries of origin. Mr. Chacón has worked, in different capacities, with Latino immigrant communities in the United States for over 20 years. Mr. Chacón was a founder of the Salvadoran American National Network (SANN), an advocacy umbrella organization of Central American community-based organizations founded in 1992. He served as SANN's president for several years. He is also a founding member of the National Alliance of Latin American and Caribbean Communities, an umbrella organization founded in 2004.

THOMAS J. DONOHUE is the President and CEO of the US Chamber of Commerce. Prior to his current post, Mr. Donohue served for 13 years as President and CEO of the American Trucking Association. Mr. Donohue has built the US Chamber of Commerce into a lobbying and political force with expanded influence across the globe. Under Mr. Donohue's leadership, the chamber has emerged as a major player in election politics, helping elect congressional pro-business candidates through financial support, voter activism, and turnout generated through the chamber's grassroots organization, VoteForBusiness.com. Mr. Donohue is also President of the Center for International Private Enterprise, a program of the National Endowment for Democracy dedicated to the development of market-oriented institutions around the world. In addition, he is a member of the President's Council on the 21st Century Workforce as well as the President's Advisory Committee for Trade Policy and Negotiations.

JEFF FLAKE is serving his third term in Congress representing the Sixth Congressional District of Arizona. The district includes parts of Mesa and Chandler and all of Gilbert, Queen Creek, and Apache Junction. Congressman Flake serves on the Committee on the Judiciary, the Committee on International Relations, and the Committee on Resources. Mr. Flake started his career at a public affairs firm in Washington, DC, in 1987. Soon after, he moved to the southern African nation of Namibia. As the Executive Director of the Foundation for Democracy, a foundation monitoring Namibia's independence process, he saw the nation usher in freedom and democracy. In 1992, Mr. Flake and his family moved back to Arizona where he was named Executive Director of the Goldwater Institute. In this role, he worked to promote a conservative philosophy of less government, more freedom, and individual responsibility.

FERNANDO GARCIA is Founding Director of the Border Network for Human Rights (BNHR). The BNHR supports immigrant border communities in the promotion of their human rights and demands humane immigration reform that is consistent with human rights. As Director, Mr. Garcia is responsible for facilitating the creation of Human Rights Community-Based Committees and the training of Human Rights Promoters in Southern New Mexico; West Texas; Arizona; Houston; Dallas; San Jose, CA; and New Jersey. In 2001, he became the National Coordinator of the National Movement for Legalization and Human Rights, an alliance of community based immigrant groups and organizations in the United States. Under Mr. Garcia's coordination, the Border Network for Human Rights has also worked closely with local elected officials and community organizations to develop city council resolutions in El Paso, Texas to oppose the militarization of the border, a call for comprehensive immigration reform, and against the presence of groups in the border region such as the minutemen.

BILL ONG HING is a Professor of Law and Asian American Studies at the University of California at Davis, and also serves as the Director of Asian American Studies. He teaches Judicial Process, Negotiations, Public Service Strategies, Asian American History, and directs the law school's clinical program. Throughout his career, he has pursued social justice by combining community work, litigation, and scholarship. He is the author of numerous academic and practice-oriented books and articles on immigration policy and race relations. His books include *Defining America Through Immigration Policy* (Temple Univ. Press, 2004), *Making and Remaking Asian America Through Immigration Policy* (Stanford Press, 1993), *Handling Immigration Cases* (Aspen Publishers, 1995), and *Immigration and the Law—A Dictionary* (ABC-CLIO, 1999). His book, *To Be An*

American, Cultural Pluralism and the Rhetoric of Assimilation (NYU Press, 1997), received the award for Outstanding Academic Book in 1997 by the librarians' journal *Choice.* He was also co-counsel in the precedent-setting Supreme Court asylum case, *INS v. Cardoza-Fonseca* (1987). Professor Hing is the founder of, and continues to volunteer as General Counsel for, the Immigrant Legal Resource Center in San Francisco. He is on the board of directors of the Asian Law Caucus and the Migration Policy Institute. He also serves on the National Advisory Council of the Asian American Justice Center in Washington, DC.

TAMAR JACOBY is a Senior Fellow at Manhattan Institute and writes extensively on immigration, citizenship, ethnicity, and race. Her 1998 book, *Someone Else's House: America's Unfinished Struggle for Integration,* tells the story of race relations in three American cities. Her newest book, *Reinventing the Melting Pot: The New Immigrants and What It Means to Be American,* is a collection of essays that argues that we as a nation need to find new ways to talk about and encourage assimilation. From 1987 to 1989, she was a Senior Writer and Justice Editor for *Newsweek.* Between 1981 and 1987, she was the Deputy Editor of *The New York Times* op-ed page. Before that, she was Assistant to the Editor of *The New York Review of Books.* In 2004, she was confirmed by the US Senate to serve on the National Council on the Humanities, the advisory board of the National Endowment for the Humanities.

JULIETTE KAYYEM is a Lecturer in Public Policy and faculty affiliate at the Belfer Center for Science and International Affairs at Harvard University's Kennedy School of Government. Since 2001, Ms. Kayyem has been a resident scholar at the Belfer Center, serving most recently as Executive Director for Research, overseeing the center's substantive activities in international security, environment, and energy policy. She is an expert in homeland security and terrorism, with a particular focus on the intersection of democracy and counter-terrorism policies. From 1999-2000, she served as House Minority Leader Richard Gephardt's appointee to the National Commission on Terrorism. She also served as a legal adviser to then Attorney General Janet Reno, in which capacity she worked on a variety of national security and terrorism cases.

Senator **EDWARD M. KENNEDY** has represented Massachusetts in the US Senate since he was elected in 1962 to finish the term of his brother, President John F. Kennedy. Re-elected seven times, he is the second most senior member of the Senate. Recent achievements include the Health Insurance Portability and Accountability Act of 1996 and the law that created the Children's Health Insurance Program in 1997. Mr. Kennedy is the senior Democrat on the Health, Education, Labor and Pensions Committee in the Senate. He also serves on the Judiciary Committee, where he is the senior Democrat on the Immigration Subcommittee, and the Armed Services Committee, where he is the senior Democrat on the Seapower Subcommittee.

Senator **JOHN McCAIN** is the senior Senator from Arizona. He was elected to the US Senate in 1986. After graduating from the Naval Academy in 1958, Mr. McCain began his career as a Naval aviator. In 1982, he was elected to Congress representing what was then the first congressional district of Arizona. In 2000,

Mr. McCain ran unsuccessfully for the Republican nomination for President of the United States. He is currently the Chairman of the Senate Committee on Indian Affairs, and serves on the Armed Services, and Commerce, Science, and Transportation Committees.

JANET MURGUÍA is the President and CEO of the National Council of La Raza. Ms. Murguía began her career in Washington, DC, as Legislative Counsel to former Kansas Congressman Jim Slattery, serving for seven years. She then worked at the White House in various capacities from 1994 to 2000, ultimately serving as Deputy Assistant to President Clinton and Deputy Director of Legislative Affairs, the senior White House liaison to Congress. She also served as Deputy Campaign Manager and Director of Constituency Outreach for the Gore/Lieberman presidential campaign.

LEON PANETTA chairs the board and co-directs the Leon & Sylvia Panetta Institute for Public Policy with a particular focus on inspiring young men and women to lives of leadership and public service. He represented the central coast area of California in the US Congress for sixteen years. During much of that time he also served as a member and Chair of the House Budget Committee. President Clinton appointed him Director of the US Office of Management and Budget from 1993 to 1994, and he served as Chief of Staff to the President from 1994 to 1997. He serves on many public policy and corporate boards, including as Co-Chair of the California Council on Base Support and Retention; Chair of the Pew Oceans Commission; membership on the Fleishman-Hillard International Advisory Board; the Board of Directors of Blue Shield of California; IDT Telecom, Inc.; Zenith Insurance Company; Connetics; and Santa Clara University.

STEVEN J. RAUSCHENBERGER was elected in 1992 to the Illinois State Senate. Now the Deputy Republican leader, he specializes in tax relief and welfare reform. He is the former Chairman of the Illinois State Senate Appropriations committee. Senator Rauschenberger has recently finished his term as the President of the National Conference of State Legislatures. As the first freshman legislator ever appointed Chairman of the Appropriations Committee, Senator Rauschenberger negotiated multi-billion-dollar budgets that provided funds to schools, senior citizen services, infrastructure improvements, and other vital programs—all without a tax increase. An advocate for taxpayers, Senator Rauschenberger has supported tax caps and increasing the income tax exemption. He also has been the Senate negotiator of KidCare, the state health insurance program for children of low-income, working families.

ROBERT D. REISCHAUER began his tenure as the second President of the Urban Institute in February 2000. From 1989 to 1995, he served as the Director of the nonpartisan Congressional Budget Office (CBO), and is a nationally known expert on the federal budget, Medicare, and Social Security. Mr. Reischauer served as the Urban Institute's Senior Vice President from 1981 to 1986. He is a member of the Harvard Corporation and serves on the boards of several educational and nonprofit organizations. He serves as Vice Chair of the Medicare Payment Advisory Commission. He was a Senior Fellow of Economic Studies at the Brookings Institution from 1995 to 2000.

KURT L. SCHMOKE serves as Dean of the Howard University School of Law. Elected in 1987, he served three terms as Mayor of Baltimore, becoming the first African American voted into that office. During his terms, Mayor Schmoke established a cabinet-level agency and a private foundation to fund, coordinate, and expand adult literacy programs throughout the city. He also strongly supported educational innovation and led a successful campaign to win more state funding through a landmark city – state partnership. In addition to education, Mayor Schmoke made housing a top priority of his administration. Baltimore became a national model for neighborhood revitalization. Mayor Schmoke also worked aggressively to retain and expand existing businesses, while working to attract new businesses to spur economic development.

FRANK SHARRY is the Executive Director of the National Immigration Forum. The Forum's mission is to embrace and uphold America's tradition as a nation of immigrants. Since becoming the Forum's Executive Director in 1990, Mr. Sharry has emerged as a leading spokesperson for pro-immigrant policies in the United States. Prior to joining the Forum, Mr. Sharry was Executive Director of Centro Presente, an agency that helps Central American refugees in the Boston area. He also led efforts to resettle refugees from Vietnam, Cuba, and elsewhere for a national organization now called Immigration and Refugee Services of America. In 1994, Mr. Sharry took a leave of absence from the Forum to work in the campaign against Proposition 187, the anti-immigrant California ballot initiative.

DEBRA W. STEWART is President of the Council of Graduate Schools, the leading national organization dedicated to the improvement and advancement of graduate education. Until July 2000, Dr. Stewart was Vice Chancellor and Dean of the Graduate School at North Carolina State University. She also served as Interim Chancellor at the University of North Carolina at Greensboro. Dr. Stewart has been an active leader in higher education nationally as Chair of the Board of Directors of the Council of Graduate Schools, the Graduate Record Examination Board, the Council on Research Policy and Graduate Education, and the Board of Directors of Oak Ridge Associated Universities. She also served as Vice Chair of the Board of Trustees of the Educational Testing Service and as a trustee of the Triangle University Center for Advanced Studies.

C. STEWART VERDERY, JR., joined Mehlman Vogel Castagnetti in March 2005, following over a decade of high-level positions in the Executive Branch, Congress, and the private sector. Mr. Verdery has extensive experience delivering public policy results to clients and the public in a wide range of fields, including homeland security and law enforcement, technology and telecommunications, intellectual property, election law and legal reform. Prior to joining MVC, Mr. Verdery served as Assistant Secretary for Homeland Security, following his confirmation by the US Senate in 2003. Mr. Verdery led efforts by the Department of Homeland Security to develop and implement policies related to immigration, visas, and travel facilitation; cargo security and international trade; transportation security; and counternarcotics and other law enforcement priorities. Prior to his service at DHS, Mr. Verdery served as General Counsel to Sen. Don Nickles (R-OK), the Assistant Senate Majority Leader, from 1998 until 2002. He served as counsel to Chairman Orrin Hatch (R-UT) on the Judiciary Committee's crime unit in 1998, and, while at the Committee on Rules and Administration from 1996–1998, he worked for Chairman John Warner (R-VA) to investigate the contested Louisiana Senate election. In addition to his government service, Mr. Verdery was the Senior Legislative Counsel for Vivendi Universal Entertainment, focusing on telecommunications and intellectual property issues. He was also an associate at the Washington office of the law firm Baker & Hostetler, concentrating on antitrust and litigation. Mr. Verdery is a graduate of Williams College and the University of Virginia School of Law.

JOHN W. WILHELM is President/Hospitality Industry of UNITE HERE, an organization created by the merger in 2004 of the Hotel Employees and Restaurant Employees International Union (HERE) and UNITE. Mr. Wilhelm began working with HERE as an organizer and business agent, and was elected President in 1998. During his presidency, HERE furthered its reputation as an organizing union, and achieved net growth after more than 25 years of membership decline. The union also substantially diversified its national leadership and became the first union in the modern era to be released from government supervision. Previously, Mr. Wilhelm served as AFL-CIO Vice President; and from 1999 to 2005, he chaired the AFL-CIO Immigration Committee, which achieved unanimous approval from the AFL-CIO Executive Council in 2000 for a historic reversal of the AFL-CIO's policy on immigration. The new policy developed by the Immigration Committee calls for legalization for immigrant workers in the United States, repeal of the dysfunctional I-9 employer sanction system of workplace immigration enforcement, criminalization of willful employer recruitment of illegal immigrants, whistleblower protection for immigrants who assert their workplace rights, and expanded training for immigrants and other workers. Since then, Mr. Wilhelm has been a leader in pressing for reform of US immigration law.

JAMES ZIGLAR has served in a variety of positions in the federal government, totaling more than sixteen years. Most recently, he was appointed by President George W. Bush to serve as Commissioner of the Immigration and Naturalization Services (INS), where he faced some of the INS's greatest challenges in the wake of September 11. Prior to this appointment, Mr. Ziglar was unanimously elected Sergeant of Arms of the US Senate, where he served as the Senate's Chief Administrative, Protocol, and Security Officer. He also served in the Reagan Administration as Assistant Secretary of the Interior for Water and Science. Mr. Ziglar began his legal career as law clerk to US Supreme Court Associate Justice Harry A. Blackmun during the Supreme Court's 1972 term. He practiced law for seven years and was in the investment banking business for more than sixteen years, including over ten years as a Managing Director of UBS Financial Services in New York City. He also has been a fellow at the John F. Kennedy School's Institute of Politics at Harvard University, and a Distinguished Visiting Professor of Law at The George Washington University Law School. Mr. Ziglar presently serves as President and CEO of Cross Match Technologies, Inc., a multinational biometrics technology company headquartered in Palm Beach Gardens, Florida.

Ex officio members

MALCOLM BROWN, Assistant Deputy Minister, Strategic and Program Policy, Citizenship and Immigration Canada

JEAN LOUIS DE BROUWER, Director, Directorate B - Immigration, Asylum, and Borders, European Commission Directorate General for Justice, Freedom and Security

JEFF GORSKY, Chief, Legal Advisory Opinion Section, Visa Office, US Department of State

GERÓNIMO GUTIÉRREZ FERNÁNDEZ, Undersecretary for North America, Ministry of Foreign Affairs, Mexico

Observers

THOR ARNE AASS, Director General, Department of Migration, Ministry of Labour and Social Inclusion, Norway

CARLOS DE ICAZA, Ambassador to the United States of America, Mexico

ALEXANDROS ZAVOS, President, Hellenic Migration Policy Institute

APPENDIX I: Temporary Visa Categories and Admission Numbers for Fiscal Year 2004

Visa Category	2004 Admissions
A: Ambassadors (A-1), other government officials (A-2), and employees (A-3)	152,649
B: Business visitors (B-1) or tourists (B-2)	11,537,896
C: Transit visa (pass-through at an airport or seaport) (C1-4)	338,171
D: Crewmember (air or sea) (D1-2)	ND
E: Treaty-Traders (E-1) or Treaty-Investors (E-2) from countries where the United States has a treaty of commerce and investment	182,934
F: Students (F-1) and spouses (F-2)	613,221
G: Employees of International Organizations (IMF, IPIC, OAS, IRC, etc.) (G1-5)	109,355
H: Temporary Workers	
H-1A: Registered Nurses	7,795
H-1B: Specialty occupations	386,821
H-1B1: Chile/Singapore Free Trade Agreement	326
H-1C: Registered nurses participating in Nurse Relief for Disadvantaged Areas	70
H-2A: Agricultural workers	22,141
H-2B: Non-agricultural workers	86,958
H-3: Industrial trainees	2,226
H-4: Spouses and children of H-1, H-2, and H-3 workers	130,847
I: Representatives of international media and families (I-1)	37,108
J: Exchange visitors (J-1) (educational exchange students, au pairs, graduate medical trainees, practical training students, professors and researchers, short-term scholars, camp counselors) and spouses (J-2)	360,777
K: Fiancés and fiancées (K-1); spouses of US citizens (K-3), and children (K-2 and K-4)	33,061
L: Intracompany transferees (L-1A and L-1B) (executives, managers, persons with proprietary knowledge) and families (L-2)	456,583
M: Language and vocational students (M-1) and families (M-2)	7,381
NATO: NATO officials and employees (NATO1-6) and families (NATO-7)	
N: Parents or children of special immigrants (N8-9)	54
O: Extraordinary ability aliens in science, arts, business, and athletics (O-1), families (O2-3)	22,178
P: Athletes, entertainment groups, support personnel (P1-3), and spouses (P-4)	39,308
Q: Cultural exchange visitors (Q1-2) and spouses (Q-3)	2,481
R: Religious workers (R-1) and families (R-2)	21,571
S: Criminal informants (S5-6)	ND
T: Victims of international trafficking in persons (T-1) and families (T2-4)	1,079
U: Victims of spousal or child abuse (U-1) and families (U2-4)	298
V: Spouses and minor children of permanent residents with pending green cards (V1-3)	48,661
TN: Professional workers NAFTA and families (TD)	78,802
TC: Professional workers US-Canada Free Trade Agreement and families (TB)	52
TOTAL	**14,680,804**

Source: US Department of Homeland Security, *Yearbook of Immigration Statistics: 2004* (Washington, DC: US Department of Homeland Security Office of Immigration Statistics, 2006).

APPENDIX II: Legal Immigration Preference System (Family and Employment)

	Category	Numerical Limit
	Total family-sponsored immigrants	480,000; limit can be pierced should the immediate relatives category exceed 254,000 in a given year
Immediate relatives	Aliens who are the spouses and unmarried minor children of US citizens and the parents of adult US citizens	Unlimited
	Family-sponsored preference immigrants	Worldwide level 226,000
1st preference	Unmarried adult sons and daughters of citizens	23,400 plus visas not required for 4th preference
2nd preference	(A) Spouses and children of LPRs (B) Unmarried adult sons and daughters of LPRs	114,200 plus visas not required for 1st preference
3rd preference	Married adult sons and daughters of citizens	23,400 plus visas not required for 1st or 2nd preference
4th preference	Siblings of adult (age 21 and over) US citizens	65,000 plus visas not required for 1st, 2nd, or 3rd preference
	Employment-based preference immigrants	Worldwide level 140,000
1st preference	Priority workers: persons of extraordinary ability in the arts, science, education, business, or athletics; outstanding professors and researchers; and certain multinational executives and managers	28.6 percent of worldwide limit plus unused 4th and 5th preference
2nd preference	Members of the professions holding advanced degrees or persons of exceptional abilities in the sciences, art, or business	28.6 percent of worldwide limit plus unused 1st preference
3rd preference – skilled	Skilled shortage workers with at least two years training or experience, professionals with bachelor's degrees	28.6 percent of worldwide limit plus unused 1st or 2nd preference
3rd preference - "other"	Unskilled shortage workers	5,000* (taken from the total available for 3rd preference)
4th preference	"Special immigrants," including ministers of religion, religious workers other than ministers, certain employees of the US government abroad, and others	7.1 percent of worldwide limit; religious workers limited to 5,000
5th preference	Employment creation investors who invest at least $1 million (amount may vary in rural areas or areas of high unemployment) which will create at least ten new jobs	7.1 percent of worldwide limit; 3,000 minimum reserved for investors in rural or high unemployment areas

* Under statute, the limit is 10,000, but 5,000 are taken away temporarily by the Nicaraguan Adjustment and Central American Relief Act (NACARA), until all NACARA applicants are processed.

Source: Congressional Research Service summary of §203(a), §203(b), and §204 of INA; 8 U.S.C. 1153, in Ruth Ellen Wasem, "U.S. Immigration Policy on Permanent Admissions," Congressional Research Service Report for Congress, Library of Congress, February 18, 2004.

APPENDIX III-A: Summary of a Proposed Simplified Temporary and Provisional Visa System

The framework outlined below streamlines the 24 current nonimmigrant visa categories into just seven and reduces the subcategories from 70 to 25. By grouping individuals according to their reason for entry, this design inserts transparency into a sprawling and opaque system and benefits users. Most travelers to the United States would receive the Visitor visa. The new Provisional Immigrant category encompasses the full range of skill sets in demand and recognizes the frequent, though not automatic, connection between temporary and permanent immigration. This new visa provides workers and employers with greater flexibility to make the decisions that work best for both of them. Graduate students would be eligible to adjust to permanent status following completion of their degrees and two years of work in the United States, allowing qualified foreign-born talent in areas of high demand to stay in the United States. Ready access to Seasonal and Short-term Work visas should reduce the entry by and hiring of unauthorized workers and reintroduce circular migration for such work at all skill levels.

Main Categories	Who is Included	Current Mode of Entry
V Visas: Visitors	Tourists; Visitors for Business; Persons in Transit; and Crew Members	B, C, D, GB, GT, WB, WT
R Visa: Representatives	Representatives of foreign governments; Representatives of international organizations; Attendants, servants, and personal employees of both of the above; Foreign media; and Dependents of representatives and foreign media	A, G, I, N
S Visa: Students/ Trainees	Students in graduate degree programs; Students in undergraduate degree programs; Students in primary or secondary schools; Vocational students; Trainees; and Dependents of all of the above	F, H-3, some J, M
W Visa: Seasonal and Short-Term Workers	Seasonal workers in industries with peak load, seasonal, or intermittent needs; Short-term workers of all skill levels for work of up to 12 months	Some H-1B, H-2A, some H-2B, some J, some L, some O, P, most Q, some R, some who now come illegally
T Visa: Treaty and Reciprocal Exchange	Treaty traders; Treaty investors; Trade agreement workers; Those entering under reciprocal exchange agreements; and Dependents of the above	E, H-1B1, some J, TN, TD, some Q
P Visa: Provisional Immigrants	Workers with extraordinary ability in permanent jobs; Workers in jobs expected to last for more than one year that require a BA or more; Workers in jobs expected to last more than one year that require less than a BA; and Dependents of all of the above	Most H-1B, some H-2B, some J, some L, O-1, some O-2, some R, some who now come illegally
O Visa: Other Provisional	Fiancees; Victims of trafficking or criminal activities; Government informants; and other foreigners whom the government may wish to admit for humanitarian, security, foreign policy, or other reasons.	K, S, T, U

Notes: Nothing in this simplification implies changing terms for any category for which provisions are treaty or reciprocity-based. The spouses and minor children of LPRs who currently enter on V nonimmigrant visas would be able to enter the United States directly through the permanent immigration system, as indicated in Appendix III-B.

Details of a Proposed Simplified Temporary and Provisional Visa System

SHADING INDICATES A CHANGE FROM CURRENT REQUIREMENTS

Visa Type		Must Prove Intent to Return?	Length of Visa	Renewable from Within Country?	May Bring Dependents?[1]	Able to Work? / Labor Market Protections?[2]	Cap on Admissions?	Direct Route to LPR w/ Self Petition?[3]
V (Visitors)	V-1 Business	Y	Length of Business	N	N	N	N	N
	V-2 Tourist	Y	Up to 6 months	N	N	N	N	N
	V-3 Transit	Y	Up to 29 days	N	N	N	N	N
R (Representatives)	R-1 Reps of Foreign Govts	Current law	Length of Assignment	Y	Y	Y / N	N	N
	R-2 Reps of Internat'l Orgs	Current law	Length of Assignment	Y	Y	Y / N	N	N
	R-3 Foreign Media	Current law	Length of Assignment	Y	Y	Y / N	N	N
	R-4 Attendants, Servants, and Personal Employees of R-1-2	Current law	Current law	Y	N	Y / N	N	N
	R-D Dependent of R-1-3	Current law	Like Principal	Y	-	Y / N	N	N
S (Students/Trainees)	S-1 Grad Student	N	Duration of Study[4]	N	Y	On Campus[13]/N	N	Y,[5] capped[6]
	S-2 Undergrad Student	N	Duration of Study[4]	N	Y	On Campus[13]/N	N	N
	S-3 Primary or Secondary Student	Y	Duration of Study[4]	N	-	-	N	N
	S-4 Vocational Student	Y	Duration of Study[4]	N	Y	On Campus[13]/N	N	N
	S-5 Trainee	Y	Duration of Study[4]	N	Y	N[14] / N	N	N
	S-D Dependent of S-1-5	Like Principal	Like Principal	N	-	N / N	N	Like Principal
W (Seasonal & Short-Term Workers)	W-1 Seasonal Worker	Y	Up to 9 months	N	N	Y / N[7]	N	N
	W-2 Short-Term Worker, all skill levels	Y	Up to 12 months[15]	N	N[10]	Y / Y	N	N
T (Treaty and Reciprocal Exchange)	T-1 Treaty Trader, Treaty Investor, Trade Agreement Worker, Reciprocal Exchange Visitor	As stipulated by treaty/agreement	As stipulated by treaty/agreement	As stipulated by treaty/agreement	As stipulated by treaty/agreement	As stipulated by treaty/agreement	As stipulated by treaty/agreement	N
	T-D Dependent of T-1	Y	Like Principal	Like Principal	-	N	N	N

P (Provisional Immigrants)								
P-1 Wrkr with Extraordinary Ability[12]	N	3 Years	Y, Once	Y / N	Y	N	N	Y, no cap
P-2 Wrkr in Job requiring BA or more	N	3 Years	Y, Once	Y / Y	Y	Y[8]	Y[8]	Y, capped[6]
P-3 Wrkr in Job requiring < BA	N	3 Years	Y, Once	Y / Y	Y	Y[8]	Y[8]	Y, capped[6]
P-D Dependent of P-1-3	N	Like Principal	Y, Once		-	N	N	Y[9] no cap
O (Other Provisional)								
O-1 Fiancee	N	Current law	N	Y / N	Y	N	N	N
O-2 Victim of Trafficking, Crime, Govt Informant, Other humanitarian or security-based entrants	N	Per government requirements	Per govt requirements	Y / Y	Y	N	N	N[11], no cap
O-D Dependent of O-1-2	N	Like Principal	Like Principal		-	N	N	Like Principal

[1] This category describes whether each visa type confers the ability to bring spouses and children in a derivative status. However, spouses and children may always come to the United States if they obtain their own visas.

[2] Employers would either be pre-certified to sponsor temporary or provisional migrants or would file individual attestations with the Department of Labor. Further details on worker protections can be found in chapter VI.

[3] Persons with these visas may adjust to LPR status if they qualify based on evidence of continued employment (or an employment offer, in the case of graduate students) in the occupation or field for which the applicant's educational or professional credentials served as the basis for the provisional visa, ability to speak English, renewed clearance of a security and background check, and payment of relevant fees.

[4] "Duration of study" includes optional practical training (OPT) for those categories of students who currently have this option. The maximum length of the OPT will be extended from one to two years.

[5] May adjust after completion of study and two years of work. Dependents will obtain derivative LPR status. Students holding US or foreign-government sponsored scholarships who currently have a two-year residency abroad requirement will retain that requirement unless waived, and will not have an automatic path to LPR status. They will still be able to adjust through the family or employment-based permanent visa systems, if eligible, once they have completed their residency requirement. Waiver requirements would be made more flexible.

[6] An overall annual cap of 300,000 will be set for S-1, P-1, P-2, and P-3 adjustments. There will be no per-country limits on adjustments. We developed this cap assuming that in addition to P-2 admissions (capped at 315,000) and P-3 admissions (capped at 105,000), an estimated 10,000 P-1s and 90,000 S-1s would enter each year in the early years of the new system. These estimates are based on current demand for O-1 visas and current levels of foreign graduate student admissions in fields of study desired by US employers. This adds up to 430,000 yearly admissions of provisional immigrants, and 90,000 admissions of graduate students. We estimate that roughly 60 percent of P-1s, P-2s, and P-3s may choose and qualify to adjust to permanent status. For S-1 entrants, we expect about a 50 percent adjustment rate. We set the initial cap on adjustments at 300,000 per year.

[7] In order to facilitate employer participation in the Seasonal Worker program we require neither a labor market test nor a cap on visas for W-1 workers initially, just as H-2A visas are uncapped under current law. Instead, employers will register and attest that they will comply with all relevant workplace regulations. Workers will receive the same wages and protections as US workers. Uncapped access to seasonal workers combined with enhanced worksite enforcement efforts will encourage reliance on a legal workforce.

[8] P-2 admissions will have an initial cap of 105,000 and P-3 admissions an initial cap of 315,000 principals, not subject to per-country limits. We arrived at these caps by estimating demand for certain current work visas. Between FY 2001 and 2005, an average of about 130,000 persons entered on H-1Bs each year. Under the new system, H-1Bs could obtain either P-2 visas or SWP visas in the direct permanent system, so we set the P-2 cap at 105,000. To calculate the P-3 cap, we looked at the number of H-2Bs who currently enter (an average of about 72,000 a year) who would obtain P-3 visas under our system. We also considered the net flow of unauthorized immigrant workers, who would also obtain P-3 visas under our system. Each year a net of 500,000 unauthorized immigrants enter the country, and roughly 60 percent of them find work, meaning that the number of unauthorized workers in the US workforce increases by as much as 300,000 each year. However, with new options to come legally and work temporarily, we project that some current H-2Bs and some unauthorized immigrants who now settle permanently would instead choose to come temporarily. Therefore, we set the initial cap somewhat below the current number of 372,000 at 315,000.

[9] P-D visa holders may obtain LPR status only if the principal adjusts to LPR status (unless adjusting through existing employer or family-sponsored channels). When P visa principals adjust to LPR status, P-D holders receive derivative LPR status.

[10] Those entering under the Irish Peace Process Cultural and Training Program (current Q-2) may bring their dependents (current Q-3). We do not expect that program to be of infinite duration.

[11] O-2 visa holders require permission from the government to adjust to LPR status, based on their compliance with the conditions of their provisional visa. O-2 visa holders are not subject to LPR adjustment requirements outlined in note 3.

[12] Workers of extraordinary ability do not require an employer sponsor for their visa, unlike all other temporary or provisional workers.

[13] Students and trainees may work on campus or off-campus if they receive authorization based on economic need.

[14] Trainees may work only if the work is incidental to and necessary for the training.

[15] The length of visa is a change for some, but not all, categories of workers who would be included in this category. Currently, some groups considered temporary workers are able to stay for a few years; under the revised system, seasonal or short-term status would be limited to those filling jobs that are truly of limited duration.

APPENDIX III-B: Summary of Proposed Changes in Redesigned Permanent Immigration System

The redesigned immigration selection system presented here was developed to meet five main goals:

- better deliver on promises of family unification and fulfillment of labor market needs;

- create space within the permanent immigration system for immigrants of various skill levels to be accommodated either directly or after a probationary period;

- allocate numbers that more accurately reflect the actual annual flows;

- maximize the visa choices available to immigrants and their sponsors; and

- enhance system flexibility to adapt and adjust to changing labor market needs.

Family

The most significant change with regard to family-based immigration is securing the prompt reunification of the spouses and minor children of lawful permanent residents (LPRs). This is accomplished by exempting them from numerical or per-country limits, thus treating the spouses and minor children of LPRs and citizens alike. In addition to speeding reunification, this change would reduce backlogs that undermine important US values. Backlogs in the remaining family preference categories for the largest migrant-sending countries would also be reduced by raising the per-country limit from 7 to 15 percent.

Other changes eliminate the current categories for adult unmarried children of LPRs (they would still be eligible for sponsorship once their parents gain citizenship) and siblings of US citizens, categories that experience waiting times of between one decade and more than 23 years. While these are difficult decisions, ultimately tradeoffs must be made when attempting to rationalize the system and better deliver on the most important priorities without simply opening immigration up to ever-growing numbers. Under this redesigned system, we estimate that the total annual number of family-based immigrants would remain at current levels, but in addition, significant numbers of family members would enter as the dependents of direct permanent and provisional immigrants. Actual numbers, however, are likely to fluctuate.

Importantly, these changes presume that a backlog clearance program will be implemented prior to elimination of any categories, as it is only fair to keep the promises made to those who have waited their turn and followed the rules. According to estimates by the Department of State, such a program could eliminate existing backlogs within six years — prior to the time that the redesigned system proposed by the Task Force would be fully implemented. In addition, given the way in which social networks and labor markets function, the greater numbers of direct employment-based visas, and the creation of the new Provisional Immigrant categories, it is highly likely that adult children, siblings, and even other family members would immigrate to the United States through employment-based visas. In fact, they are likely to do so far more quickly than they would have through the existing family sponsorship arrangements.

Employment

The redesigned system increases employment-based immigration to account for roughly half of total legal immigration, rather than the 17 or so percent it has averaged over the last five years. It expands the number of permanent visas available for highly qualified professionals whose presence benefits the United States. Uncapped numbers are available for the new Strategic Growth visa to entice extremely talented individuals in strategically important disciplines, persons of extraordinary ability, and outstanding professors and researchers to put their skills and education to work for the United States. The redesign also makes substantial numbers available for multinational executives or managers and skilled workers and professionals with a college degree or higher. These visa categories would boost the country's competitive strength in an increasingly knowledge-based global economy, and meet the demand for specialized workers as it arises. The redesign also eliminates per-country caps for the Strategic Growth visa and raises them to 10 percent (from the current 7 percent) for multinational executives and managers and skilled workers and professionals. This change would reduce backlogs from high-demand countries and facilitate employers' ability to hire foreign workers with needed skills without undue delay. Although this proposal suggests an initial allocation of visas for employment categories, such determinations ultimately would rest with The Standing Commission.

The second way in which the proposed system facilitates the immigration of needed workers is through the creation of the new Provisional Immigrant category. Individuals who qualify for that visa would be able to adjust to LPR status directly from their provisional visas. Provisional immigrants would account for about 80 percent of all permanent employment-based visas, allowing workers and employers to test each other prior to making a more permanent commitment. Provisional Immigrant adjustments to permanent status would not be subject to per-country limits and would include workers at all skill levels, as well as foreign students with qualifying advanced degrees. The number of visas available for workers with less than a bachelor's degree would be significantly expanded from current levels, allowing legal entry for many of the workers who now enter the country without authorization or overstay their visas.

By providing multiple paths for legal entry, this re-design increases the choices available both to potential workers and employers, regardless of skill levels, and better reflects the nature of the US labor market and interests. The total number of employment-based immigrants (principals and dependents) estimated to enter under this system once it is fully operational would be about 750,000, compared to an annual average of nearly 168,000 in each of the last five years. We estimate that the total annual number of new LPRs would initially be at about 1.5 million.

APPENDIX III-B: Comparison of Current and Redesigned Permanent Immigration Systems

CURRENT SYSTEM (average annual admissions FY 2001 to FY 2005)	Annual Number of New LPRs
Approximation of actual annual visa demand*	1,805,064
Total admissions under the current system	**980,478**
Family (principals + dependents)	**621,878**
Immediate family of US citizens (no overall cap, no per-country limit)	**420,791**
Spouses	252,284
Minor children	87,594
Parents	80,913
Family-sponsored immigrants (floor=226,000, per-country limit of 7%)	**201,086**
Principals	122,880
1 Adult unmarried children of US citizens	18,323
2A Spouses/minor children of LPRs	59,059
2B Adult unmarried children of LPRs	15,259
3 Adult married children of US citizens	7,643
4 Siblings of US citizens	22,595
Dependents of family-sponsored principals	78,207
1 Adult unmarried children of US citizens	6,333
2A Spouses/minor children of LPRs	6,429
2B Adult unmarried children of LPRs	8,072
3 Adult unmarried children of US citizens	17,337
4 Siblings of US citizens	40,036
Employment (principals + dependents)	**167,701**
Employment-based immigrants (cap=140,000 on principals & dependents, per-country limit of 7%)	
Principals	77,259
1-1 Aliens with extraordinary ability	2,993
1-2 Outstanding professors or researchers	3,278
1-3 Multinational executives or managers	8,973
2 Professionals with advanced degrees/persons with exceptional ability	17,037
3 Skilled workers, professionals, other workers	41,369
4 Special immigrants	3,547
5 Employment creation	61
Dependents	90,442
1 Priority workers	22,119
2 Professionals with advanced degrees/persons with exceptional ability	18,499
3 Skilled workers, professionals, other workers	45,884
4 Special immigrants	3,825
5 Employment creation	115
Remaining immigrants	**190,899**
Refugees and asylees	98,742
Legalized under IRCA	135
Diversity (cap=50,000)	45,502
Other immigrants	46,521

REDESIGNED SYSTEM	Annual Number of New LPRs
Total admissions under proposed system	**1,530,533**
(Beginning in Year 7)	[7]
Family (principals + dependents)	**620,791**
Immediate family of US citizens and LPRs (no overall cap, no per-country limit)	**520,791**
Spouses of US citizens	252,284
Minor children of US citizens	87,594
Spouses/minor children of LPRs (former 2A)	100,000 [1]
Parents of US citizens	80,913
Family-sponsored immigrants (cap=50,000 for principals, no cap on dependents, per-country limit of 15%)	**100,000**
Principals	50,000 [2]
AUC Adult unmarried children of US citizens	35,000
AMC Adult married children of US citizens	15,000
Dependents of family-sponsored principals	50,000 [6]
Employment (principals + dependents)	**750,000**
Direct Permanent (cap=65,000 for principals, no cap on dependents, per-country limit 10% for MEM and SWP visas)	150,000
Principals	75,000 [2]
SG Strategic growth	15,000 [3,5]
MEM Multinational executives and managers	10,000 [4]
SWP Skilled workers and professionals w/BA degree or higher	50,000 [4]
Dependents	75,000 [6]
Provisional Immigrant (cap=300,000 for principals, no cap on dependents, no per-country limits)	600,000
P-visa Principals and S-1 Advanced degree students	300,000 [2,8]
P-1 Workers w/extraordinary ability	10,000 [5]
P-2 Workers in jobs requiring a BA or more	60,000
P-3 Workers in jobs requiring less than a BA	190,000
S-1 Advanced degree foreign students	40,000
P-D Dependents of P and S-1	300,000 [6]
Remaining immigrants	**159,742**
Refugees and asylees	98,742
Diversity	0
Other immigrants	25,000 [9]
O Other Provisional	36,000

[1]   We assume this number will be about 70 percent greater than the average 2A admissions between FY 2001 and 2005.

[2]   All category caps represent initial levels that would then be adjusted by The Standing Commission on Immigration and Labor Markets.

[3]   Strategic growth visas would include workers with extraordinary ability and outstanding professors or researchers who currently come under the EB-1 visa, those currently coming under the EB-5 visa, and persons in strategic industries as determined by The Standing Commission. Eligible persons could self-sponsor for SG visas or be sponsored by an employer. There would be no labor market test for such workers.

[4]   The MEM visa would include multinational executives and managers who currently come under the EB-1 visa. The SWP visa would include those who currently come under EB-2 visas, skilled workers under EB-3, and some under EB-4 visas. MEM and SWP visas would require an employer sponsor and a streamlined labor certification process.

[5]   SG and P-1 visa numbers would not be limited. However, their numbers would be counted against the overall caps on Direct Employment visas for principals and adjustments to LPR status of Provisional Immigrant principals, respectively.

[6]   We assume a rate of one dependent per principal.

[7]   During the first three years of implementation of this system no one would be eligible to adjust through the Provisional Immigrant system. Some Provisional Immigrants would not adjust until after their second three-year period. During the first three years, therefore, admissions under this preference system would total about 930,533, and would remain lower than 1.5 million between years three and six. This figure excludes admissions resulting from the backlog clearance program that would be implemented during this time.

[8]   300,000 is the number of people we think would likely seek to adjust from Provisional Immigrant to LPR status. This figure includes approximately 60 percent of Provisional Immigrant admissions (430,000) plus about 50 percent of the 90,000 annual admissions of graduate students (S-1s). The 430,000 figure is composed of 105,000 P-2s, 315,000 P-3s, and an estimated 10,000 (uncapped) P-1s. There are no recent estimates of the rate of adjustment to LPR status by persons in various nonimmigrant categories or by nonimmigrants in general. The only available estimate is that about 50 percent of H-1B workers adjusted to LPR status in the late 1990s. We believe that under the proposed system, as many as 60 percent of Provisional Immigrants may seek and qualify to adjust to LPR status, and, based on rates of graduate study in fields desired by US employers, that about 50 percent of foreign graduate students will seek and qualify to adjust to LPR status.

[9]   Other Immigrants includes many of the immigration categories currently under EB-4 (excluding religious workers/ministers), as well as immigrants currently falling under the Other immigrants category such as parolees, NACARA immigrants, cancellation of removal, HRIFA adjustments, private bill adjustments, and others. Many of these programs are of finite duration and we expect that such entries will continue to taper off, falling to only about half the current number by the time seven years have passed under this system.

APPENDIX IV: Innovative Approaches to Promoting Health Coverage for New Immigrants[1]

1. **Encourage new insurance programs that pool risk.** The government could encourage new insurance programs and products that allow employers who do not currently offer health insurance to band together to purchase group coverage, thus pooling their risk more efficiently. This option would especially benefit small businesses, and it would reach both US natives and immigrants who are uninsured. New immigrants (and employers that sponsor temporary or provisional immigrants) could be required to participate.

2. **Create an insurance buy-in option.** The government could require all new temporary and provisional immigrants to enroll in a health coverage program, such as employer-based insurance, state employee health insurance, Medicaid, or Medicare. Enrollees would pay a premium at the group rate to join a program. The generally healthy incoming immigrants would likely strengthen the solvency of existing programs.

3. **Develop bilateral agreements with sending countries to provide health care.** The federal government could ask sending countries that have nationals working in the United States to help subsidize the health care of their citizens. These funds might be used to support existing public safety net providers in areas where nationals from one country are concentrated.

4. **Channel temporary immigrants' Social Security and Medicare tax payments toward health care coverage.**
Temporary immigrants in a new immigration system would be unlikely to ever collect Social Security and Medicare. Therefore, the federal government could use a share of temporary immigrants' tax payments toward these programs to subsidize health care for those who do not have employer-sponsored benefits. Alternately, the government might allow employers to channel a portion of the Medicare and Social Security taxes they pay on behalf of temporary immigrant workers toward health insurance benefits.

5. **Establish a "medical home" for new immigrants.** Temporary or provisional immigrants could be required to undergo an initial health screening at a designated "medical home" — a safety net community medical provider, such as a public clinic or federally qualified community health center. Introducing immigrants to a medical home would establish an affordable location for early care and potentially reduce uninsured immigrants' reliance on emergency rooms. The medical home could screen immigrants for public insurance program eligibility and charge those who would not qualify a discounted rate (as providers do for other low-income Americans) for care. Higher income immigrants could be required to purchase private health insurance or enroll in employer-sponsored plans.

---

[1] A key consideration in promoting health care coverage is doing so in ways that contain or reduce costs to federal, state, and local governments. This appendix has been adapted from policy options proposed by Leighton Ku and Demetrios Papademetriou, "Access to Health Care and Health Insurance: Immigrants and Immigration Reform," and Adam Gurvitch, "Access to Health Care after Immigration Reform — Practical Considerations for Policymakers." For a more detailed analysis of these options' strengths and weaknesses, see these pieces in the forthcoming volume *Securing the Future: The US Immigrant Integration Policy Agenda*, ed. Michael Fix (Washington, DC: Migration Policy Institute, 2006).

APPENDIX V: List of Acronyms

BIA	Board of Immigration Appeals
CBP	Customs and Border Protection
DHS	Department of Homeland Security
DOL	Department of Labor
FAST	Free and Secure Trade program
FY	fiscal year
GAO	Government Accountability Office (Called the General Accounting Office until July 2004)
GDP	Gross Domestic Product
ICE	Immigration and Customs Enforcement
IG	Inspector General
INA	the Immigration and Nationality Act of 1952
IRCA	the Immigration Reform and Control Act of 1986
LCA	labor condition attestation
LEP	limited English proficient
LPR	lawful permanent resident
NAFTA	North American Free Trade Agreement
NCLB	No Child Left Behind Act of 2001
REAL ID	The REAL ID Act of 2005
SBI	Secure Border Initiative
SENTRI	Secure Electronic Network for Travelers Rapid Inspection
SEVIS	Student and Exchange Visitor Information System
SLIAG	State Legalization Impact Assistance Grants
SSA	Social Security Administration
USCIS	US Citizenship and Immigration Services
US-VISIT	United States Visitor and Immigrant Status Indicator Technology
UAV	unmanned aerial vehicle

APPENDIX VI: Who Does What in US Immigration

Most of the policy and implementation functions of the former Immigration and Naturalization Service (INS), which was abolished in March 2003, landed within one of three bureaus of the newly created Department of Homeland Security (DHS).

Nevertheless, as outlined below, a variety of other agencies have immigration-related functions, and some have immigrant integration-related responsibilities even though the United States has no formal integration policy or a dedicated agency for integration. Currently, no single agency or bureau develops immigration policy, coordinates the work, and assesses the effectiveness of various federal agencies in performing their immigration functions.

The federal agencies listed below are responsible for implementing, supporting, and enforcing the immigration and integration laws made by the legislative branch. *Note: These agencies have other functions as well, but only those related to immigrants are described here.*

Department of Homeland Security (DHS)

- **US Citizenship and Immigration Services (USCIS).** USCIS is responsible for providing immigration-related services such as processing immigrant and nonimmigrant benefits; adjudicating refugee, asylee, and naturalization petitions; and granting or denying work authorization.

- **US Customs and Border Protection (CBP).** CBP is charged with securing US borders at and between ports of entry and facilitating legitimate trade and travel. It includes Border Patrol agents, as well as inspectors enforcing immigration, customs, and agriculture laws.

- **US Immigration and Customs Enforcement (ICE).** ICE handles the interior investigative and enforcement responsibilities of immigration and customs, including detention and deportation. ICE focuses on national security, financial, and smuggling violations to target the support behind terrorist and criminal activities.

- **US-VISIT.** This is a stand-alone program office responsible for implementing the program that uses biometric indicators to track the entry and exit of nonimmigrant visa holders at US air, land, and sea ports of entry.

- **Office of Immigration Statistics (OIS).** OIS is responsible for developing, analyzing, and disseminating immigration-related statistical information, including the annual *Yearbook of Immigration Statistics.*

Department of State (DOS)

- **Bureau of Population, Refugees, and Migration (PRM).** PRM is responsible for formulating policies on population, refugees, and migration, as well as administering US refugee assistance and admission programs.

- **Bureau of Consular Affairs (CA).** CA interprets visa laws and regulations and serves as a liaison between the Department of State and overseas embassies and consulates on visa matters. Oversight of visa policy now rests within DHS. Consular officials issue visas and passports and provide services to US citizens abroad.

Department of Justice (DOJ)

- **Executive Office for Immigration Review (EOIR).** EOIR is responsible for adjudicating immigration cases and for the interpretation and administration of immigration law. Its components include:
    - **Board of Immigration Appeals (BIA).** BIA is the highest administrative body for interpreting and applying immigration laws. It has nationwide jurisdiction and is responsible for hearing appeals of decisions rendered by immigration judges or DHS district directors.
    - **Office of the Chief Immigration Judge (OCIJ).** This office is responsible for conducting formal court proceedings related to immigration cases. Their decisions are final unless sent to the BIA.
    - **Office of the Chief Administrative Hearing Officer (OCAHO).** OCAHO oversees the administrative law judges who adjudicate employer sanctions, document fraud, and IRCA-related discrimination cases.
- **Office of Immigration Litigation (OIL).** This office holds jurisdiction over all civil immigration litigation and is responsible for coordinating immigration matters before the federal district courts and circuit court of appeals.
- **Office of Special Counsel for Unfair Immigration-Related Employment Practices (OSC).** OSC investigates and prosecutes employment discrimination based on citizenship status, national origin, document abuse, or retaliation. It also engages in outreach and education regarding employer sanctions' antidiscrimination provisions.

Department of Labor (DOL)

- **Bureau of International Labor Affairs (ILAB).** ILAB carries out DOL's international responsibilities by conducting research on economic, trade, immigration, and labor policies.
- **Employment Standards Administration (ESA).** ESA's Wage and Hour Division ensures compliance with minimum wage, overtime, and child protection laws; the Migrant and Seasonal Agricultural Worker Protection Act; and the protections of temporary worker programs. It also conducts inspections of I-9 forms.
- **Employment and Training Administration (ETA).** Prior to an employer petitioning USCIS for a foreign-born worker, ETA's Office of Foreign Labor Certification must first certify that requirements for that visa classification have been met, such as attempted recruitment of US workers and payment of specified wage levels.

Department of Education (ED)

- **Office of English Language Acquisition, Language Enhancement, and Academic Achievement for Limited English Proficient Students (OELA).** OELA ensures that limited English proficient children, including immigrants, attain English proficiency and meet the same standards as all other students.

- **Office of Migrant Education.** This office administers grant programs that provide academic and other services to the children of migrant workers whose parents work in the agricultural, fishing, and timber industries.

- **Office of Vocational and Adult Education (OVAE).** OVAE supports national research, evaluation, demonstration, technical assistance, and capacity building activities. Included in its program are adult literacy and the Center for Adult English Language Acquisition.

Department of Health and Human Services (HHS)

- **Office of Refugee Resettlement (ORR).** ORR provides funds to states, public and private entities, and nonprofit voluntary agencies to assist refugees and asylees in resettling in the United States and attaining self-sufficiency. The office also recently was tasked with overseeing the care of unaccompanied minors.

- **Migrant Head Start Program.** The migrant component of this national program modifies delivery to meet the unique needs of migrant farm-worker families. The program provides services to low-income, preschool-age children and their families. Its goals are related to education, health, parental involvement, and social services.

- **Migrant Health Program.** This program under the Health Resources and Services Administration provides grants to community nonprofit organizations for culturally and linguistically appropriate primary and preventive medical services for migrant and seasonal farm workers and their families.

Source: Megan Davy, Deborah W. Meyers, and Jeanne Batalova, "Who Does What in US Immigration," *Migration Information Source,* December 1, 2005.

Appendix VII: Task Force Meeting Speakers, Commentators, and Resources

Session I: May 17, 2005
Upholding the Rule of Law: The Unauthorized Population

SPEAKERS & DISCUSSANTS

Frank Bean
Co-Director
Center for Research on Immigration,
Population, and Public Policy
University of California-Irvine

Jeanne Butterfield
President
American Immigration Lawyers
Association

Congressman Jeff Flake*
(R) Member of Congress, Arizona

Senator Kennedy*
(D) Senator, Massachusetts

Senator McCain*
(R) Senator, Arizona

Demetrios Papademetriou
President
Migration Policy Institute

Jeffrey Passel
Senior Research Associate
Pew Hispanic Center

Steven J. Rauschenberger*
Senator, State of Illinois;
President-Elect, National Conference of
State Legislators;
Deputy Republican Leader and
Former Chairman of the Illinois State
Appropriations Committee

*Task Force Member

RESOURCES

"Immigration." Chap. 4 in *Economic Report of the President.* Washington, DC:
United States Government Printing Office. 2005.

"Immigrant Families and Workers." Facts and Perspectives Brief No. 2.
Washington, DC: Urban Institute, November 2002.

The Chicago Council on Foreign Relations Independent Task Force. *Keeping the
Promise: Immigration Proposals from the Heartland.* Chicago: The Chicago Council
on Foreign Relations, 2004, 12–32.

Cooper, Betsy and Kevin O'Neil. "Lessons From The Immigration Reform and
Control Act of 1986." Task Force Policy Brief No. 3. Washington, DC: Migration
Policy Institute, April 2005.

Grieco, Elizabeth. "Characteristics of the Foreign Born in the United States: Results from Census 2000." *Migration Information Source,* December 1, 2002. http://www.migrationinformation.org/USfocus/display.cfm?id = 71.

Fix, Michael, Doris Meissner, and Demetrios Papademetriou. "Independent Task Force on Immigration and America's Future: The Roadmap." Task Force Policy Brief No. 1. Washington, DC: Migration Policy Institute, June 2005.

Martin, David A. "Twilight Statuses: A Closer Examination of the Unauthorized Population." Task Force Policy Brief No. 2. Washington, DC: Migration Policy Institute, June 2005.

Meyers, Deborah and Jennifer Yau. "US Immigration Statistics in 2003." *Migration Information Source,* November 1, 2004. http://www.migrationinformation.org/Feature/display.cfm?id = 263.

Passel, Jeffrey S. *Unauthorized Migrants: Numbers and Characteristics.* Prepared for the Independent Task Force on Immigration and America's Future. Washington, DC: Pew Hispanic Center, May 4, 2005.

Papademetriou, Demetrios G. "Reflections on Restoring Integrity to the United States Immigration System: A Personal Vision." Task Force Policy Brief Insight No. 5. Washington, DC: Migration Policy Institute, September 2005.

Papademetriou, Demetrios G. "The 'Regularization' Option in Managing Illegal Migration More Effectively: A Comparative Perspective." Task Force Policy Brief No. 4. Washington, DC: Migration Policy Institute, September 2005.

Wassem, Ruth Ellen. "US Immigration Policy on Permanent Admissions." Congressional Research Service Report for Congress. Washington, DC: Congressional Research Service, February 18, 2004.

UNPUBLISHED RESOURCES

"The Secure America and Orderly Immigration Act of 2005 (McCain, Kennedy, Kolbe, Flake, Gutierrez) Bill at a Glance." Prepared for the Independent Task Force for Immigration and America's Future, Washington, DC, May 12, 2005.

"McCain/Kennedy/Kolbe/Flake/Gutierrez The Secure America and Orderly Immigration Act Section by Section Analysis." May 12, 2005. Prepared for the Independent Task Force for Immigration and America's Future, Washington, DC, May 12, 2005.

Session II: September 21, 2005
Meeting Immigration Enforcement and National Security Imperatives

SPEAKERS & DISCUSSANTS

Tamar Jacoby*
Senior Fellow
Manhattan Institute

Randel Johnson
Vice President
Labor, Immigration, and Employee
Benefits, US Chamber of Commerce

Juliette Kayyem*
Lecturer in Public Policy
John F. Kennedy School of Government at
Harvard University;
Former member of the National
Commission on Terrorism

Admiral James M. Loy
Former Deputy Secretary
US Department of Homeland Security

*Task Force Member

RESOURCES

Commission of the European Communities. "Green Paper on an EU Approach to Managing Economic Migration." (COM 2004) 811. Brussels: Commission of the European Communities, January 2005.

Dixon, David and Julia Gelatt. "Immigration Facts: Immigration Enforcement Spending Since IRCA." Task Force Fact Sheet No. 10. Washington, DC: Migration Policy Institute, November 2005.

Ginsburg, Susan. *Countering Terrorist Mobility: Shaping an Operational Strategy.* Prepared for the Independent Task Force on Immigration and America's Future. Washington, DC: Migration Policy Institute, 2006.

Jacoby, Tamar. "An Idea Whose Time Has Finally Come? The Case for Employment Verification." Task Force Policy Brief No. 9. Washington, DC: Migration Policy Institute, November 2005.

Jernegan, Kevin. "Documentation Provisions of the Real ID Act." Task Force Backgrounder No. 11. Washington, DC: Migration Policy Institute, November 2005.

Jernegan, Kevin. "Eligible to Work: Experiments in Verifying Work Authorization." Task Force Insight No. 8. Washington, DC: Migration Policy Institute, November 2005.

Meyers, Deborah W. "US Border Enforcement: From Horseback to High-Tech." Task Force Policy Brief No. 7. Washington, DC: Migration Policy Institute, November 2005.

Rosenblum, Marc R. "Immigration Enforcement at the Worksite: Making it Work." Task Force Policy Brief No. 6. Washington, DC: Migration Policy Institute, November 2005.

Turner, Eliot. "Major Immigration Legislation Pending in the 109th Congress Side-by-Side Chart" published as part of "Solving the Unauthorized Migrant Problem: Proposed Legislation in the US." Migration Information Source, November 1, 2005. http://www.migrationinformation.org/Feature/mpi_legislative_proposals.pdf.

UNPUBLISHED RESOURCES

Gelatt, Julia. "IRCA's Employer Sanctions: Legal Status as a Labor Standard." Prepared for the Independent Task Force for Immigration and America's Future, Washington, DC, September 21, 2005.

Government of Canada. "Brief Overview of Canada's Policies on Meeting Immigration Enforcement and National Security Imperatives." Provided to the Independent Task Force on Immigration and America's Future, Washington, DC, September 21, 2005.

Session III: November 30, 2005
Labor Markets and the Immigration System

SPEAKERS & DISCUSSANTS

David T. Ellwood
*Dean and Scott M. Black Professor of
Political Economy
John F. Kennedy School of Government,
Harvard University*

Demetrios Papademetriou
*President
Migration Policy Institute*

Susan Martin
*Director
Institute for the Study of International
Migration, Georgetown University*

RESOURCES

Batalova, Jeanne. "The Growing Connection Between Temporary and Permanent Immigration Systems." Task Force Insight No. 14. Washington, DC: Migration Policy Institute, January 2006.

Capps, Randy, Michael Fix, Jeffrey S. Passel, Jason Ost, and Dan Perez-Lopez. "A Profile of the Low-Wage Immigrant Workforce." Facts and Perspectives Brief No. 4. Washington, DC: Urban Institute, November 2003.

Fix, Michael and Neeraj Kaushal. "The Contributions of High-Skilled Immigrants." Task Force Insight No. 16. Washington, DC: Migration Policy Institute. July 2006.

Lowell, B. Lindsey, Julia Gelatt, and Jeanne Batalova. "Immigrants and Labor Force Trends: The Future, Past, and Present." Task Force Insight No. 17. Washington, DC: Migration Policy Institute, July 2006.

Martin, Susan. "US Employment-Based Admissions: Permanent and Temporary." Task Force Policy Brief No. 15. Washington, DC: Migration Policy Institute, January 2006.

Murray, Julie, Jeanne Batalova, and Michael Fix. "The Impact of Immigration on Native Workers: A Fresh Look at the Evidence." Task Force Insight No. 18. Washington, DC: Migration Policy Institute. July 2006.

Meyers, Deborah W. "Temporary Worker Programs: A Patchwork Policy Response." Task Force Insight No. 12. Washington, DC: Migration Policy Institute, January 2006.

Rosenblum, Marc. "'Comprehensive' Legislation vs. Fundamental Reform: The Limits of Current Immigration Proposals." Task Force Policy Brief No. 13. Washington, DC: Migration Policy Institute, January 2006.

Turner, Eliot, Marc R. Rosenblum, and Julia Gelatt. "Major Immigration Legislation Pending in the 109th Congress Side-by-Side Chart" published as part of "Solving the Unauthorized Migrant Problem: Proposed Legislation in the US." *Migration Information Source*, November 1, 2005. http://www.migrationinformation.org/Feature/mpi_legislative_proposals.pdf.

UNPUBLISHED RESOURCES

Davy, Megan and Deborah W. Meyers. "Immigration System Basic Facts." Prepared for the Independent Task Force on Immigration and America's Future, Washington, DC, November 30, 2006.

Fischel, Stephen. "Employment-Based Visa Facts." Prepared for the Independent Task Force on Immigration and America's Future, Washington, DC, November 30, 2006.

Government of Canada. "Selecting Permanent and Temporary Immigrants to Enhance Economic Prosperity and Social Well-Being." Provided to the Independent Task Force on Immigration and America's Future, Washington, DC, November 30, 2006.

Government of Mexico "Non-Paper." Provided to the Independent Task Force on Immigration and America's Future, Washington, DC, November 30, 2006.

Government of Mexico "Fact Sheet: Law Enforcement, Fight against Organized Crime and Border Security." Provided to the Independent Task Force on Immigration and America's Future, Washington, DC, November 30, 2006.

Session IV: February 28 – March 1, 2006
Immigrant Integration and Discussion of Final Recommendations

SPEAKERS & DISCUSSANTS

Michael Fix
Vice President and Director of Studies
Migration Policy Institute

Leighton Ku
Senior Fellow
Center on Budget and Policy Priorities

Tamar Jacoby*
Senior Fellow
Manhattan Institute

David Martin
Nonresident Fellow
Migration Policy Institute;
Warner-Booker Distinguished Professor of
International Law
University of Virginia

Cecilia Muñoz
Vice President
Office of Research, Advocacy, and
Legislation
National Council of La Raza

Demetrios Papademetriou
President
Migration Policy Institute

*Task Force Member

RESOURCES

Fix, Michael, ed. *Securing the Future: The US Immigrant Integration Policy Agenda.* Washington, DC: Migration Policy Institute, forthcoming, 2006.

Note: The volume's chapters, listed below, were originally prepared as resources for the Task Force on Immigration and America's Future.

Beeler, Amy and Julie Murray. "Improving Immigrant Workers' Economic Prospects: A Review of the Literature." Chap. 8.

Garvey, Deborah L. "Designing and Impact Aid Program for Immigrant Settlement." Chap. 10.

Gelatt, Julia and Michael Fix. "Targeted Federal Spending on the Integration of Immigrant Families." Chap. 6.

Gurvitch, Adam. "Access to Health Care after Immigration Reform — Practical Considerations for Policymakers." Appendix II.

Fix, Michael. "Immigrant Integration and Comprehensive Immigration Reform: An Overview." Chap. 1.

Jacoby, Tamar. "Immigrant Integration — The American Experience." Chap. 2.

Johnson, Mary Helen, Michael Fix, and Julie Murray. "New Americans: Facts on Naturalization and Birthright Citizenship." Appendix III.

Kerwin, Donald. "The Role of Rights in Immigrant Integration." Chap. 5.

Ku, Leighton and Demetrios Papademetriou. "Access to Health Care and Health Insurance: Immigrants and Immigration Reform." Chap. 7.

Murguía, Janet and Cecilia Muñoz. "From Immigrant to Citizen." Chap. 3.

Murray, Julie, Jeanne Batalova, and Michael Fix. "Educating the Children of Immigrants." Chap. 9.

Waldinger, Roger and Renee Reichl. "Today's Second Generation: Getting Ahead or Falling Behind?" Chap. 4.

UNPUBLISHED RESOURCES

Rauschenberger, Steven J., letter to Task Force Director Doris Meissner, February 7, 2006.

Government of Canada. "Immigrant Integration in the Canadian Context." Provided to the Independent Task Force on Immigration and America's Future, Washington, DC, November 30, 2006.

Commission of the European Communities. "Commission Staff Working Document Annex to the Communication from the Commission Policy Plan on Legal Migration Impact Assessment." (COM 2005) 669.

Mexican Secretary of Foreign Relations, "Mexico and the Migration Phenomenon," (February 2006), http://www.sre.gob.mx/eventos/fenomenomigratorio/docs/mexmigrationpheno.pdf.

MEMBER COMMENTS

Oscar A. Chacón

I want to congratulate the team of writers who put together the "Report of the Independent Task Force on Immigration and America's Future." It is a major undertaking and largely represents the many hours of deliberation held during the several meetings of the Task Force. However, I find the report fails to provide a vision for recasting the relationship between immigration and America's future. In my opinion, the report needed to go much farther to articulate the interdependent nature of today's migration phenomenon with other major issues such as economic globalization. Today's migration is profoundly impacted by the ever more globalized economic, social, cultural, and political dynamics affecting every corner of the planet. Although we often celebrate the fact that we live in a world without borders in terms of trade and investment, the very opposite is increasingly true when it comes to people's migration and labor mobility. By glossing over this historical context, the report misses a key opportunity to promote multi-lateral and cooperative approaches to managing migration in the context of new approaches to sustainable and equitable development.

While I endorse the essence of the recommendations made by the report, I am not entirely comfortable with many sections of the overall report. Nor do I support the specific focus given to several of the chief recommendations. In the service of brevity, I would like to fully endorse the dissenting opinions and/or comments made by Bill Hing, Fernando Garcia, Janet Murguía, and John Wilhelm. In as far as a specific area of dissent of mine, I would like to emphatically point out that in today's interdependent world it is not practical to suggest that developing country governments must bear the full responsibility for improving economic opportunity in migrant-sending countries. While it is certainly true that governments in the global south may need to elevate the creation of local economic opportunity on their respective political agendas, it would be disingenuous to ignore the historical patterns in which the most economically powerful nations manage to "persuade" economically impoverished nations to embrace development strategies that often prove to be ineffective in transforming for the better the economic, social, and cultural standard of life for the majority of the population.

In my opinion, powerful nations such as the United States of America must shoulder a significant degree of responsibility for helping to identify and support new development paradigms that develop the human resources of developing countries as more than just low-wage workers. Such a new paradigm would require the collective creativity and political will of both economically enriched and economically impoverished nations. In any event, even an ideal development scenario in the global south will not eliminate migration from the face of the earth, but it will make it much easier to manage. I wish the report had taken this perspective closer to heart in its final recommendations.

Thomas J. Donohue

The US Chamber of Commerce is pleased to support the vast majority of conclusions and recommendations in this report. But we recognize that it is a consensus document and therefore, that there are some aspects of which we cannot support and deserve clarification as to our views. Among other areas these include the following points.

Workplace Advisory Board

The Task Force, under Recommendation #3 proposes the creation of a new Workplace Advisory Board, and there needs to be clarification as to what exactly this new board will do. Two agencies — the Department of Homeland Security and the Department of Labor — have power over employers and enforcing certain components of immigration laws. Further, the Department of Labor, the Equal Opportunity Employment Commission, and the National Labor Relations Board oversee enforcement of a variety of employment laws. Another body overseeing or regulating these areas would only lead to mass confusion, and furthermore, is completely unnecessary. The Chamber can support a Workplace Advisory Board whose sole mission is to ensure that the new government-run employment verification system is functioning adequately in workplaces. But, the Task Force report is unclear as to what the Workplace Advisory Board powers of "monitor[ing] the progress of new measures" would be and the Chamber would strongly oppose any extension of the authority of this board to other areas.

Private Cause of Action

The report contains a discussion on page 67 entitled "Rights on Par with US Workers," stating that "Temporary and provisional workers should have the same labor rights and protections as similarly employed US workers." The Chamber agrees. But the paragraph goes on to make extraneous commentary on existing resources and remedies which are unnecessary to the conclusion of the need for equal protections and implies, in admittedly vague language subject to interpretation, that a private cause of action in court should be added to existing immigration law, as distinguished from administrative remedies. Of course, review of administrative decisions is always available in court under a standard of review, but we would strongly disagree with any implication in this paragraph that a de novo trial in court is appropriate and would strongly oppose any such amendment to immigration law.

Standing Commission on Immigration and Labor Markets

The Chamber agrees with the report that the current situation under immigration law which requires appealing to Congress any time a change in immigration levels is necessary has proven to be a difficult, politically driven, process, which needs to be changed. Nevertheless the Chamber is unsure that the proposed Standing Commission on Immigration and Labor Markets should be given blanket power to propose new limits, which apparently must be adopted by the president unless the Congress steps in and affirmatively takes a different approach. This grant of power may be excessive and in need of further consideration. Deference to a formula based on economic conditions and past immigration patterns which indicate a need for an increase (or decrease) in immigration levels should possibly be included in the Commission's mandate.

Department of Labor Spending

The Chamber is concerned that the comment "most government agencies responsible for enforcing labor protection laws have experienced steady reductions in resources for the past 25 years" is not well supported, and could give rise to the impression that employers have not been held accountable under these laws. Resources devoted to enforcement should be seen as only one component of a larger strategy for increasing employer compliance, and lower resources for enforcement do not necessarily translate into a lower emphasis on improving compliance. Indeed, the primary source cited, in note 37, for this comment is a report from the Urban Institute issued in 2003 that describes the Department of Labor's web-based methods to assist employers in complying with various workplace protection laws such as the minimum wage and overtime, as well as workplace safety laws. The web-based compliance assistance reflects an enhanced effort by the Department of Labor to increase employer compliance with these laws. The Urban Institute report found significant use by employers (60 percent of employers contacted) of DOL web-based compliance tools to learn about the requirements of these laws. This suggests that enforcement resources and activities may no longer be (if it ever was) a reliable proxy for assessing employer compliance.

The report from NYU's Brennan Center, also cited in note 37 as support for the proposition that fewer investigators means more violations of workplace protection laws, raises an array of problems. First, the manner in which the data is presented says nothing about the trend or the conditions that give rise to it. Indeed, increased investigations and enforcement activities are often associated with expansions in the Fair Labor Standards Act and increases in the minimum wage, both of which occurred in 1974. Second, by its own admission, the report says that a "key point in interpreting these findings" is the strong anecdotal evidence of employer violations — based largely on newspaper accounts. This type of assertion is neither statistically valid, nor legally acceptable — employers are due their opportunity to defend themselves. Third, a case can be made that the data, as presented in this report, actually indicates improved enforcement with fewer resources. Compared with 1975, more back wages have been assessed even though there are fewer investigators and fewer compliance actions, but more employees and establishments are now covered. Fourth, states also have a role in enforcing their versions of these laws such as minimum wages, so looking only at federal resources spent does not tell the full story. Finally, any assertion that there is less enforcement activity should allow for the possibility that employers are actually doing a better job complying with these laws. Independent surveys conducted for the Department of Labor, including those industries where workers might not be likely to file complaints, confirm that employers are complying with these laws at a very high level.

Border Enforcement

Recommendation #7 advocates that steps should be taken "by the government to disband vigilantism of any form along the border." The US immigration system is undoubtedly broken, and this broken immigration system affects all of us. It is understandable that there is so much anger and frustration surrounding this issue, and a few civilian groups have formed to help keep watch over the border. Their frustration in the face of the absence of a federal solution is completely understandable, as is the desire to take matters into their own hands. But ultimately the answer is not in self-help, but in passage and enactment of comprehensive immigration reform, which of course must include improved border security.

Fernando Garcia

The convening and creation of the Independent Task Force on Immigration and America's Future was, without a doubt, long overdue. Through the Task Force, the Migration Policy Institute was able to open an important space of dialogue and discussion on the quite contentious and challenging issue of immigration reform, bringing together myriad perspectives. On behalf of The Border Network for Human Rights (BNHR), I acknowledge and endorse the recommendations of the Task Force report and the gigantic effort undertaken to compose this report and the constructive ideas that envision, in the long run, an overhaul of our failed immigration system. The report recognizes the historical complexity of immigration and gives credit to migrants in the development of our nation and economy. Moreover, it addresses the contributions of migrant workers for current and future socioeconomic stability. The report also acknowledges the reality of millions of immigrant workers living in the United States and provides specific ideas to legalize them and fully integrate them into our society.

However, the final report of the Task Force contains several shortfalls and critical limitations in various sections, but my concern and comment is primarily focused on the section on border enforcement and protection of human and civil rights. For the last several years, my efforts and those of the BNHR have aimed to achieve policies and practices that comprehensively combine national security, community security, and respect for human and constitutional rights. Through these efforts, we have concluded, and believe, that national security and protections of rights are not mutually exclusive, but part of the elements to build better immigration and border policies. Unfortunately, our Task Force did not see that in the long run, enforcement strategies, immigration reform, and national security policies that do not recognize and respect the rights of any sector of our society as part of the solution are doomed to fail dramatically; and, through time, these policies will only achieve the alienation of the impacted sector.

Even though the protection of rights of border communities is mentioned, the report does not escape the historical eagerness to overlook and ignore the need to create a clear and specific accountability process for law enforcement. This is particularly evident along the US/Mexico border, where migrant deaths continue to rise dramatically every year and where law enforcement misconduct is becoming a part of our daily reality. Border communities and residents live in an environment where law enforcement agencies bluntly disregard constitutional and human rights under the obnoxious pretext of protecting our national security.

The report enthusiastically supports the creation of new structures for the implementation of the recommendations to achieve comprehensive immigration reform (Standing Commission on Immigration and Labor Markets, the Office of Immigrant Integration, a White House coordinator for immigration policy, etc.), but when it came to the establishment of an Independent Oversight and Monitoring Commission that would review the impacts of immigration law enforcement on life, rights, and well-being of communities, the Task Force dismissed it. The recommendation was not included in the final report even though several members of the Task Force supported it. In my opinion, this was a fundamental error.

In finalizing my comments about the report, the BNHR and I strongly agree with the concerns on family visas, employment verification, and labor protections presented by Janet Murguía of the National Council of La Raza. All these issues must be thoroughly discussed to be able to reach real and effective comprehensive immigration reform.

Tamar Jacoby

I endorse the Task Force's recommendations and believe the report makes a valuable contribution to the immigration debate. But as a conservative wary of excessive government interference with market forces, I have serious reservations about putting immigration decisions — particularly all-important decisions about annual quotas — in the hands of a new, potentially politicized Commission on Immigration and Labor Markets. In the interest of consensus, I have decided not to file a full-fledged dissent from the Task Force's recommendation of such a commission. But I believe the recommendation should be qualified in a number of ways.

As the Task Force recognizes in general terms, the current surge in immigration is largely the product of economic changes, both here and abroad, and the United States needs a flexible immigration policy that respects this de facto equilibrium of supply and demand. Of course, as in any sovereign nation, the state must be responsible for who and how many foreigners we admit, and few would argue that the market can be allowed to operate unfettered in this or any other realm. Nevertheless, here as elsewhere, there is a fine line between reasonable protections and overregulation. What's needed is a policy that reflects and responds to market forces, moderating their excesses, but not ignoring them, or worse, trying futilely to defeat them, as current policy does.

This is necessary not only for economic reasons but also to preserve the rule of law. As we have learned all too vividly in recent decades, an unrealistic system — immigration quotas out of sync with the much more powerful laws of supply and demand — is ultimately unenforceable: a recipe for endemic illegality and the security risks that come with it. Bottom line: The system must be realistic, and it must be flexible enough to accommodate the inevitable ups and downs of the business cycle — our intake of immigrants should expand when the economy is expanding and shrink when employment growth is flat or slowing.

The question is *how* to adjust our quotas so that intake rises and falls with the market. Governments are notoriously bad at making such determinations; nothing can be worse for an economy than heavy-handed decisions by a sclerotic bureaucracy. And, when it comes to setting immigration quotas, it is plainly a mistake to leave the task to Congress, which for political reasons has failed repeatedly to adjust the flow as needed.

But would a standing commission do any better? That seems far from clear.

Certainly, if the nation were to entrust these decisions to a commission, its mission must be clearly defined and its scope limited.

First, it ought to be clear that while family and humanitarian concerns play a part in setting immigration ceilings, the overriding goal of policy — and the commission's primary task — is to approximate the annual flow generated by market forces.

Second, the commission ought not operate in a vacuum or with unfettered power, but rather on the basis of fairly strict guidelines tying its decisions to empirical data. One of the best ideas to emerge from the 2006 Senate debate on immigration was a clause that would have linked temporary worker quotas to labor market conditions — in that case, to the number of bona fide employment-based applications filed in a given period. The rationale behind such a formula was that it would act as a kind of thermostat, regulating the flow automatically and without intervention, eliminating the need for politically driven meddling by government. And to the degree possible, the standing commission ought to be required to defer to such a legislated formula, departing from it only in exceptional circumstances — and in such cases, members should be responsible for justifying those departures to the public.

Finally and most important, every effort must be made to insulate the commission from undue political buffeting, while also ensuring that it remains accountable to the democratic process. This is a difficult balance to strike, but I am concerned that the structure proposed by the Task Force would ultimately fail on *both* counts. Among other problems, the bureaucracy strikes me as bloated; ten years is far too long a term for commissioners. And certainly, there should be an even rather than odd number of commission members — so that neither party would ever have a controlling majority.

The Task Force isn't wrong: the market alone cannot be allowed to set our immigration policy. But nor can one political party or a group of faceless bureaucrats answerable to no one.

Janet Murguía and John Wilhelm

The nation badly needs good policymaking in the area of immigration, and the political compromises which have produced immigration law for the last 20 or more years have not produced this result. This is the premise of the Task Force on Migration and America's Future, and we agree wholeheartedly with it. There is much to commend in the Task Force's recommendations, and we therefore endorse them. However, we have deep reservations about several of the recommendations of the report and the language which supports them. The report does not fully reflect our views on several critical issues in the debate, and it does not outline critical protections for immigrants and American workers that are essential to the success of a reformed immigration policy.

In particular, the report does not go far enough in expressing the benefits of family-sponsored immigration both in demonstrating our country's most deeply held values, and in supplying workers at every skill level who benefit the nation economically. This nation has been and continues to be extremely well served by making it a priority to allow US citizens and legal permanent residents to reunite with their closest family members. Family reunification should continue to be the basis for our nation's immigration policy; it upholds cherished values while also fulfilling strategic labor force needs. In the last two decades, there have been at least two failed legislative attempts to decimate the family preference system by eliminating categories or stemming the flow of visas to these categories; such proposals are misguided and we would object vigorously to any suggestion that the Task Force report justifies further such attempts.

In addition, we have deep reservations about the section of the report calling for an employer verification system and for the elevation of the Social Security card into a *de facto* identity document. We have supported the former in legislation which recently passed the Senate, but only on the condition that there are clear protections against employment discrimination, and against the likelihood that authorized workers would be denied the ability to work because of database errors. Two decades of experience with employer sanctions have demonstrated a clear need for such protections; there is a strong likelihood that the expansion of verification programs and the enhancement of the Social Security card will alleviate some forms of discrimination while exacerbating others. The latter is an unacceptable policy outcome, and vigorous steps to prevent discrimination before it happens and address it efficiently afterwards are an essential part of the policy equation. We have presented detailed language regarding these protections to the Task Force, and though it was received without objection, our views are not sufficiently reflected in the final report.

Similarly, in its discussion of temporary and provisional visas, the Task Force report does not make sufficient mention of the labor protections required to ensure that these new worker visas do not undercut the wages and working conditions of the US workforce. While we have supported the creation of new and revised temporary worker streams in the legislative debate, we cannot support them in the absence of strong and well-enforced worker protections. We believe that any policy which advances temporary and provisional visas without such protections is counterproductive, dangerous, and misguided.

Finally, we strongly associate ourselves with the comments provided by Fernando Garcia of the Border Network for Human Rights regarding the strengthening of the report's language with respect to human and civil rights protections in the conduct of border enforcement. These are essential to a sound immigration policy consistent with our nation's highest values.

Frank Sharry

I salute the work of the Migration Policy Institute for its groundbreaking Task Force report, and I endorse the recommendations it makes.

The depth and breadth of the report and its recommendations underscore the need for a thorough and thoughtful modernization of our nation's immigration system. Too often, policy makers and interested parties work to reform our nation's immigration system through the advancement and enactment of piecemeal measures. Unfortunately, such measures often result in a patchwork of confusing and often contradictory policies. In contrast, the Task Force's report and recommendations rightly recognize that the system is in need of a multi-faceted overhaul in which all of the elements of the comprehensive reform hang together and work together.

This commendation and concern is the source of this modest comment. I want to be on record that my endorsement for the recommendations relates to the interrelated and integrated nature of the recommendations taken as a whole. Attempts by policy makers to move forward on some of the elements while ignoring other elements might well shift my position from one of support to one of opposition. For example, my support for the kind of electronic worker verification system recommended by the Task Force is dependent on the enactment of a reformed legal admissions system and a practical solution for the 11 to 12 million immigrants residing in the United States without authorization. In the absence of a comprehensive overhaul, I fear that the introduction of a new employment verification system would make the dysfunctional status quo even worse.

Similarly, the recommendation that the nation review and revise our legal admissions priorities and categories makes sense to me only in the context of an expanded, workable, and properly regulated legal immigration system combined with a set of sensible integration strategies. Such a system needs to simultaneously deal with current family reunification backlogs, continue a robust family reunification category, expand legal channels for needed workers, properly protect both US and immigrant workers, target enforcement strategies consistent with a reformed immigration system and respect for civil rights, due process, and accountability, and expand integration efforts aimed at the incorporation and social mobility of new Americans.

Because the recommendations speak to all of these key elements, I endorse the report. Because politics often forces trade-offs, divide-and-conquer tactics, and compromises that do not, I respectfully submit this comment.

DISSENTING COMMENT

Bill Ong Hing

For the reasons set forth below, the drafting process of the report, and the problems identified with the report in the supplemental statements provided by Fernando Garcia, Oscar Chacón, and Janet Murguía, I cannot endorse the broad themes or recommendations of the Task Force report.

Although the text claims to not emphasize employment-based immigration at the expense of family reunification, the proposal as to annual immigration states that for family immigration to remain "timely" for immediate relatives of US citizens and permanent residents, consideration should be given to eliminating the family category for siblings. This troubles me because at our meeting on February 28–March 1, 2006, the sentiment of those speaking on this topic expressed strong support for retaining the family categories. Yet on the eve of its publication, the report urged consideration of eliminating both the sibling category and the category for adult sons and daughters of citizens only to be revised at the last minute. All that was done by staff without deliberation by the Task Force. Significantly, recent legislation passed by the Senate retains all the family categories and contains a bi-partisan proposal that would clear the backlogs permanently. In my discussion with staff on this issue, a difference in vision was clear; those who drafted this proposal and I have different starting points when it comes to priorities in the admissions system. Staff's claim is that to help the economy, more jobs and skilled-based criteria should be used. My position is that the nation and its employers would continue to do quite well economically by expanding the family numbers throughout all categories. What's noteworthy here is that the Task Force was never asked to debate that fundamental difference in values that could have led to a wholly different selection proposal. If we had discussed what values are important to us as a nation in terms of human rights, moral obligations, and social responsibility, quite a different report could have emerged.

The Task Force has missed an opportunity to make a bold statement on immigration and to reframe the debate. I choose to believe that most Americans are decent, well-meaning individuals with a solid sense of right and wrong, who often are silenced by a vocal minority. Americans who have had the opportunity to work or socialize with people of other backgrounds come to realize how much we all have in common. I believe that the vast majority of Americans, if given the choice, would not endorse the mistreatment of immigrants — documented and undocumented — but they sense no immediate way to intervene in uncivil immigration enforcement methods. As with many other policy debates, the "fervor and activism of [a] small minority greatly magnify their influence, especially within the U.S. Congress,"[1] in the area of immigration policy and enforcement.

When it comes to the treatment of our fellow human beings who have crossed boundaries into our territory, we should consider what has driven or attracted them here before we become too judgmental. There is a reason why Chinese immigrants in the 1800s referred to the United States as *Gold Mountain*. Many such immigrants initially may have been lured by the stories of the discovery of gold, but eventually the attraction of gold was a metaphor — not to be underestimated — for the vast opportunities that the new world presented.

The new American empire also cannot be underestimated. As US culture, economic influence, political power, and military presence affect the far reaches of the globe, we cannot be too surprised at the attraction that Old Glory holds throughout the world. While I agree with many commentators that the cost of aggressive military actions has created more enemies for the United States, this power aspect of American empire attracts newcomers as well. Coupled with the ubiquity of American culture throughout the world, American empire appeals to would-be immigrants and refugees who seek the American dream of freedom, prosperity, and consumerism. Migrant workers, refugees, high-tech workers, multi-national executives, and relatives (both from the working class and the professions) all respond. Thus, American empire is responsible for luring countless migrants to the United States each year, as the phenomenon reinvigorates the Statue of Liberty's call to those "yearning to breathe free" and the fascination with America. Viewed in this manner, the debate over the profile of new immigrants is disingenuous. Since the nation has attracted these immigrants, the appropriate response is a commitment to integrating the newcomers in order to incorporate them into a system devoted to the political, economic, and social vitality of the nation.

We are in this together. The experiment that we call America is a test of our character and our willingness to believe that we can have a strong country that is caring and diverse. Showing compassion and fairness in our immigration policies is not a sign of weakness. Rather, those traits demonstrate a confidence in a rule of law and system of government that metes out punishment when necessary, but understands that moral obligations, rehabilitation, and opportunities to mature are essential elements of a civil society. While these traits of a civil society benefit individuals, they benefit us all as a common community. For when an individual becomes a contributing member, we all benefit — socially, emotionally, and economically.

---

1   Jimmy Carter, *Our Endangered Values: America's Moral Crisis* (New York: Simon & Schuster, 2005), 11.

ABOUT THE CONVENING INSTITUTIONS

The Migration Policy Institute

The Migration Policy Institute (MPI) is an independent, nonpartisan, nonprofit think tank dedicated to the study of the movement of people worldwide. The institute provides analysis, development, and evaluation of migration and refugee policies at the local, national, and international levels. It aims to meet the rising demand for pragmatic responses to the challenges and opportunities that migration presents in an ever more integrated world. MPI also produces the Migration Information Source, a Web-based resource at www.migrationinformation.org. www.migrationpolicy.org

The Manhattan Institute for Policy Research

For over 25 years, the Manhattan Institute for Policy Research has been an important force in shaping American political culture. The goal of the Manhattan Institute is to develop and disseminate new ideas that foster greater economic choice and individual responsibility. To meet this goal, the Manhattan Institute has supported and publicized research on our era's most challenging public policy issues, including taxes, welfare, crime, the legal system, urban life, race, education, and immigration.
www.manhattan-institute.org

The Woodrow Wilson International Center for Scholars

The Woodrow Wilson International Center for Scholars is a nonpartisan institution established by Congress in 1968 as a living national memorial to President Wilson. It commemorates his ideals and concerns by linking the worlds of ideas and policy while fostering research, study, discussion, and collaboration among a broad spectrum of individuals concerned with policy and scholarship. Opinions expressed in Center publications are those of the authors and do not necessarily reflect the views of the Center or its funders.
www.wilsoncenter.org